Getting the Left Right

Getting the Left Right

The Transformation, Decline, and Reformation of American Liberalism

THOMAS A. SPRAGENS JR.

 University Press of Kansas

© 2009 by the University Press of Kansas
All rights reserved

Published by the University Press of Kansas (Lawrence, Kansas 66045), which was organized by the Kansas Board of Regents and is operated and funded by Emporia State University, Fort Hays State University, Kansas State University, Pittsburg State University, the University of Kansas, and Wichita State University

Library of Congress Cataloging-in-Publication Data

Spragens, Thomas A.
 Getting the left right: the transformation, decline, and reformation of American liberalism / Thomas A. Spragens, Jr.
    p. cm.
  Includes index.
  ISBN 978-0-7006-1672-5 (cloth : alk. paper)
  1. Liberalism—United States. 2. United States—Politics and government. I. Title.
  JC574.2.U6S67 2009
  320.510973--dc22
                        2009018202

British Library Cataloguing-in-Publication Data is available.

Printed in the United States of America

10 9 8 7 6 5 4 3 2 1

The paper used in this publication is recycled and contains 30 percent postconsumer waste. It is acid free and meets the minimum requirements of the American National Standard for Permanence of Paper for Printed Library Materials Z39.48-1992.

In Memoriam
Robert F. Kennedy
Christopher Lasch
Wilson Carey McWilliams

Contents

Introduction / ix

1 My/Traditional American Liberalism: A Recollection of Recurrent Themes / 1

2 The New Face of American Liberalism / 47

3 Why Did It Happen? / 93

4 The Deontology Trap / 146

5 New Democratic Vistas / 214

Afterword: Queries and Responses / 263

Notes / 297

Index / 323

Introduction

This book is not a work of disinterested scholarship so much as it is a political treatise informed by scholarly resources. My subject is American liberalism, its animating purposes, its changes, its problems, and its future. By liberalism, I here mean what that term signifies in conventional American political discourse rather than what it signifies in the academic discourse of political theory: that is, I am concerned with the public philosophy of the mainstream left in American politics and not the broader modern political and moral outlook centered on liberty and equality that originated in Europe in the seventeenth and eighteenth centuries. American liberalism here is understood to mean the socially "progressive" and antihierarchical orientation in American politics from Thomas Jefferson and Andrew Jackson through twentieth-century Progressivism, the New Deal, the New Frontier, the Great Society, and contemporary social justice–oriented liberalism.

Because my argument proceeds from a political point of view and has political purposes, it may be helpful to contextualize my concerns genealogically—to provide a brief account of the political biography and the political prejudices (in the literal sense of prejudgments) that have motivated my inquiry.

Voting behavior studies have made it clear that our partisan leanings are heavily influenced by our familial background and experiences. And this finding is hardly surprising—or for that matter even a novel discovery. Gilbert and Sullivan marveled sardonically long before the tools of modern survey research were

INTRODUCTION

developed how it was that every Englishman alive was, mirabile dictu, "born a little liberal or a little conservative." This is not so much a function of parental indoctrination, I think. All of us who have parented know well the limited power of such efforts. It is instead a result of habituation into a particular moral imaginary and the prereflective social attitudes and responses that derive from it. So we have those "to the manor born" political aristocrats and "red diaper babies."

In the same way, I was an early habituated American liberal. My first specifically partisan political memory is my father's outrage at Richard Nixon's Checkers speech. I proudly wore one of a handful of Adlai Stevenson buttons to school in our upper-class California suburb amid a sea of "I like Ike" regalia. I watched with admiration my father's insistence before assuming the presidency of a border state college in the fifties that its board of trustees commit itself to the admission of African American students. I cast my first vote at eighteen for John Fitzgerald Kennedy and worried about the safety of southern-born professors at my New England college who went back home as Freedom Riders.

These early prejudices and sympathies not only survived but were confirmed and deepened by my forays into political theory and American history. What I found intuitively attractive on the liberal side of the American political spectrum now appeared to me as the closest contemporary embodiment of those social hopes and moral principles that led Abraham Lincoln to pronounce American democracy as "the last best hope of mankind." These hopes and principles come more or less from the confluence of Enlightenment liberalism, civic republicanism, and Protestant progressivism. Foremost among those principles are the Enlightenment norm of universal respect for the dignity of persons captured in Immanuel Kant's conception of the "kingdom of ends," Thomas Jefferson's insistence that all people are created equal and should be accorded fundamental rights and protections, the religious ideal of charity toward one's neighbors, the Protestant principle of liberty of conscience, and the civic republican embrace of civic equality, devotion to the common good, and the rule of law. Foremost among those hopes are G. W. F. Hegel's insistence upon the conviction that "all can be free," John Stuart Mill's belief in the mental and moral progress of the people, and the belief that the members of a democratic society can successfully govern themselves instead of being ruled by some kind of aristocratic or oligarchic elite.

My reading of American history, moreover, led me to believe that it was the party of the Left that did most of the creative work of pushing our policies and institutions toward the achievement of these ideals. The party of the Right had its useful functions: it could serve as repository and defender of important traditions, it could offer stable governance when the party of the Left became corrupt or chaotic, and it could serve to consolidate and accord the imprimatur of partisan consensus upon previously contested social advances. But when we consider the creative adaptations that have improved the polity and brought it closer to achieving the deeper moral aspirations of democratic liberalism, it seems clear that these usually have originated on the left side of the aisle: the democratization of political power during the nineteenth century, the harnessing of buccaneer capitalism, the reforms of Progressivism, the creation of the social safety net of the New Deal, the landmark civil rights legislation of the 1960s, and so on.

As fortune would have it, I found myself heading to Chicago in the summer of 1968 to attend the Democratic National Convention. My father, who had, under the duress of the controversy over the Vietnam War, abandoned the partisan neutrality generally adopted by college presidents as a prudential necessity, was a delegate committed to the insurgent candidacy of Eugene McCarthy and had offered to take his progeny along to see the show. I had expected to witness important decisions being made, but I had not anticipated having a ringside seat at the implosion of the New Deal version of the Democratic Party. That implosion took place not only inside the convention hall, where Richard Daley and his minions sat front and center shaking their fists at Senator

INTRODUCTION

Abraham Ribicoff, but even more dramatically and violently in Grant Park, where the Chicago police set upon student demonstrators and associated others with their billy clubs. As the tear gas wafted over the park and students with bleeding heads staggered into adjoining hotels, I was filled with dismay and anger. This was a police riot, outrageous and unacceptable. But I also found myself experiencing a disquieting sense of ambivalence about the protagonists. I obviously sympathized most with the students who had been brutalized. They were, after all, on my side. But I had also found myself unpleasantly surprised and put off by the attitudes and behavior of some of the activists, who seemed to delight in expressions of their disdain for the patriotic and religious values of the local ethnic population. However much they may have styled themselves as valiant resisters against an oppressive establishment, their taunting of the "pigs" had an unmistakable flavor of upper-class toffs out to flaunt their superiority to the common throng and their presumably benighted allegiance to conventional social norms.

As American liberalism took on something of a new identity in the aftermath of the civil rights revolution, under the strain of divisions over Vietnam, and under the influence of the cultural changes of the seventies, the ambivalence created in me by the battle of Grant Park persisted and deepened. Some parts of the New Left social agenda seemed valuable to me, for example, but other parts of it were considerably less attractive. On the positive side of the ledger, the authors of the Port Huron Statement were right in their insistence that liberalism in the '50s had—under the duress of the Cold War and the fixation on rebuilding the post–World War II economy—gone complacent and conservative. The ostensibly more democratic party was in thrall to its southern oligarchic wing, which effectively inhibited it from its progressive mission of bringing greater freedom and opportunity to the socially oppressed and the economically disadvantaged. These early Students for a Democratic Society sought to recall liberalism to its historical mission to promote civil rights and social equality against the resistance of entrenched hierarchies. Moreover, in making an appeal for a more participatory form of public life, they recalled to a Lockean nation some of the larger moral purposes of democracy that John Stuart Mill had championed in his defense of representative government and that Walt Whitman had eulogized as central to the deeper aspirations of a democratic society: they sought to remind their compatriots that the purposes of democracy are not exhausted by the defense of property and individual freedom but extend to the personal development fostered by successfully taking on the challenges of self-rule.

Also valuable in the culture of the New Left, I would argue, was a welcome challenge to the dominant postwar ethos of success/achievement/productivity/social conformity/status-seeking. This was the social ethos that produced the character types characterized and perhaps caricatured in the sociologists' archetypes of the "lonely crowd," the "organization man," and the "man in the grey flannel suit." At a deeper level, this New Left challenge arguably embodied a spiritual revolt against imprisonment within what Max Weber famously styled as the "iron cage" of a society driven by the potent imperatives of technocratic rationalization. In Weber's version of this air-conditioned nightmare, the intertwined compulsions of scientific, economic, and bureaucratic rationalization create a way of life in which, as one of his interpreters has put it, "the world loses its savor. The spontaneous affections of the heart, the hatreds of the moment, the comely and honorable ways of tradition are all forbidden. Reason illuminates all being with a shadowless and clinical light before which fly poetry, faith, and myth."[1] Against the backdrop of these deprivations of the heart, the New Left's quest to build a counterculture represented, in Theodore Roszak's words, "the spontaneous urge to counter the joyless, rapacious, and egomaniacal order of our technological society."[2]

The New Left had its more unattractive features, however, which have arguably played a role in the declining moral purchase of liberalism. Noteworthy among these problematic features are the inclinations fostered by the New Left toward a fairly straightforward if romanticized hedonism, a tendency to convert the principled restraints of tolerance into the abandonment of moral discrimination, and an ironic tropism toward social snobbery.

As it turned out, the counterculture's resistance to the Apollonian ethic of what Herbert Marcuse called the "performance principle"—that is, the success/achievement/work ethic—of a technicist and economizing rationalism reenacted the ambiguities and multiple destinations found in Jean-Jacques Rousseau's reaction against the Enlightenment. The flight from a cool and cerebral self-denial that is experienced as repressive can run in different directions. Celebration of the passions and reasons of the heart may be invoked to elevate the prereflective moral intuitions of common folk above the calculations of the learned, or it may serve to legitimize the uninhibited self-indulgences of the son above the prudent consequentialism of the father. Dionysiac ec-stasis can be achieved both in the mystic's communion with the divine and in riotous drunkenness. Given the academic and late adolescent demographic axis of the New Left persuasion, it is perhaps unsurprising that the cultural manifestations and legacy of the New Left wound up being more about unleashing the id than about reaching for the ineffable and sublime. As Alan Watts complained as early as 1958, the counterculture used Zen largely as a "pretext for license." The point can indeed be generalized. The religious and philosophical doctrines found attractive by the countercultural Left—including not only Eastern religion but also Rousseau's paean to authenticity, Charles Fourier's lionizing of the natural passions, and Marcuse's embrace of what he calls the "great refusal" of the instincts to acquiesce in their subordination to social imperatives—all "look very much," as Roszak wrote, "like middle-class permissiveness reaching out for a religious sanction, finding it, and making the most of it."[3]

It was one of the defining features and the political genius of the self-interpretation of the New Left—and Charles Reich's account in *The Greening of America* is particularly clear and explicit in this respect—to insist that its partisans served the public good and were beneficently revolutionizing society simply by "doing their own thing." One could do as he or she pleased and simultaneously claim the garland of political heroism, for it was the insistence upon personal indulgence and the refusal of all social discipline that would subvert the repressive establishment and bring about the greening of America. Bob Dylan was not merely a troubadour or even a prophetic social critic, Reich counseled: he was the exemplar of New Left political activism. "Bob Dylan did what he wanted to do, lived his own life, and incidentally changed the world," wrote Reich.[4] More than a faulty strategy for social change, more than a soft and defective account of civic virtue, this formulation allowed those who affirmed it the unique capacity to claim the pleasures of self-indulgence and self-righteousness simultaneously.

However unattractive this self-romanticizing may have been and however damaging it may have been to our grasp of the demands of democratic civic virtue, perhaps the most problematic feature of the New Left was its entanglement within and its resultant fostering of a kind of social insularity and snobbery that has been important to what I want to call the decline of American liberalism. For although Reich overtly and focally depicted the several kinds of consciousness he fastened upon as crucial to his political critique—Con I, Con II, and Con III—as representing chronological stages in a pattern of social development, one need not probe too deeply into his text to see that these normatively charged characterizations represent a tendentious account of cultural commitments and values associated with different social classes. If the avatars of Con III were the upper-class youth Reich rubbed shoulders with at Yale, Con II represented the ethos of their allegedly acquisitive and status-seeking parents along with upwardly mobile and upper-middle-class types more generally. And Con I represented the mind-set of those simple folk who, Reich sneered, "believe that the American dream is still possible and that success is determined by character, morality, hard work, and self-denial."⁵ Reich pointedly claimed that the most deluded segment of American society is the lower middle classes. "False consciousness," he wrote, "is most readily described in terms of a lower middle class family."⁶ If that be so and if the road to progress must come through "revolution by consciousness," the lesson here was clear. Despite Reich's determination to present a scenario of benign revolution without social conflict, the logical consequence of his analysis was to identify the beliefs, the values, the desires, and the social goals of the working and lower middle classes as the principal obstacle to progress. In terms of the political alignment of the social classes, this conclusion was momentous in its implications. For if the old liberalism saw its mission largely in terms of championing the interests of the working and lower middle classes, the new liberalism would on this account have to take as a critical part of its mission the destruction or transformation of the culture of these classes.

Although many of the most distinctive elements of New Left politics, culture, and ideology have faded into a hazy historical curiosity along with bell-bottoms and tie-dyed shirts, this new class disarticulation between liberal reformism and the lower middle class became a persistent and troubling feature of the American political landscape. Whether one canvasses the dominant public philosophy of post-1970 academic liberalism or the partisan alignments and interest-group affiliations of the post–George McGovern Democratic Party, what seems notably subordinated is any focal concern with the social aspirations and animating ideals of the "common people" who figured so prominently in the rhetoric of an earlier liberalism. This aftermath of the New Left is one contributing factor in a complex process leading to a situation in which, as Michael Tomasky succinctly puts it, "the left is anything but populist."⁷ It will be one of the concerns of this book to substantiate that claim, to consider the causes and consequences of the state of affairs it describes, and to argue that this pattern represents a weakness and anomaly within contemporary American liberalism requiring attention and remediation if that liberalism is to recover and retain its legitimacy and vitality for the twenty-first century.

Indeed, one of the central convictions animating this book is the insistence that American liberalism needs to recover its populist heart. Because populism is a label that has accrued multiple meanings, I want to be clear about what I mean in saying this. Populism as I understand and endorse it does not mean a belief that the voice of the people is the voice of God. Moreover, I do not mean to endorse a politics centered entirely on class-based interests and animosities. What I mean here by populism is a passionate and principled commitment to the ideal of government "of the people, by the people, and for the people." It means devotion to the never-ending task of creating and re-creating a strong and self-reliant people who govern themselves individually and collectively in their private pursuit of happiness, in the multiple venues and institutions of a vital and complex civil society, and through their ultimate control and supervision of the agencies of government proper. It means the recognition that you cannot have democracy without a strong, competent, and virtuous (in the civic republican sense of that term) citizenry who conduct their multifarious social enterprises with an ethos of good craftsmanship.[8] It means understanding democracy as a way of life and a philosophy of governance—not merely as a set of policy outcomes congruent with a prespecified standard of equality.

Since the 1970s, it seems to me, American liberalism has largely abandoned these populist aspirations—or at least has subordinated them to other concerns. This has resulted in part from its tendency to base its politics upon an overgeneralization of a somewhat narrow and misleading understanding of the goals and politics of the civil rights revolution. In some quarters—more often in the academy—this has meant an insistence upon constructing this country as "Amerika": a basically oppressive, disciplinary, and racist society. The politics of this American version of a Foucauldian dystopic sociology has been ambiguous and multiform. At its most useful, it has helped fuel resistance against

INTRODUCTION

racial and gender hierarchies and the normalizing pressures that stem both from those sources and from the workplace regimes of industrial modernity. On the other side of the ledger, this is a political orientation that has contributed to political alienation and to the kinds of ethnic chauvinism and divisions that characteristically undermine social reform coalitions.

The more mainstream version of postseventies American liberalism, whose academic avatar is John Rawls rather than Michel Foucault, also seemed to me to base its social goals and build its public philosophy upon its own understanding of the civil rights revolution. It has taken its central mission to be the pursuit of distributive justice and has understood the content of that justice in terms of equality and individual rights. Remembering the role of judicial strategy and executive decrees in furthering the goals of civil rights, this liberalism became comfortable with pursuing a mode of governance that emphasizes reform from the top via these channels—a conception of liberal governance and reform that one commentator has characterized as "juridical democracy."[9] What gets lost or subordinated here are other social goals that were quite important to Jeffersonian democratic ideals, to civic republican conceptions of democracy, and to the Progressive movement. Among these goals are those related to the personal development of democratic citizens, the creation of democratic communities, energetic self-governance by a competent democratic public, and the electoral formation of legislative majorities.

The worries and dissatisfactions with the current state of American liberalism that provided the impetus for this book were consolidated and sharpened for me by an insightful commentary of Harry Boyte and Nancy Kari on the striking contrast they observed between the public works art of the New Deal period and the retrospective representation of that same period in the FDR Memorial on the Washington Mall. The art of the New Deal period they saw on display at the National Archives depicted a strong, competent, and active citizenry. This New Deal art, they wrote, "explicitly challenged elitist views. Artistic themes focused on the dignity and energy of common men and women in the midst of hardship. They stressed the contributions that ordinary people made through their work to build the commonwealth." In contrast, they note, the FDR Memorial depicts ordinary citizens as weak and passive. "The citizens are drained of energy. Their faces are vacant and spiritless, their posture is drooped. The overwhelming impression is that FDR—and by extension, government—single-handedly saved the nation." What is on display in these starkly contrasting artistic representations, Boyte and Kari argue, is "how radically our public culture has eroded in the years [between them]." The recently built FDR Memorial "is a window into modern liberalism's views of government and the citizenry. It conveys an image of the New Deal through the prism of our time. Professionals deliver the goods to passive clients. The government is the center of the action. Political leaders are the source of energy and initiative. The people are reduced to a kind of Greek chorus, expressing gratitude."[10]

My sense is that the change and the contrast Boyte and Kari find embodied in these works of public art are real ones. They represent, moreover, an important feature of a transformation in the dominant public philosophy of American liberalism over the last half of the twentieth century. Although the relevant philosophical and ideological landscape is by no means simple or dichotomous, American liberalism in its progressivist and New Deal incarnations exhibited a considerable degree of trust in the basic competency and goodwill of the people as a whole and a corresponding dedication to procedural norms of democratic self-governance and popular sovereignty. Moreover, although this version of liberal public philosophy was committed to social justice, that goal was understood largely as the attainment of equal opportunity and equal rights, and a good deal more emphasis was placed upon the goal of allowing all citizens to have a "good life" in a larger sense—with something akin to what John Stuart Mill called "mental and moral development" constituting an important feature of the good life. In these respects, this form

INTRODUCTION

of early twentieth-century public philosophy was basically continuous with the understanding of democratic purposes found in Jefferson, the apologists for Jacksonian democracy, Lincoln, Whitman, and the Progressives. In contrast to this account of democratic ideals, recent American liberalism has lacked a populist spirit and has correspondingly been much less dedicated to procedural norms of democratic legitimacy. Substantive goals of expressive liberty and social and economic equality have been the centerpiece, with procedural norms subordinated or shouldered aside. The goal of social justice, moreover, has assumed a more capacious, demanding, and specific form, while aspirations for universal personal development seem to have faded or even to have become vaguely illegitimate.

In the pages that follow, I have several related purposes. In the next two chapters, I want to provide a more specific and detailed account of the contrast between the older and more recent versions of liberal public philosophy adumbrated in the preceding couple of paragraphs. I try to identify what I regard as the enduring themes and commitments within what I call "traditional" American liberalism. Granting myself a certain degree of hermeneutic license, I then try to integrate these themes and commitments into an ideal type in the Weberian sense of that term. Although happy to concede the limitations and the contestability of this model, I will argue that it represents a rough but faithful archetype useful both for analytic purposes and for the sake of prompting critical reflection. I then turn to examine some of the more important norms and judgments that have a prominent place within the public philosophy of contemporary liberalism. Particular attention will be given in this context to some of the core themes in John Rawls's theories of social justice and political liberalism. According some pride of place to Rawls seems both unavoidable and appropriate, given that he is widely acknowledged as the leading theorist of today's "high liberalism."[11] Moreover, I believe that the basic moral claims and judgments articulated and championed by Rawls provide us with the most explicit and forthcoming theoretical account of the dominant moral imaginary animating contemporary American liberalism.

I then venture into what for a political theorist is the less familiar terrain of political history, sociology, and empirical social science to consider what I regard as some of the contributory causes of the political philosophical transformation I describe. Some of these causes are themselves theoretical in origin. Others are the kinds of historical contingencies that produce changes in political preoccupations and that disrupt prevailing political coalitions.

Finally, having characterized and tried to explain the ways in which contemporary liberalism has become both a politically and philosophically different animal than the liberalism that preceded it, I offer my assessment of whether this transformation has been a desirable one. Although I happily acknowledge that contemporary American liberalism has its heart in the right place and exhibits many healthy impulses, I shall focus on what I regard as its problematic aspects. This focus on the problematic runs the risk of creating a critical imbalance, but the reasons for it are purely pragmatic: whether it comes to our bodies, our automobiles, or our political norms and practices, it's the parts that aren't working all that well that need our attention.

I conclude the book by offering some thoughts on remediation and a look forward. In doing so, I shall not be so foolish as to try to develop a novel public philosophy or to dictate a specific political program. Instead, I shall try to argue that it would be both philosophically viable and politically advantageous for American liberals to transcend their recent preoccupation with social justice, reincorporating their legitimate distributive concerns within the larger and more traditional liberal dedication to popular self-rule and universal self-realization. For if American liberalism in the twenty-first century defines itself by seeking to answer the question "How can we reallocate the social resources at our collective disposal so that all have as equal a share as possible?" it will doom itself to political futility and defeat. If, instead, American liberalism can constructively address the question "How can we—in the

INTRODUCTION

context of a large, diverse, postindustrial nation—create a society in which all of us can become capable democratic citizens able to rule ourselves and flourish as, in Walt Whitman's phrase, "separate and complete subjects for freedom?" it has the opportunity to create a bright new chapter in its illustrious historical career.

My dedication of this work to the memory of Robert Kennedy, Christopher Lasch, and Carey McWilliams is not motivated simply by my admiration for these three people, each of whom it was my good fortune to meet. It also recognizes that each of them advocated or represented important features of the kind of American liberalism I want to endorse. Robert Kennedy well understood that a just and effective liberal politics had to champion the interests of both dispossessed minorities and the white working class. Had he lived and become president in 1968, American liberalism—and American society more generally—would almost surely have developed in different and better ways. Christopher Lasch understood that in order to flourish, American liberalism needed to retain its connections to midwestern progressivism and to what he referred to as the values of the petty bourgeoisie. Carey McWilliams reminded us that democracy at its best cannot be only about interests and justice but also about civic friendship and good citizens. I am honored to remember each of them here.

1 My/Traditional American Liberalism

A Recollection of Recurrent Themes

Anyone who wants to speak of transformation or decline must provide a description of the old order by reference to which the alleged changes can be perceived and measured. We need a baseline. Edward Gibbon has to tell us something about the glories of Rome at its peak for us to see its decline and fall. Alexis de Tocqueville has to delineate the structural characteristics of the Old Regime for us to see the distinctiveness of postrevolutionary France. Benjamin Constant has to tell us something about how the ancients construed liberty for us to recognize the novel features of the modern take on political freedom. Given my title, then, it is incumbent upon me to provide a credible account of some earlier form of liberalism that contrasts with the dominant form of liberalism today. What are the core features of this older or traditional American liberalism that have been abandoned or transformed over the past several decades?

Any attempt to meet this requirement encounters immediate difficulties. The fundamental problem is that there simply is no such thing as a single, coherent, universally accepted social doctrine that could claim to be the "traditional theory" of American liberalism or progressivism. There is no accepted catechism. Instead of offering the basis for some clear and unequivocal conception of socially progressive goals and practices in this country, the historical record provides us with a panoply of perspectives that overlap but also diverge in significant ways. Any philosopher with reasonable standards of intellectual coherence and consistency would see polyphony rather than unanimity. American political progressives have invoked and often synthesized in a rough-and-ready fashion ideas that derive from varied constructions of Lockean liberalism, civic republicanism, Protestantism, midwestern populism, Whiggism, Enlightenment humanism, native pragmatism, and syncretic versions of socialism. Only a fool, it seems, would rush into this philosophical quagmire with any intent of finding something that could plausibly be presented as the "traditional beliefs" of mainstream American progressivism.

Foolhardy as it may be, however, some such attempt must be made. Unless we do so, however imperfectly, any account of the course of American progressivism dissolves into an itemization of unrelated particulars, and whatever might be distinctive and novel in contemporary forms of political liberalism becomes difficult to see. With all the attendant perils of such an enterprise duly acknowledged, moreover, useful things can be said about some deep and persistent thematic continuities within American reform liberalism. For despite the polyglot form and the philosophically mongrel heritage of American political progressivism, there are enough recurrent themes to create the kind of "family resemblance" that Ludwig Wittgenstein argued was the justification for any categorical term, such as—to take one of his examples here—*game*. As he noted, we call such diverse enterprises as football, chess, and courtship *games* although they exhibit only the kind of multiple and partial resemblances one might encounter in an extended family. It is what seem to me to be the most pertinent of such elements of resemblance among the various strands of American progressivism that I want to identify here and to gather into something approximating a broad but reasonably coherent political orientation.

The best analogy of the task at hand and its methodology is that of a bird building its nest. This is a creative enterprise involving a certain degree of discretion. The feathered fabricator enjoys the hermeneutic license, as it were, to shape the nest in a way he or she finds commodious. But the component parts are not themselves created anew. Instead, they are pillaged and appropriated from bits and pieces of material that someone else has left lying around. In like manner, the rough intellectual construct I seek to fashion here will be the product of this kind of semicreative bricolage. I bear the responsibility for the shape of the model, but the contents of the model are not themselves original. Rather, they are taken from the stock of ideas that appear and reappear in the writings of American political theorists and political leaders of broadly liberal or progressive sympathies. Thus the odd hybrid title of this chapter. This is an account of what can be characterized as "traditional" American liberalism because all the pieces are taken from the relevant historical stock. But it is also "my" liberalism because I acknowledge the hermeneutic license I have used in identifying the various thematic elements and in assembling them into a kind of ideal type construct.

Recent debates about the liberal tradition in America have centered in large measure on competing accounts of the ideology of the American Revolution. For a long time, it was taken largely for granted that American liberalism was deeply imbued with and predicated upon Lockean premises. Louis Hartz and Carl Becker gave paradigmatic expression to this characterization in their accounts of principles of the American founding, as manifested particularly in the Declaration, and of the later course of American political thought. The American polity has been, Hartz averred, a national articulation of Lockean thought in which the Lockean principles are so deeply ensconced that most people don't even see them as explicitly involved. If they are beyond contestation, they are hardly visible, but their power is all the greater as a result.[1] In support of this interpretation, it is easy and pertinent to reference the appropriation of Lockean concepts and phrases by Jefferson and the wide and deep acceptance in America of norms of limited government, property rights, rule of law, and the other core notions that composed John Locke's account of "the true original, end, and extent of civil government."

CHAPTER ONE

A few decades ago, however, this depiction of the Lockean provenance of the American democratic project was subjected to a frontal assault by the intellectual historians Bernard Bailyn, Gordon Wood, and J. G. A. Pocock. In their telling of the American story and reading of the American mind, Lockeanism figured hardly at all—or at least was profoundly subordinated to other sources and another political tradition. The colonists' challenge to British rule—and hence, it was implied, the principles animating the American founding—were inspired on this recounting not by Lockean liberalism but by the civic republicanism putatively espoused by figures such as Algernon Sydney, James Harrington, and the authors of *Cato's Letters*, John Trenchard and Thomas Gordon. Bailyn surveyed the pamphlet literature during the pre-Revolutionary era to support his case, while Pocock provided an intellectual genealogy of the transmission of republican ideas from ancient Greece through Renaissance Italy and seventeenth-century England into eighteenth-century America.[2] The burden of this historiographic revisionism and the "republican synthesis" it engendered was that the American political tradition cannot properly be understood as a libertarian, individualist, and capitalist one but should instead be seen as embodying the republican aspirations for civic equality, virtue, and solidarity.

This scholarly controversy has provided much valuable illumination regarding the multiple sources of the American political imagination in the eighteenth century. Moreover, it has usefully pointed us toward important sources of the more communitarian—as contrasted with the individualist—strands of American political ideals and aspirations. No doubt, this latter purpose was part of the impetus for the revisionist interpretation from the onset. Historical reinterpretation is often driven by contemporary ideological imperatives. And for the revisionists, a belief in the exclusively Lockean and liberal provenance of American political values seemed to threaten a libertarian and hypercapitalist understanding of these core values. Despite the contributions of this scholarly literature to our understanding of the ideological origins of the American Revolution, however, the focus upon and the prominence of this particular debate in recent years have come with a price. It has introduced distortions of its own into our understanding of the reception of Locke and of the republican tradition in America. And it has arguably confined scholarly attention to, if not the wrong place, at least too narrow a place to look for the larger aspirations of traditional American liberalism.

The substantive distortions generated in the course of this debate about America's ideological origins derive in the first place from what is arguably a misunderstanding of Locke's political philosophy and correlatively from what is almost surely a misunderstanding of how eighteenth-century Americans would have read Locke. The "Locke" whose American influence the revisionists insisted had been vastly overstated was "Locke" as seen through the eyes of the neo-Marxist C. B. Macpherson and the classical conservative Leo Strauss. Like Karl Marx and Thomas Carlyle coinciding in their reading of bourgeois society as one where relations among citizens were reduced to a cash nexus, so Macpherson and Strauss depicted Locke as an apologist for capitalist acquisitiveness and an exponent of hedonistic individualism. But, as Steven Dworetz has persuasively argued, this interpretation represents a retrospective misconstruction that strips away the sociological and philosophic-religious context of Locke's thought.[3] This is an interpretation that assimilates Locke to a later, more secular, and more individualistic tradition running from Herbert Spencer and William Graham Sumner to Milton Friedman and Ludwig von Mises. Locke could hardly have understood his ideas in this way, and the American colonists certainly did not see him that way.

What is largely missing in the Macpherson-Strauss construction of Lockeanism is the Protestant sensibility and moral persuasion that inform and contextualize its politics. As John Dunn has written, "An extremely high proportion of Locke's arguments [depend] for their very intelligibility, let alone plausibility, on a series of theological commitments."[4] And even were that admonition not well warranted, the American colonists' reception and

CHAPTER ONE

deployment of Lockean ideas would have had to have been mediated by and rendered compatible with the dominant and pervasive Protestant sensibilities of the era. That means that they took Locke's invocation of the constraints of the natural law quite seriously—rather than seeing it as the lip service to conventional pieties that Strauss depicts it as being. And it means that they took with similar seriousness Locke's acknowledgment that we are all "God's property"—an acknowledgment that leaves his account of property rights constrained by the doctrine of Christian stewardship and by the obligations of Christian charity. For the colonists, the famous fifth chapter of Locke's *Second Treatise*, "Of Property," would have been read as consistent with the account of property rights given by John Winthrop in his lay sermon "A Model of Christian Charity," which he delivered aboard the *Arbella* on its journey to New England (separated by only sixty years from Locke's work), rather than being consistent with Herbert Spencer's *Social Statics* (written almost two centuries after Locke's work).

In like manner, the colonists' construction of republicanism was also mediated by a Protestant understanding of political morality. John Adams's republicanism is a case in point. Adams invokes with great regularity the republican language of civic virtue, public spirit, and the fear of corruption. But his model citizen is not the Machiavellian neo-Roman citizen-soldier so much as it is the diligent and law-abiding Puritan. The law he obeys is not only civil law but God's law, his public spirit is Christian *caritas* (charity) and neighborliness, and the corruption that worries him includes sins such as sloth and gluttony. And because both Lockean liberalism and civic republicanism were seen through the eyes of Protestant parishioners for the most part, the colonists were relatively oblivious to the allegedly deep tension between liberalism and republicanism insisted upon by many twentieth-century intellectual historians. This is a tension that comes into sharp relief only when Lockean liberalism is stripped of its theological commitments and when republican civic virtue is similarly secularized—and when both are contextualized within an industrial political economy. Only then can the relationship between Lockean liberalism and republicanism turn into a clash between a worldly and libertarian rugged individualism, on the one hand, and an equally worldly egalitarian communalism, on the other. If we want to understand the way that the protagonists of the American Revolution understood themselves and their political ideals, however, we need to understand that they could not have seen things that way.[5]

Even more important for my purpose here than the distortions induced by this scholarly debate over the ideological origins of the American Revolution is the distraction produced by the dominant role it has played in recent constructions of American political ideals and aspirations. In one sense, the concentration on these debates is understandable: it is routine for all manner of protagonists in contemporary ideological controversies to rake through the ashes of the founding era to find arguments they can display as authoritative endorsement of their favored views. Where better to look for authoritative understanding of the purposes of a political society than at the intentions of its founders? But in another sense, this is an inappropriate and misleading place to look, especially when such a founding took place against the backdrop of a rebellion against established authority and when the arguments being examined were penned as justifications for that act of rebellion. For in such circumstances, the argument in question will understandably be dominated by a single, overriding theoretical question: what are the grounds and extent of legitimate political authority? And the answer given to that question will not by itself serve as an answer to the much broader and more teleological question: what are the purposes and goals of our political association? It is crucial, of course, that the regime being founded be legitimate, but knowing why a form of government is legitimate doesn't give us a full answer to the question of what the society is supposed to accomplish.

To look to the arguments of the protagonists of the Revolutionary era for a full and broad sense of what people have conceived

CHAPTER ONE

to be the ultimate goals and aspirations of American democracy, I am suggesting, is to look in the wrong place. It is only after independence has been achieved, only after the legitimacy and basic integrity of the new order have been established, that people can and must turn to reflect seriously about what they seek to achieve through their political association. To understand the animating purposes of the liberal and progressive tradition in American politics, we need to canvass not so much the ideas of Locke and pre-Revolutionary ideology in England but the ideas and arguments of post-Revolutionary political leaders and democratic visionaries.

That is particularly the case here, moreover, because of the widespread sense shared by these leaders and visionaries that American democracy was something genuinely new under the sun, a *novus ordo seclorum*. Having consolidated their successful revolution, the leaders of the new regime realized that they were in important respects sailing uncharted waters. That recognition was less marked among the conservative members of the political elite, who saw their fundamental challenges in more traditional terms. The old Federalists and the Hamiltonians were exemplary in this regard. For them, the tasks of the newly established regime were not themselves so novel: to consolidate political order and authority and to lay the institutional foundations needed to enable the new country to become powerful and wealthy. This would be a liberal regime, in the sense that civil liberties would be respected and there would be a private domain of family, religion, and economic enterprise. It would be a democratic regime, in the sense that the electorate could choose its leaders and, if it so chose, cashier them at designated intervals. But the basic purposes of this regime would be the same as those common to all political regimes: to protect the persons and properties of the citizenry, to regulate social conflict by law and the police power, and to provide an institutional setting to facilitate commerce. As for who was to govern, moreover, it was assumed that it would still be the usual elites of wealth and power—even if the common folk could pick and choose among them from time to time. And this, for the conservative post-Revolutionary leaders and thinkers, was all as it should be and had to be.

It was the genius of the founders of what I am calling the liberal tradition in America—principally Jefferson and the Jacksonians—to perceive and embrace some broader, more novel and radical aspirations for American democracy. What these leaders and visionaries recognized was fundamentally what Hegel was recognizing and expressing in his own metaphysical fashion at just about that same time. They recognized, that is, that they were standing on the cusp of a new era in political history, an era in which not one, not the few, but all people were coming to see themselves as entitled to be "free"—in the sense not merely of what we now call, following Sir Isaiah Berlin, "negative freedom" but in the sense that they were able to become and entitled to be treated as self-actualizing agents and not merely as the subservient vehicles of the life projects of the rich and powerful. This was a new and radical set of expectations and attendant demands. Ultimately, as Hegel saw, it developed in large measure out of the Reformation attack on the hierarchical authority of the church and upon its insistence on the priesthood of all believers. It also received a boost from the Enlightenment spirit whose core admonition, as Kant put it, was *sapere aude*: dare to use your own intelligence. Indeed, it was the convergence of the Reformation and the Enlightenment upon the validation of the epistemic competence of the average human mind that produced some odd bedfellows at times: for example, the Marquis de Condorcet, the archrationalist, cited the same Martin Luther who called reason a whore as a heroic precursor of Enlightenment because Luther challenged the "insolent despotism" of the pope over those "who were his equals" (Condorcet's words) and called upon believers to read scripture and seek God without mediation from self-described authorities. Although Hegel declared that it was "the Germanic peoples" who came to the realization, through Christianity, that all were free, Jefferson and the Jacksonians believed that it was

CHAPTER ONE

in America—largely unshackled from the legally entrenched hierarchies of the Continent—where this radical new insistence was most powerful and where the institutional, sociological, and geographic setting was most conducive to its political and cultural incarnation. Their intuition, moreover, was seconded by Tocqueville. Like Hegel, Tocqueville looked back over the course of history and claimed that "for seven hundred years we shall scarcely find a single great event which has not promoted equality of condition." Also like Hegel, he construed this "irresistible revolution which has advanced for centuries in spite of every obstacle" as "a Providential fact."[6] But when he endeavored to see close up the leading edge of this irresistible revolution, he did not travel overland to Hegel's Prussia. He got on a ship and sailed to America.

Tocqueville confessed to being in the grip of what he called a "religious dread" as he contemplated the enormity, the providential quality, the inevitability, and the potential implications of the course of democratization. There was, he thought, much in this drama to applaud, much to view with trepidation. What has divided the liberal or progressive and the conservative political traditions in America politics, it could be said, is that they have gravitated toward the opposing judgments whose simultaneous embrace by Tocqueville produced his own ambivalence toward the democratic project. The American old Federalists accepted the democratic or what they would have called the republican principle of legitimacy. But they were greatly alarmed by Shays' rebellion and dismayed by the spectacle of those muddy boots on the White House chairs at Andy Jackson's inauguration. Republicanism for them meant the demise of royal prerogative but not the end of social, political, and economic hierarchies, which they regarded in Burkean fashion as both natural and generally benign. Prudence would have kept them from speaking with Edmund Burke's candid disdain for commoners, but they would have agreed with his insistence that "the occupation of a hairdresser or of a working tallow-chandler cannot be a matter of honor to any person—to say nothing of a number of other more servile employments. Such descriptions of men ought not to suffer oppression from the state; but the state suffers oppression if such as they, either individually or collectively, are permitted to rule."[7]

The liberal/progressive persuasion in American politics, in my reading, was composed of those who shared and embraced the import of Hegel's belief that the ultimate destination of human affairs and the deeper meaning of democracy is that *all* are destined to be free. And what freedom here means is not merely what Burke conceded—that working commoners not be oppressed by the state—but that these same commoners are destined and entitled to be what Walt Whitman aptly called "separate and complete subjects for freedom, worldly thrift and happiness, and for a fair chance for growth." Profoundly moved by the dignity and extraordinary courage of the wounded soldiers he saw in the military hospitals of the Civil War ("I realize that it is finally from what I learned personally mixing in such scenes that I am now penning these pages," he wrote), Whitman responded as if directly to Burke's deprecation of the average run of humankind:

> I myself see clearly enough the crude, defective streaks in all the strata of the common people; the specimens and vast collections of the ignorant, the credulous, the unfit and uncouth, the incapable, and the very low and poor. The eminent person just mentioned sneeringly asks whether we expect to elevate and improve a nation's politics by absorbing such morbid collections and qualities therein. . . . Our answer is general, and is involved in the scope and letter of this essay. We believe the ulterior object of political and all government . . . to be . . . not merely to rule, to repress disorder, and so on, but to develop, to open up to cultivation, to encourage the possibilities of all beneficent and manly outcroppage, and of that independence, and the pride and self-respect latent in all characters.[8]

CHAPTER ONE

What Whitman recognized as well as anyone and what he articulated with unmatched ardor if not with great philosophical clarity or sophistication was that the heart and soul of America's distinctive brand of political progressivism was "populist." As he insisted, it was Lincoln who captured this core dimension of America's democratic aspirations most succinctly and memorably in the peroration to his Gettysburg Address: "That phrase, THE GOVERNMENT OF THE PEOPLE, BY THE PEOPLE, FOR THE PEOPLE, which we inherit from the lips of Abraham Lincoln," wrote Whitman, is "a formula whose verbal shape is homely wit, but whose scope includes both the totality and all minutiae of the lesson."[9] It is also important to note here that Whitman adds that "few probably are the minds, even in these republican States, that fully comprehend" the full meaning and significance of that phrase. In so saying, Whitman is alerting us to the fact this "populism" is not the simplistic form of unrefined and unmediated majoritarianism or class politics with which it is often confused—sometimes by its friends and often by its enemies. Instead, it is a much more complex and nuanced set of procedural norms and substantive goals covering the source of democratic authority, the proper modalities of democratic decisionmaking, and the larger aspirations of a truly democratic society. In the remainder of this chapter, then, I want to develop with somewhat greater specificity what I regard as this more complex and nuanced version of democratic populism, invoking along the way the words and proposals of various contributors to the liberal tradition in America. I do this for two fundamental reasons. First, I want to argue that Whitman's vision well captures what progressive politics in America has been, at its best, all about. And second, it is the core concern of this book to argue that contemporary American liberalism would vastly enhance both its moral legitimacy and its political viability if it would subordinate its more recent fixation upon a particular rendering of social justice to a deeper dedication to the kind of democratic flourishing Whitman envisions.

Whitman can maintain that the populist formula of government of, by, and for the people "includes both the totality and all minutiae of the lesson" of democratic governance because it incorporates a principle of legitimacy, a principle for decisionmaking, and a principle regarding the ultimate purpose of democracy. These three principles can be characterized as the principles of consent (of the people), self-rule (by the people), and self-realization or development (for the people). These principles come close to embodying the traditional American liberal answers to the questions Locke posed in the subtitle of his *Second Treatise on Civil Government*: the questions of the "true original, extent, and end of civil government." The principle of legitimate authority answers the question about the "true original" (i.e., legitimate source) of government power. The principle of development answers the question about the "end" or purpose of government. And the principle of self-rule answers the question of how governance is conducted, a question Locke does not pose in his title but says a great deal about in his essay.

If similar in its form and in the issues it addresses, the core claims encapsulated in the phrase "of, by, and for the people" overlap with but also depart from (or significantly expand and enlarge) the constructive claims of Lockean politics. The greatest overlap comes in the principle of legitimate authority, where Whitman's populist norm coincides with Locke's insistence that all legitimate government power derives from the consent of the people. The most striking contrast comes between the populist and Lockean answers to the question about the ultimate purposes of the well-ordered society: Locke wants largely to confine these purposes to the protection of life, liberty, and estate, whereas Whitman's democracy more ambitiously seeks to go beyond these rather narrow police functions to accomplish larger goals of human flourishing. The populist principle of self-rule overlaps in part but contrasts in part with Locke's account of legitimate decisionmaking procedures. Both affirm and incorporate the principles

CHAPTER ONE

of majority rule, rule of law, and public judgment, but Whitman construes the process and the standards of self-rule more expansively than does Locke. The differences here arise principally from the fact that Locke is equally liberal but less democratic than the nineteenth-century American progressives and from Locke's determination—inspired no doubt by the Wars of Religion—to limit the public domain to matters mundane and to consign matters of the spirit and human flourishing largely to the private realm. The continuities here point to the Lockean provenance of American liberalism, which is genuine and important. But the discontinuities point to the distinctiveness and broader ambition of American liberalism by comparison with Locke's seventeenth-century vision, which was progressive for its time but which also incorporated, sometimes tacitly, residual elements of feudal hierarchy and public acquiescence in structures of private governance. Although it has Lockean roots, especially in its specifically governmental institutions, American progressivism's larger concerns and aspirations make it misleading to characterize the liberal tradition in America as nothing more than a national articulation of Locke, as Hartz suggested. And the source and content of the distinctive and more expansive political aspirations are not properly attributable to some recrudescence of a Machiavellian moment or simply to the persistence of the concerns of the anti-Federalists, who were, after all—as Cecelia Kenyon has reminded us—"men of little faith."[10] Instead, the social and philosophical inspiration for America's distinctively populist and ambitious form of liberal and democratic progressivism came from ideas and hopes generated by what some have called the Enlightenment century—from the political and economic advances produced by nineteenth-century democratization and technology and from the ideas of those who reflected upon the possibilities presented by these developments. The philosophical music that animates the political poetry of "Democratic Vistas" doesn't come from the pens of Locke or Harrington or Sydney so much as it comes from people such as John Stuart Mill and G. W. F. Hegel.

The phrase "of the people, by the people, for the people" embodies, then, the three core principles of democratic consent, democratic self-rule, and democratic self-realization or development. These three principles answer the questions from where, by what means, and for what purpose does democratic government come. These core principles depend for their validity and feasibility upon a crucial animating assumption: a faith in the dignity and competency of the average human being. They in turn inform the content of the core democratic norms of liberty, equality, and participation. They carry important implications for legitimate political institutions and procedures. And they generate several fundamental imperatives for democratic policy. Taken together, this complex of principles, assumptions, norms, and policies constitutes the core logic and the recurrent themes of America's distinctive progressive politics, what I am calling "traditional American liberalism." In the remainder of this chapter, I will briefly delineate these constituent components/themes of this political persuasion and then offer a few concluding reflections about how we should situate it within the topography of political philosophy.

In Lincoln's justly famed democratic mantra, "of the people" represents the principle of consent, answering the question "From whence comes legitimate political authority?" Of the three elements of the mantra, this one is the most common and the least controversial. It is also the principle with the oldest lineage, antedating the piecemeal democratic revolution of the nineteenth and twentieth centuries. It was arguably prefigured in the Protestant validation of individual conscience above the authority claims of a clerical hierarchy, the reason that a liberal rationalist such as Condorcet could salute the dramatically less liberal or rationalist Luther as a spiritual forebear. And its basic logic was well articulated by classical liberals and republicans such as Locke, Rousseau, and Jefferson.

The logical case is a straightforward one. Traditionally, the exercise of political authority was justified by appeals to force, to nature, or to God. But none of these appeals is convincing, and each can be dismissed in turn. Candidly stated, appeals to force are exercises in cynical willfulness. Consider here the memorable Melian dialogue in Thucydides. People may, like the abject citizens of Melos, be compelled to submit to strength, but the compulsion involved is purely physical and prudential. No moral obligation is involved unless strength can be transformed into right and obedience into duty, as Rousseau observes, and any argumentative attempt to derive right and obligation from the bare fact of the possession of power results in "a mass of inexplicable nonsense."[11]

As for claims to ground political authority upon its alleged conferral by God, these also are unpersuasive. Rousseau offers here a sardonic quip: "All power comes from God, I admit; but so does all sickness: does this mean that we are forbidden to call in the doctor?"[12] Locke in contrast provides a serious, if by now largely otiose, argument against such claims of divinely based political authority in his *First Treatise of Civil Government*. All power comes from God, the ruler and creator of us all, he acknowledges, no antitheist he. The difficulty, however, is that no plausible case can be made that God conferred his own unquestionable authority over us upon some human vice-regent. So although God is the fount of all right and power, no specific human political authority can be derived from that source.

The claims of those who would ground political authority upon differential natural capacities are likewise unavailing. Though people indeed differ greatly in their natural abilities, these distinctions do not translate into legitimate political rights to compel or obligations to obey. These are no "slaves by nature" as Aristotle and others maintained, nor any morally requisite political subjection of any sort derivable from nature. Instead, Locke averred, there is "nothing more evident" than the "equality of men by nature" in terms of political status—that so far as their natural standing is concerned, they "should be equal one amongst another, without subordination or subjection."[13] Rousseau concurred that "no man has a natural authority over his fellow."[14] And as Jefferson explained in memorable words written only days before his death, this was the meaning of his insistence in the Declaration that all men are created equal: "that the mass of mankind has not been born with saddles on their backs, nor a favored few booted and spurred, ready to ride them legitimately by the grace of God."[15]

If neither force, nor God (in any direct sense), nor nature creates and legitimates any authority of some human beings over others, then the logical inference must be that drawn by Rousseau: "We must conclude that conventions form the basis of all legitimate authority among men."[16] It must be the (initially) free and equal parties to the body politic who themselves are the authors of legitimate political power. It is their own creation, of their own doing, of their own free will. In short, the people are sovereign, and all the legitimate powers of government arise from the consent of the governed. This is what government "of the people" signifies.

It may be worth noting, parenthetically, that this moral logic and the principles of consent and popular sovereignty it generates do not imply or require adherence to any existentialist notions of moral decisionism or dreadful freedom, as in Max Weber or Jean-Paul Sartre. Nor does it imply or require acceptance of postmodernist notions of moral aestheticism—of "strong poets" who create from whole cloth the shape and meaning of their lives. These twentieth-century moral and anthropological notions would have astonished the seventeenth-, eighteenth-, and nineteenth-century apostles of the principle of consent. Their claim was not that God or nature did not create real and important dynamics and imperatives of human relations that carry significant repercussions for ordering political society. Their point instead was that these dynamics and imperatives had to be validated and affirmed by the will and conscience—the hearts and minds, as it were—of the human beings whose lives they shaped in order for them to become governmentally legitimate. To put this in terminology pertinent to

CHAPTER ONE

contemporary democratic theory and familiar to its practitioners, the principle of consent did not presuppose that the consenting selves were "unsituated" subjects who created their own identities. Instead, the principle insisted only that the subjects in question, who were presumably constituted by much beyond their own choosing—by God and/or by nature and/or by their social historicity—had the right to create their political societies and their terms of association. It was not the subjects of consent that were works of artifice but their political institutions.

The second element in Lincoln's phrase, government "by the people," embodies a more distinctive, more novel, and more radical democratic principle: the principle of self-rule. It was largely beyond the ken of someone historically situated in John Locke's time to conceive of the people actually governing themselves in any significant or meaningful sense. He spoke of natural equality and may have affirmed that precept with utter sincerity as a moral norm, but his society was quite hierarchical, and he assumed that these patterns of functional inequality were largely natural, normal, and hence politically unproblematic. He insisted upon the propriety of parliamentary supremacy, but the parliament in question was essentially a confabulation of the lords of the realm. It was only in the nineteenth century, with the emergence of a larger middle class and with the democratizing of suffrage, that English political thinkers could think seriously about democratic self-government rather than simply about government that was in some general way responsible and responsive to the people. The contrast between Locke's *Second Treatise* and Mill's *Considerations on Representative Government* is illustrative here.

The idea that self-rule was a central aspiration of democracy appeared earlier in America as a consequence of America's distinctive political sociology and its attendant practices. Tocqueville understood this phenomenon clearly and insisted upon its importance in the opening chapters of *Democracy in America*. Apart from the Native Americans, who were pushed aside rather than incorporated into the colonial regimes, colonial New England was a political *terra rasa* (blank slate). The new order could begin unencumbered by entrenched feudal hierarchies. And both the doctrines and the sociology of the Puritan newcomers were decidedly democratic. As Tocqueville noted, Puritanism "was not merely a religious doctrine, but it corresponded in many points with the most absolute democratic and republican theories." Both in its doctrine of religious authority and in its norms of church governance, reform Protestantism was as a matter of principle distinctly and explicitly antihierarchical. The sociology of the New England colonies reinforced this doctrinal egalitarianism. As Tocqueville observed, "In England the stronghold of Puritanism continued to be in the middle classes; and it was from the middle classes that most of the emigrants came." As a result, "the settlers who established themselves on the shores of New England all belonged to the more independent classes of their native country. Their union on the soil of America presented the singular phenomenon of a society containing neither lords nor common people, and we may almost say, neither rich nor poor." Politically, the consequences of this confluence of democratic doctrine and middle-class egalitarian sociology were quite remarkable. As Tocqueville put it, at a time when democratic principles "were scorned or unknown by the nations of Europe," they "were proclaimed in the deserts of the New World, and . . . were reduced to practice by a community so humble that not a statesman condescended to attend to it. . . . A democracy, more perfect than antiquity had dared to dream of, started in full size and panoply from the midst of an ancient feudal society."[17]

If this pattern of democratic precocity was the product of historical accident, it was also recognized, embraced, and perpetuated as a matter of conscious principle and purpose. In *Albion's Seed*, historian David Hackett Fisher reports an interesting and amusing episode that makes this quite clear. After the Massachusetts Bay Colony had established its viability, it received a missive from several English Puritans of noble standing who were interested in coming to the New World. In contemplating such a

CHAPTER ONE

move, they wrote their New World brethren to assure themselves that their social rank would be recognized on this side of the Atlantic. The Massachusetts authorities replied very diplomatically to the effect that the newcomers would be accorded the respect attending their social status but that no special political rights or privileges would be given them—in keeping with the norms and practices of the colony. The prospective emigrants decided to stay in England.[18]

In the present context, the most important feature of this system, one that was in Tocqueville's phrase "produced offhand," was that it made self-rule not only a principle but a reality. As a matter of both necessity and principle, the emigrants "continually exercised the rights of sovereignty."[19] With no authority above them and no agency beyond them, the colonists as a body of equals chose their own magistrates, established their own institutions, passed their own legislation. Popular sovereignty, not only in the sense of the people as ultimate repository of power but in the sense of the people as the executors of governance, was here not pure aspiration but fact. Moreover, this instantiation of the principle of self-rule, of government "by the people," had a dual dimension: it involved the self-rule of each and the self-rule of all.

For the embodiment of the self-governance of all, one need look no further than to the same New England town meetings Tocqueville had in mind when he spoke of the Puritans exercising their popular sovereignty. "The republic was already established in every township," he wrote, and "the affairs of the community were discussed, as at Athens, in the marketplace, by a general assembly of the citizens."[20] The ability of the New England township to embody the principle of communal self-rule was one basis for Jefferson's vision of dividing his state of Virginia into a multitude of "wards" whose inhabitants could meet and manage their local governance on their own. As he wrote to John Adams, he proposed that the Virginia legislature "divide every county into wards of five or six miles square, like your townships." His proposal "had for a further object," he continued, "to impart to these wards those portions of self-government for which they are best qualified, by confiding to them the care of their poor, their roads, police, elections, the nomination of jurors, administration of justice in small cases, elementary exercises of militia; in short to have made them little republics."[21]

When politics went beyond the local scale of township and ward, the principle of collective self-rule required, as Whitman insisted, universal suffrage. It is "democracy's rule," he wrote, "that men, the nation, as a common aggregate of living identities . . . for a fair chance for growth, and for protection in citizenship, must, to the political extent of the suffrage, or vote, if no further, be placed in each and in the whole, on one broad, primary, universal, common platform."[22]

The self-rule of all, moreover, was not seen as confined to the realm of formal governmental institutions. Instead, as Robert Putnam and other contemporary students of what makes democracy work have been reminding us recently, collective self-governance in democratic societies depends in part upon the creation of voluntary civic associations that grow up around common needs and purposes. The phenomenon of what Tocqueville called these "extemporaneous assemblies" is no mere sociological curiosity. It is an essential mode of self-governance in democratic times. If democratic citizens act entirely on their own as individuals, they are feeble and ineffectual. But if they depend for their collective pursuits solely upon the agencies of a large and powerful government, "their independence would be in great jeopardy."[23] The institutional requisites of democratic self-rule thus include elections with universal suffrage, vital agencies of local self-governance, and a healthy and flourishing panoply of civic associations.

The second dimension of government "by the people" on this account is the self-rule of each: the exercise of autonomy over one's own life project. The capacity for and the exercise of personal self-rule were seen as both a right and a responsibility. The self-rule of each was a right, in the sense of being a necessary component of a full and free human life, for reasons set out by republican liberals such as Adam Smith and liberal republicans such as Algernon Sydney. Without the leave and capacity for personal self-rule, people were ultimately no better than slaves. "Liberty," wrote Sydney, "is to live upon one's own terms; Slavery is to live at the mere mercy of another" and hence liberty "consists in an independency upon the will of another."[24] And Smith writes in a similar vein that "nothing tends so much to corrupt and enervate and debase the mind as dependency, and nothing gives such noble and generous notions of probity as freedom and independency."[25] If personal self-rule was a right whose enjoyment was needful for human freedom, dignity, and self-actualization, it was also a responsibility whose exercise was important to the democratic community and one's fellows. Ralph Waldo Emerson thus both lyricized the life of nonconforming self-reliance to an extent that carried overtones of Nietzschean self-creation and Thoreauvian anarchism and at the same time insisted that this deep form of personal self-rule was essential to the success of the free and democratic society whose mission it was for America to create. The "self-helping man" is "welcome evermore to gods and men"[26] because the activity of the self-reliant provides the energy for social progress and because those who are not "self-sufficing" are a drag upon and a burden to society. Thus, he said, "the face which character wears to me is self-sufficingness." And "the tendencies of the time favor the idea of self-government [by which he means what I am calling here the self-rule of each] and leave the individual . . . to the rewards and penalties of his own constitution, which work with more energy than we believe."[27]

Moreover, as Jefferson recognized and emphasized, the two dimensions of self-rule—the personal self-rule of each and the collective self-rule of all—are causally implicated with each other. Citizens who lack the capacity for personal self-rule or a social setting in which they can actualize it will soon become incapable of collective self-governance. They could be subjects but not members of a competent democratic sovereign people. This recognition lay at the heart of Jefferson's agrarianism. The yeoman farmer, he thought, made the ideal democratic citizen because the circumstances of his life kept him from degenerating into a state of dependency, "which begets subservience and venality."[28] It is a crucial part of the tradition of American progressivism that it praised and hoped to perpetuate the very same agricultural petty bourgeoisie that Vladimir Lenin and Joseph Stalin sought to liquidate and for exactly the same reason: these people possessed the character and wherewithal to be self-reliant and independent, and they could therefore be counted upon to resist servitude and the designs of despotic regimes.

The last component of Lincoln's formula, government "for the people," is the most ambiguous of the three and lends itself to alternative interpretations. It tells us who is to receive the benefits of government, namely, the whole people rather than the members of a ruling class or political aristocracy, but it says nothing about what these benefits are understood to consist of. Presumably, government "for the people" means government devoted to the "general welfare" or to the "public interest," but these commonly deployed terms—as, for example, in the Preamble to the Constitution or in James Madison's invocation of the "public good" and the "permanent and aggregate interests of the community" in *Federalist* #10—are largely indeterminate as to content. The best interpretation of the understanding of the ultimate purposes of a democratic society—what democratic government is for—that seemed to animate the larger aspirations of the more democratic and progressive political thinkers in the nineteenth century, I would argue, is tipped off by Jefferson's reference to the "pursuit of happiness" in the Declaration. From the common formulations of the day, one would have expected Jefferson to have followed his reference to the right to life and liberty with a reference to property rights. He chose instead his somewhat distinctive and, in context, anomalous invocation of a right to pursue happiness for several reasons. First, he sought to demote property from its place of special privilege to subsume it under larger goals. Second, the word *pursuit* is used to acknowledge that neither government nor society has the authority to define or the obligation and capability to deliver whatever it is that will fulfill the life plans of individual citizens and thus produce their contentment. Finally, *happiness* is meant to convey his conviction that the ultimate purpose of democratic government was not limited to the protection of person and property against the depredation of others and to providing the framework for commercial prosperity. Instead, the ultimate purpose was to create a social setting within which all the members of society could live lives that they found meaningful and fulfilling. Jefferson's notion of happiness, I am supposing, owed much to Aristotle, whose *Politics* he kept at one point on his bedside table, and nothing to Jeremy Bentham, whom he could not have read by the year 1776. It meant *eudaemonia*, or what moral philosophers these days tend to render as "flourishing," rather than simple pleasure, utility, or preference satisfaction. It meant what Aristotle characterized as "an activity of soul in accordance with its goodness" or particular excellence.[29] Put differently, it is the full development and satisfying deployment of all the abilities and capacities that define and characterize human beings in both their universality and their particularity. In a word, then, "for the people" embodies, first, a commitment to the principle of development and, second, the insistence that is applicable to all the members of society.

The phrase "for the people" captures the grand democratic hope, again referencing Hegel's account of the deeper telos of historical development, that all can be free—with freedom here meaning what it did in Hegel's philosophical vocabulary: self-realization. It is Whitman, again, who perhaps expresses this high aspiration best. Democracy, he says, is "the grand experiment of development, whose end (perhaps requiring several generations) may be the forming of a full-grown man or woman—that *is* something." The "ulterior object of political and all other government" is, therefore, "not merely to rule, to repress disorder, etc., but to develop, to open up to cultivation, to encourage the possibilities of all manly outcroppage, and of that aspiration for independence, and the pride and respect latent in all characters."[30] The ultimate end of democracy is, according to this hopeful anticipation at the heart of America's progressivism, the creation of something unprecedented in history, something so novel that its very characterization sounds like an oxymoron: what Benjamin Barber (who quite fittingly in this context occupied the Walt Whitman Chair in Political Science at Rutgers when he wrote the phrase) has called "an aristocracy of everyone." If an aristocracy comprises a subset of a political society who live a freer and happier (in Aristotle's sense) existence than the rest on account of their social position and privilege, then obviously by definition not everyone could be an aristocrat. But if the essence of being an aristocrat is absolute rather than relative, if the substantive meaning of that status is being properly situated and equipped to live as "a separate and complete subject for freedom," as Whitman put it, then it is entirely conceivable even if unprecedentedly ambitious to imagine that someday we could fashion our society in a manner that would allow every one of us to be an "aristocrat." In what I'm calling my/traditional American liberalism, the phrase "government for the people" is meant to convey precisely this outrageous ambition.

Each of the three elements of Lincoln's phrase, "of, by, and for the people," captures something different and distinctive in the vision of America's progressivism, but they are also interrelated both conceptually and empirically, so that the omission of any one of them would alter and weaken the others. Of specific significance in this regard, the middle term serves to validate the first and to supply an important impetus to the latter. "By" validates "of" in the following way. At the outset of liberalism, liberal theorists sought to establish the content of democratic consent hypothetically. In the absence of anything resembling a genuine public sphere, or a genuine "tribunal" (Condorcet's term) of public opinion, or a genuinely sovereign democratic electorate, it was necessary by default to conjure the substance of consent by a feat of imagination. Thus the state-of-nature thought experiments of

CHAPTER ONE

Locke, Thomas Hobbes, and Rousseau: a way to find by hypothetical inference what it was that a free, equal, and rational people would in fact agree to. With the development of media of political communication, the spread of education, and the extension of the franchise through the eighteenth and nineteenth centuries, the incomplete and imperfect but nonetheless very real and important institutionalization of a democratic public proceeded apace. At some point in this process, then, it becomes increasingly unnecessary and even improper to ascertain the norm of consent by imaginative construction and more and more possible and proper to ascertain it empirically.[31] What people consented to would be embodied in and ascertained by attending to and respecting what they actually did: how they acted in their representative assemblies, how they voted, and how they responded to public opinion surveys. The government of the people is seen in and validated through governance by the people.

Government "by the people" is also tied both conceptually and empirically to government "for the people." If government for the people means a form of governance that will conduce to the fullest development of the capacities of all its members, then it must entail practices of democratic self-rule. Among the highest and most definitive capacities of those who lead a distinctively human life are the capacities for deliberation, judgment, and rational action. These capacities are preeminently manifested in the process of forming and carrying out a "plan of life" because human beings qua human beings can fully develop into Whitman's "separate and complete subjects for freedom" only when they are self-governing. If others determine for us and enforce upon us what our life goals and activities are to be, we become less than fully developed human beings—becoming instead creatures who (to borrow here from Mill's rhetoric about "automatons" and "ape-like imitation" in chapter 3 of *On Liberty*) resemble machines or animals more than men and women. The several parts of Lincoln's famous phrase—the "of," "by," and "for"—are thus not an itemization of separate particulars but instead serve to designate the interrelated core features of a single coherent and ambitious normative conception of democratic society and its purposes.

This "populist" political idealism that resides at the heart of traditional American progressivism manifests and presupposes a crucial empirical assumption about the extent and distribution of human talent and intelligence. It requires a faith in the dignity, the competence, and the potential of the "common man"—the average member of a democratic society. The words *empirical* and *faith* are both important here, for this logically essential belief that average human beings have what it takes to become and act as "separate and complete subjects of freedom" was based in part upon existing evidence and in part upon a hopeful anticipation of future possibilities.

This faith had to be affirmed in the face of and in contradiction to what had arguably been the conventional wisdom among both political leaders and political theorists for centuries: to wit, the conviction that the average run of humankind were fit only to function socially as "subjects" in the political sense of "my loyal subjects" rather than as "subjects for freedom" in Hegel's and Whitman's sense. The little people, the common folk, the lower orders, the hoi polloi, the mob were destined to be ruled—fodder for dynastic ambition, sheep to be sheared and guided. The progressivism of Jefferson, Lincoln, Whitman, and others who shared their democratic idealism depended for its plausibility upon denying that the demos were and could only amount to the creatures of appetite memorably depicted by Plato. It required denying that people needed rulers like frogs needed storks, as Luther claimed. It required rejecting Niccolò Machiavelli's intimations that the common throng were basically credulous and venal loose cannon on the ship of state who needed to be forcefully tied down by successful princes. It meant rejecting Burke's sneer about the unnaturalness and abnormality of expecting those of "servile employment" to be able to play a part in their own governance. It meant opposition to the assumption of the Hamiltonians and old Federalists that the political hierarchy would continue to track the

CHAPTER ONE

traditional social hierarchy and that the lower orders would remain politically subservient to their betters. It meant instead sharing the insistence of the anti-Federalist Melancton Smith that in a democracy, it was crucial for the "respectable yeomanry" to have a place at the table where decisions were being made.

In his debate with Hamilton at the New York ratifying convention in 1788, Smith spoke eloquently about the competence and reliability of "the common people" and about the dangerous presumptions of the great. "Those in middling circumstance," he said,

> are inclined by habit and the company with whom they associate to set bounds to their passions and appetites—if this is not sufficient, the want of means to gratify them will be a restraint—they are obliged to employ their time in their respective callings—hence the substantial yeomanry of the country are more temperate, of better morals and less ambition than the great. The latter do not feel for the poor and middling class; the reasons are obvious—they are not obliged to use the pains and labor to procure property as the other. They feel not the inconveniences arising from the payment of small sums. The great consider themselves above the common people—entitled to more respect—do not associate with them—they fancy themselves to have a right of pre-eminence in every thing. In short, they possess the same feeling, and are under the influence of the same motives, as an hereditary nobility.

Hence, he argued, "it has been the principal care of free governments to guard against the encroachments of the great," and it should be so here. The great should by no means be excluded from power, but the legislative body should include "a sufficient number of the middling class to control them. . . . A representative body composed principally of respectable yeomanry is the best possible security to liberty."[32]

In the context of the somewhat novel political sociology of the new nation, there was some empirical evidence that the common folk were capable of rising to the challenges of self-governance. The success of township governance in New England in the absence of any effectual supervision from above was certainly relevant in this regard. As Tocqueville wrote, in these townships, "power has been disseminated with admirable skill," and the results were good. In these townships, "the people were always sovereign" and "the government really emanates from those it governs." The result was not only that "the conduct of local business is easy" but also that "the political education of the people has long been complete."[33] In like manner, the highly important area of church government also was conducted very democratically, especially within the dominant Protestant sects. "Congregationalism" was not simply a denomination but a form of governance that seemed competent and efficacious in practice. The spirit of democratic self-governance is strikingly evident, for example, in the Congregationalist minister John Wise's 1717 work, *A Vindication of the Governance of New England Churches*, which argues that "an aristocracy is a dangerous constitution in the Church of Christ" and that "if there be any of the regular government settled in the Church of God it must needs be a democracy."[34]

For Walt Whitman, the empirical evidence of the competence and even nobility of America's commoners came from his experiences in the military hospitals of the Civil War. He saw there, he said, "august spectacles of fortitude and dedication and resolution." Seeing how "the gist of this fiercest and most resolute of the world's war-like contentions resided exclusively in the unnamed, unknown rank and file, and how the brunt of its labor of death was, to all essential purposes, volunteered," provided for him the "last needed proof of democracy." These events and the remarkable response to them by the ordinary run of the American people gave evidence that "the popular democracy, whatever its faults and dangers, practically justifies itself beyond the proudest claims and wildest hope of its enthusiasts."[35]

The evidence was mixed, however. As Whitman acknowledged, "I myself see clearly enough the crude, defective streaks in all the strata of the common people; the specimens and vast collections of the ignorant, the credulous, the unfit and uncouth, the incapable, and the very low and poor." The doubt that it is possible to "expect to elevate and improve a nation's politics by absorbing such morbid collections and qualities therein," he conceded, "is a formidable one."[36] The political convictions and aspirations of democratic progressivism therefore had to acknowledge that the sovereign demos was in some respect very much a work in progress and had to incorporate a faith in the continued improvement of the people. What Mill called "utility in the largest sense," namely, the "mental and moral improvement of the people," was not only the ultimate purpose of democratic society but also the necessary condition of its survival and prosperity. Democracy may have had its roots firmly established by this time, Whitman believed, but it was "at present in its embryo condition," and its "fruition . . . resides altogether in the future."[37]

To speak of "the people" is language at its most unspecific. It is important to understand, therefore, that the people in whom Jefferson and Whitman placed their faith were not an undifferentiated mob. Indeed, Jefferson was quite convinced that if American sociodynamics were to end up producing a kind of illiterate and anarchic lumpen proletariat like the one he was dismayed to find in Paris during his time as an American envoy, the democratic experiment in this country would not have a felicitous outcome. And Whitman took a similar view. "Ungracious as it may sound, and a paradox after what we have been saying, democracy looks with suspicious, ill-satisfied eye upon the very poor, the ignorant, and those out of business. She asks for men and women with occupations, well-off, owners of houses and acres, and with cash in the bank—and with some cravings for literature, too; and must have them, and hastens to make them."[38] "The people" are, to invoke Melancton Smith's term once more, the *respectable* yeomanry. To put it in sociological terms, America's democratic progressivism placed its bets upon the emergent petty bourgeoisie: the class of small, independent farmers, artisans, and merchants who were the most numerous stratum of nineteenth-century society, who worked hard, supported themselves and their families, obeyed the law, had material and even cultural aspirations, and saw themselves as having some stake in the social order. Often disdained today by the wealthy for their Ritz cracker tastes, disparaged by the intelligentsia for their seeking of creature comforts and their reading of *Reader's Digest,* and reviled by utopian revolutionaries for their moral traditionalism and their recalcitrant resistance to collectivist central authority, these are the people upon whose unleashed energy and future potential traditional American liberalism pinned its fondest hopes.

This idealistic and populist brand of democratic progressivism not only incorporated the acceptance and endorsement of the central liberal norms of liberty, equality, participation, and deliberation but also carried implications for the interpretation of these ambiguous and multivalent political norms.

Liberty within this framework encompassed both what Benjamin Constant famously distinguished as the liberty of the ancients and the liberty of the moderns. The liberty of the ancients corresponded to the principle of the self-rule of all, the democratic principle that "here the people rule." The liberty of the moderns, which referred to the right of individual members of society to some area of sanctuary against the intrusion of collective governance upon their personal pursuits, corresponded to the self-rule of each. These are different, but they were both deemed important. If there were tensions between them—manifested in contestations over the proper line between public and private—they were by no means seen as incompatible.

The liberty enshrined in this brand of democratic liberalism, it should also be observed, was not what philosophers call a "maximizing goal." It was not the simple "absence of impediment" in Hobbes's definition. And it was not the "absence of laws" as in Sir Robert Filmer's conception. As self-rule, this was liberty as autonomous and hence not without law or opposed to law. This was James Harrington's liberty by the laws or Katharine Lee Bates's ("America the Beautiful") "liberty in law."[39] As Whitman insisted, democratic liberty had to incorporate both law and conscience, which it perfected rather than negated. "Many suppose," he wrote, ". . . that [democracy] means a throwing aside of law, and running riot." But the truth is that "democracy too is law, and of the strictest, amplest kind." Individual freedom does not escape from but rather occurs within the constraints of "Conscience, the primary moral element. If I were to specify in what quarter lie the grounds of darkest dread, respecting America of our hopes, I should have to point to this particular. I should demand the invariable application, this day and any day, of that old, ever-true plumb-rule of persons, eras, nations."[40]

The heart of the democratic equality championed by this populist progressivism was a steadfast resistance to any political aristocracy of the feudal sort. Its essence was antielitism, antipaternalism, and antidomination. This understanding of the content and the point of social equality within traditional American liberalism accords with Jefferson's explication of the meaning of his famous phrase about everyone being "created equal." It coheres with the devotion of the civic republican tradition to what Philip Pettit calls "structural egalitarianism."[41] And it arguably coheres with Michael Walzer's conception of "complex equality."[42] The commitment to equality here does not mean subscribing to the delusion that all have equal talent. And it does not expect or demand that everyone shall wind up possessed of the same level of economic resources. It means instead that political society must be organized in such a manner that the various ways in which people begin or wind up unequal are not convertible into a capacity for political dominance. The opposite of democratic equality is what Madison once called the very definition of tyranny—the concentration of powers, all sources of unequal standing, into the same hands. This progressivism hoped for what Mickey Kaus calls "civic equality": where citizens stand on the same footing in the public sphere and in public spaces and where, as George Orwell said admiringly of revolutionary Barcelona, no one had to bow and scrape before any others.[43]

Institutionalized political elites customarily had based their dominance upon birth, wealth, and/or knowledge. With the absence of feudal ranks and stations in America, unequal birth was much less a concern here than in the Old World. The worry about unequal wealth and its convertibility into political domination was more of a threat. Indeed, the concern Tocqueville expressed about what he called a "manufacturing aristocracy" became, in the latter nineteenth century, a proper and overriding preoccupation of America's populist progressivism. Worries about a politically self-aggrandizing aristocracy of knowledge were much less intense. The natural homes of such an aristocracy of knowledge—especially where no titled landed aristocracy could pretend to be a legitimately privileged repository of wisdom and virtue—are an established church and a powerful "scientific estate."[44] But the American church was not established and was in any case too pluralistic and libertarian in its structure to be much of a threat in this context, and a powerful educational or scientific establishment was barely on the horizon. When Whitman complained about elites of the intelligentsia, it was more on account of what he perceived as their irrelevance, their effeteness, and their fetishistic absorption in European culture—not in any great worries about their political menace.[45] The same principle applied, however, in opposition to any claims of the clever or the learned to political authority on that account. That denial of political dominance based upon a putatively superior intellect, for example, provided the basis for Lincoln's pointed reductio ad absurdum in the context of justifications offered for slavery: "You mean the whites are *intellectually* the superiors of the blacks, and, therefore have the right to enslave them? Take care again. By this rule, you are to be slave to the first man you meet with an intellect superior to your own."[46]

CHAPTER ONE

Egalitarian both in moral temperament and in their political aspirations, American progressives from Jefferson through the New Deal nonetheless recognized the naturalness and the moral propriety of some inequalities of wealth and knowledge. Some people are brighter than others. Some are more commercially adept. And some work hard while others seek leisure and rest at every opportunity. There was such a thing, as Jefferson famously averred, as a "natural aristocracy." The proper concern of a progressive politics was not to try to delegitimize, much less abolish, such inequality—an attempt that would be futile and destructive.[47] The point instead was to devise institutions and policies that would base membership in this natural aristocracy upon merit, would constrain the extent of economic disparities resulting from it, and would direct the exertions of this aristocracy to the promotion of the public interest. That is why Jefferson was so proud of his role in ending primogeniture and modifying the law of entail by introducing laws of partible inheritance. And that was why he was also so intent upon creating a system of public education open to all. Through these policies, neither vast wealth nor access to learning would be determined by inheritance. His natural aristocracy would depend on talent rather than birth and would constitute itself anew with every generation.

As for the third element in the Enlightenment liberal trilogy, namely, fraternity, America's populist progressives, for the most part, did not have a great deal to say. But it nonetheless makes an appearance on their radar screen, and that appearance is worth noting for two reasons: first, to acknowledge that this goal did play at least some role in the democratic vision of traditional American liberalism, and second, to establish the baseline for comparison with the construction of this goal in contemporary liberalism.

As Carey McWilliams observed in his comprehensive study entitled *The Idea of Fraternity in America*, "Political thinkers in America have spoken of liberty and equality, decentralization and bureaucracy, law and violence, but they have rarely spoken of fraternity." And in this respect, they could be said to have mirrored more than deviated from the pattern in France, where the ideal of fraternity was indelibly enshrined in the lexicon of revolutionary politics. McWilliams notes: "Kingsley Martin's *French Liberal Thought in the Eighteenth Century* refers to fraternity in its first chapter, as any work dealing with the creed of 1789 must. The terms discussed throughout the book, however, are liberty and equality, not fraternity—and in this respect Martin is typical."[48] In France, fraternity was perhaps anticipated as a corollary side benefit derived from the breaking up of political ranks and separate estates. There is logic to sustain that assumption: as Aristotle argued in his analysis of the dynamics of friendship in his *Ethics*, "When a great gulf is fixed, as between God and man, there can be no friendship."[49] But if greater equality might conduce to friendship among those previously separated by the great gulf between different political estates, equality is only a contributory and not a sufficient cause of friendship. How the political and social leveling of the ancien régime would actually result not simply in the equal status of *citoyen* (citizen) but also in the relations of trust and affection and mutual support of friendship was not clearly articulated.

In America, even where it was discussed in its application to the political realm, the ideal of fraternity was largely grounded in and mediated by religious aspirations to "human brotherhood." That is evident, for example, in the very early exhortations of John Winthrop to his fellow Puritans: "We must be knit together in this work as one man, we must entertain each other in brotherly affection, . . . we must delight in each other, make others' conditions our own, rejoice together, mourn together, labor and suffer together, always having before our eyes our commission and community in the work, our community as members of the same body."[50] And it is similarly evident in the much more recent invocations of the ideal of "the beloved community" by Martin Luther King Jr.

Religious conceptions of human brotherhood, however, tend to move from the local—family and church—to the universal— "one great fellowship of man across the whole wide Earth," as one hymn puts it. National fraternity is left in a somewhat tenuous middle ground. And perhaps that structure accurately reflects the empirical psychodynamics of friendship. We can be friends with those we deal with face-to-face, and we can at least imagine and aspire to having *eunoia*—a settled disposition of sympathetic beneficence—to all our species. As for our compatriots, we may be friends *per accidens* or instrumentally, as in Benjamin Franklin's wry observance that we must hang together if we don't wish to hang separately. How our common national citizenship can produce ties of trust, affection, and benevolence, however, is more problematic.

Nonetheless, the aspiration for fraternity or civic friendship as a political goal is clearly visible within the tradition of American progressivism. Both Jefferson and Lincoln voiced it in presidential inaugural addresses—not coincidentally in the wake of an acrimonious campaign, on the one hand, and a fratricidal conflict, on the other. Jefferson's admonition in his first inaugural address was: "Let us, then, fellow citizens, unite with one heart and one mind. Let us restore to social intercourse that harmony and affection without which liberty and even life itself are but dreary things."[51] And Lincoln not only penned the memorable determination in his second inaugural address to act "with malice toward none; with charity for all" but wrote in his last letter, published posthumously, that his purpose was "to restore the Union, so as to make it, to use your language, a Union of hearts and hands as well as of States."[52]

In line with his neo-Hegelian historical optimism, the Jacksonian historian laureate George Bancroft looked forward to a future of unfolding and expanding freedom: "As a consequence of the tendency of the race towards unity and universality, the organization of society must more and more conform to the principle of FREEDOM." The specific content of this condition of freedom, however, presaged by the trope of "unity," was depicted by Bancroft as including fraternal affection and care:

> The love for others and for the race is as much a part of human nature as the love of self. . . . The good time is coming, when humanity will recognize all members of its family as alike entitled to care; when the heartless jargon of overproduction in the midst of want will end in a better science of distribution; when man will dwell with man as with his brother; when political institutions will rest on the basis of equality and freedom.[53]

Whitman likewise envisioned the ultimate capstone of the cosmic sweep toward democratization to be a kind of universal fraternity of free democratic spirits:

> Topping democracy, this most alluring record, that it alone can bind, and ever seeks to bind, all nations, all men, of however various and distant lands, into a brotherhood, a family. It is the old, yet ever-modern dream of earth. . . . Not that half only, individualism, which isolates. There is another half, which is adhesiveness of love, that fuses, ties, and aggregates, making the races comrades, and fraternizing all.[54]

And Whitman also offered a vision of township-scale political community, "say in some pleasant western settlement or town," where people "blossom" in their individual development as they cooperate for their common good and run their own affairs—a vision that seems to combine Pericles' idealization of Athens and Rousseau's idealization of Geneva with American representations of the virtues of small-town life.

Carey McWilliams takes a somewhat jaundiced view of Whitman's invocations of fraternity, seeing them as abstract and narcissistic.[55] There is something to be said for this negative assessment, for Whitman's Hegelian pantheism led him toward subsuming concrete persons into an abstract cosmic "personhood," and his celebration of spirit often seemed partly an infatuation with his

CHAPTER ONE

own thoughts, sentiments, and libido. But this is ultimately an unduly negative reading that distracts us from what arguably seems a genuine appreciation of the importance of bonds of civic friendship in a well-ordered society. When he gets beyond singing about himself, Whitman offers a conception of democratic fraternity that embodies some of the logic of the "democratic peace" in contemporary social science and that incorporates both traditional religious visions of community and the Enlightenment anthropological claim of John Stuart Mill that there is in humankind a "desire to be in unity with our fellow creatures, which is already a powerful principle in human nature, and happily one of those which tend to become stronger, even without express inculcation, from the influences of advancing civilization."[56] This may well be a romantic and unwarrantedly optimistic view of human inclinations and their historical trajectory. But it still is somewhat unfair and misleading to reduce all of these expressions of social idealism to shallow notions of gemütlichkeit. American progressives at their most hopeful shared the sense of France's liberal visionaries that the freedom and equality of democratic self-rule would create a social setting for increasing concord and *philia* (friendship) among democratic citizens.

Traditional American liberalism also incorporated some of the insights and logic of participatory and deliberative conceptions of democracy, which have found recent expositors and defenders.

It is probably fair to say that Americans practiced participatory democracy before it had a name and before Mill famously articulated its virtues as central to the justification of representative government. The colonists participated in running their public affairs out of necessity and perhaps as a part of the dominant culture of middle-class dissenting Protestantism. The British expatriates who dominated colonial America came from a society with a relatively advanced and institutionalized civic culture, but they did not have agencies of formal government to re-create that kind of civil society here. They therefore had to accomplish that task "spontaneously" in Friedrich von Hayek's sense, developing these organizations from the ground up. One paradigmatic example of this process were the various social and charitable societies that Benjamin Franklin helped initiate in Philadelphia. Americans had to create what Burke styled as the "little platoons" of political society on their own recognizance, and they did so in profusion. In addition, many of the tasks of formal political governance were carried out in a relatively participatory mode. In a politically decentralized and predominantly agricultural society of small towns, most of the everyday work and decisionmaking of governance went on in the town meetings and town councils scattered around the countryside. The jury system was also very important in this regard. Here, ordinary citizens chosen by lot performed important tasks of governance. The jury, Tocqueville wrote, "is the most energetic means of making the people rule." And reflecting upon what he regarded as the beneficent consequences of jury duty upon the public, Tocqueville characterized jury service as functioning in the same manner that Mill argued electoral participation and voting did. Indeed, the parallel is so close that Mill's famous account of the "ideally best polity" as "one in which the whole people participate" derives from his appreciation of Tocqueville's praise of the political virtues of the jury system. Just as Tocqueville praised the jury system as "a gratuitous public school" in the art of governance and as a mechanism of "obliging men to turn their attention to other affairs than their own," thereby "rubbing off that private selfishness which is the rust of society," Mill calls participation in public functions a "school of public spirit." He also says that it provides moral instruction for good citizenship by calling one so involved "to weigh interests not his own; to be guided, in case of conflicting claims, by another rule than his private partialities; to apply, at every turn, principles and maxims which have for their reason of existence the public good."[57]

Especially struck by the contrast with the politically and administratively centralized French state that induced French citizens to look to Paris for solving their social problems, Tocqueville wrote that in America, the spirit of participatory self-governance

CHAPTER ONE

"pervades every act of social life. If a stoppage occurs in a thoroughfare, and the circulation of vehicles is hindered, the neighbors immediately form themselves into a deliberative body; and this extemporaneous assembly gives rise to an executive power, which remedies the inconvenience before anybody has thought of recurring to a pre-existing authority superior to that of the persons immediately concerned." This habituation to self-reliance, self-governance, and spontaneous organization produces a society in which associations are formed for "public pleasure," "to resist evils which are exclusively of a moral nature," and "to promote the public safety, commerce, industry, morality, and religion."[58] In short, Jacksonian Americans did not so much produce the theory of participatory democracy as they produced the practices that led to some of the classic theoretical arguments on behalf of participatory democracy. It seems perfectly appropriate, therefore, to consider the logic and the values animating participatory democrats as de facto constituting one of the components of traditional American liberalism.

In like fashion, although nineteenth- and early twentieth-century democratic republicans, populists, and Progressives had not read Jürgen Habermas and did not have "deliberative democracy" as part of their lexicon, their rhetoric and aspirations often incorporated the tropes and aspirations found among contemporary deliberative democrats. American's populist liberalism was not a simple majoritarianism, and it did not celebrate or romanticize unreflective public will. Note, for example, that in Tocqueville's account of the propensity of the Americans to form spontaneous associations, he said that in so doing, "the neighbors immediately form themselves into a *deliberative* body." These little platoons were not political mobs but instrumentalities of communal practical reason. The exemplary formal political institutions of self-governance—the legislatures, the town meetings, and the juries—were also deliberative bodies. And underlying and sustaining these formal modalities of deliberative decisionmaking was a "public sphere" in the Habermasian sense that once again struck Tocqueville as quite remarkable. "The political activity which pervades the United States must be seen in order to be understood," he wrote.

> The great political agitation of American legislative bodies, which is the only one that attracts the attention of foreigners, is a mere episode, or a sort of continuation, of that universal movement which originates in the lowest classes of the people, and extends successively to all the ranks of society. . . . The cares of politics engross a prominent place in the occupations of a citizen in the United States; and almost the only pleasure which an American knows is to take a part in the government and to discuss its measures.

In the spirit of the sardonic remark that the problem with socialism was that it required "too many evenings," Tocqueville drolly concluded in the face of this Jacksonian spectacle that "it is impossible to spend more effort in the pursuit of happiness."[59]

It is also instructive in this context to note that the historian George Bancroft, perhaps the greatest and most archetypal defender of Jacksonian democracy, never claimed that the public will per se was the source of political legitimacy. What justifies the democratic faith in the ultimate authority of the people and what allows "true political science" to "venerate the masses," he writes, is a belief in the capacities of "the common judgment" of "the human mind in masses." Again and again, Bancroft cites not the public will but the "common mind" as the crucial force and legitimating element in popular government. It is the common mind that is "the true material for a commonwealth." The spirit of God "breathes through the combined intelligence of the people." Democracy relies upon "the sagacity of the people," based upon the assumption that "the people collectively are wiser than the most gifted individual." The ultimate authority in a democracy should be "enlightened collective reason." It is always popular reason, mind, intelligence, sagacity, and conscience that he favorably invokes, not unreflective popular will.[60]

CHAPTER ONE

For Bancroft as for Mill, then, the ultimate criterion of political success is the progressive enhancement of the intellectual and moral powers of the people. It is not, as David Hume would have it, peace and security. Nor is it, as many believe, the power and prosperity of the country. Instead, "the exact measure of the progress of civilization is the degree in which the intelligence of the common mind has prevailed over wealth and brute force; in other words, the measure of the progress of civilization is the progress of the people." The foremost political imperative is thus "universal education": "Intelligence must be diffused among the whole people."[61] If democracy is to be government by the people, they must have the requisite intellectual and moral powers to exercise their collective sovereignty effectively and responsibly. If democracy is to be government for the people, its measure must be set by what I have called the principle of development—namely, the growth and flourishing of all the members of society as free and self-governing moral persons. It is no accident, then, that from Jefferson's fixation upon a system of public education open to all talents to Bancroft to Horace Mann to John Dewey, the most important social institutions for American progressivism have been universal education and a vibrant public sphere. Governments can provide protection and markets can provide prosperity, but neither separately nor together can they create a democratic society.

It is probably fair to say that, by any reasonably demanding standard, America produced no political theorist of the first rank between James Madison and John Dewey. That leaves no one to serve as a paradigmatic expositor and interpreter of the ideals and aspirations of American political progressivism in the nineteenth century. Jefferson and Lincoln were lawyers and politicians, Walt Whitman a journalist and poet, George Bancroft a historian, Emerson an essayist and a man of letters. Seeking to produce a rough-and-ready template of traditional American liberalism, therefore, turns into a hazardous and eminently contestable hermeneutic exercise. We have to sift through the somewhat fragmentary pronouncements of the relevant thinkers to identify what seem to be the most enduring themes and then by seeing what pattern these themes assume when brought together.

My reading of these fragments and their dominant themes has led me to an endorsement of Whitman's view that Lincoln's invocation of government of, by, and for the people "includes both the totality and all minutiae of the lesson." That claim may be overstated by design for rhetorical effect, but it correctly insists upon the kind of populist perfectionism at the core of the traditional American liberal account of the meaning and purposes of a democratic society. It insists that the democratic aspirations of this political sensibility are not exhausted by the principle of consent but instead go on to incorporate the principle of self-rule and the principle of development. Embracing Lincoln's formula entails a determination to create a society wherein it can truly be said both that "here the people rule" and that here "all are free" in Hegel's ambitious meaning of that phrase.

The lineage of this populist progressivism is liberal, civic republican, and Protestant. It draws upon the Lockean account of political legitimacy and the rule of law. It incorporates republican norms of civic equality and civic virtue. And it secularizes the Protestant notion of the priesthood of all believers into the political dream of an aristocracy of all citizens. In its sum and substance, this adds up to a conception of democratic purposes that can be seen as an emphatically populist rendering of John Stuart Mill's classical theory of democracy.

That claim may seem surprising, even a bit perverse, to many readers. When looked at from the vantage point of today and within the context of today's ideological landscape, Mill tends to appear in one of two guises, neither of which would seem to associate him with the ideals and aspirations of American progressivism. On the one hand, there is Mill the libertarian individualist whose political perspective centers on the harm principle. In this form, he may appeal to civil libertarians of various stripes while becoming subject to criticism by scholars of conservative disposition as simplistic and insufficiently attuned to the moral culture of a good society.[62] On the other hand, he is seen by many contemporary liberals as an "aristocratic liberal," someone who feared democracy and sought to constrain it by various stratagems such as literacy tests, multiple votes for the educated, and the exclusion of welfare recipients from the franchise. Neither of these images of Mill seems to comport well with seeing him as someone whose political vision bore much in common with the democratic enthusiasm of people such as Jefferson, Bancroft, and Whitman. Perhaps, however, that is because neither of these retrospective characterizations of Mill adequately captures his full hopes for representative government. In any case, neither of these accounts does much to explain the noteworthy empirical fact that serves as exhibit A in support of the claim that America's traditional liberalism shares much in common with Mill's account of democratic purposes. That fact is Whitman's acknowledgment in the opening paragraph of "Democratic Vistas" that his vision of the American future was inspired by his reflections upon "John Stuart Mill's profound essay on liberty."[63]

Whitman's opening acknowledgment of his fundamental indebtedness to *On Liberty* may well seem unexpected. (I have on occasion asked a number of political theory students and faculty to name the classic text that Whitman invokes at the outset of "Democratic Vistas." So far, I have gotten no right answers and many expressions of surprise.) To understand what Whitman sees as inspirational in Mill and why he sees it as closely tied to the Lincolnian formula of government of, by, and for the people, however, it is helpful to attend to Whitman's allusions in this context. He doesn't invoke the harm principle, much less Mill's specific institutional suggestions. Instead, he speaks of "the democratic republican principle," "the theory of development and perfection," and "full play for human nature to expand itself in numberless and even conflicting directions."[64] What Whitman remembers better than some contemporary commentators is that Mill's essay—and indeed his whole theory of government—has to be understood in light of the words Mill takes from Wilhelm von Humboldt and places at the beginning of *On Liberty*: "The grand, leading principle, towards which every argument unfolded in these pages directly converges, is the absolute and essential importance of human development in its richest diversity." Just as Bancroft's Jacksonian populism leads him to argue that "the measure of the progress of civilization is the progress of the people," understood as the development of "the intellectual and moral powers," so Mill says that the "principal element" of good government is "the improvement of the people themselves," where improvement means "to promote the virtue and intelligence" of the people.[65]

Mill's argument on behalf of participatory representative government, moreover, provides the rationale for government "by the people" and ties it to the principle of development. Mill begins his defense of representative government by arguing that a despotic or paternalist regime, be it ever so benign and competent, could never be the best form of government because it would turn its subjects into passive recipients of its benefits—thereby undermining the full development and exercise of their human potential. Because "the mental and moral, like the muscular, powers are improved only by being used," the principle of development entails the principle of self-rule. That is why, in Whitman's words, the "mission of government is to train communities to rule themselves." That is why, in Mill's account, "there is no difficulty in showing that the ideally best form of government" is one in which "every citizen" has "not only . . . a voice in the exercise of that ultimate sovereignty" of the people but is also "at least occasionally called on to take an actual part in the government, by the personal discharge of some public function."[66]

These are the perceptions and aspirations that lie at the heart of Jeffersonian-Jacksonian-Linconian-populist politics. The American experiment was seen by Lincoln as "the last best hope of mankind" because it was the crucial historical experiment in popular self-government. Elites of one description or another had always ruled before, with everyone else serving as what Hegel termed "objects of history": means rather than ends, merely the raw material for historical events and political decisions to which their own ends and purposes were essentially irrelevant. The central goal of traditional American liberalism was that here, the people would instead rule in the service of their own freedom, their own flourishing. Here, the "common man," the "respectable yeomanry," was to be elevated to sovereignty and to dignity. This is by any account a radical and ambitious political faith—enough so that not only ideological conservatives but "realistic" social scientists can educe logic and evidence to deprecate it as a species of sheer utopianism. Perhaps it is this lack of supposed realism that has led contemporary liberalism to substitute for it a doctrine more demanding and egalitarian in its substantive distributive norms but less egalitarian and populist in its procedural norms.

2   The New Face of American Liberalism

Fast-forward now to the last several decades of the twentieth century. What is the current face of American liberalism? From the standpoint of political philosophy and social theory, how much does today's liberalism resemble the traditional liberalism canvassed in the previous chapter? Where there are changes, do these represent mainly changes that can be understood as tactical adaptations to new social and economic circumstances while the fundamental principles and goals remain essentially constant? Or do some of the fundamental principles and goals seem themselves to have changed? Certainly, no one could expect American liberalism to look the same in a technologically advanced and predominantly urban nation of some 300 million people as in a smaller and largely agrarian country. But has the basic creed remained intact, the basic aspirations the same? Or has the dominant orientation of those who consider themselves liberals morphed into a distinctive and historically somewhat novel conception of political purposes?

 The burden of this chapter will be to argue that contemporary American liberalism has departed from its forebears in ways that are neither purely tactical nor superficial. From the standpoint of political theory, today's liberalism exhibits notable changes in its core moral intuitions, in its philosophical anthropology, and in its normative sociology—changes that in turn carry important implications for its political goals, strategies, and alliances. In this chapter, I want to specify what some of these changes have been. In the next chapter, I explore some of the intellectual developments, sociological changes, and historical events that have helped shape these changes. And in the final two chapters, I offer an assessment of the moral and political costs and benefits of these changes, followed by an argument about how a twenty-first-century liberalism might remedy some of the weaknesses and fend off some of the pitfalls of today's liberalism—in part by recalling and reclaiming its intellectual heritage.

Just as in the case of "traditional liberalism," the hermeneutic challenge of discerning or constructing an ideal typical model of contemporary liberalism is a daunting one. Any such model is an open invitation to legitimate controversy. The American mainstream left, in the sense of the more democratic and antioligarchic side of the major partisan and ideological divide operative in today's political disputes, comprises not only a multiplicity of sometimes cooperative and other times combative groups and interests but also a range of political and moral persuasions. Contemporary American liberalism is not a univocal cadre but a family alliance—sometimes a contentious one. Will Rogers once said in wry acknowledgment of this lack of unanimity, "I belong to no organized political party. I'm a Democrat." Pari passu, there is on the American left no single catechism for analysts or critics to invoke.

There are, nonetheless, useful guideposts to which one can repair for illumination in this matter. Just as we can look to figures such as Jefferson, Whitman, Bancroft, and Lincoln to gain some purchase on the core convictions that animated the progressive politics of the nineteenth century, so we can look at contemporary theorists of comparable stature who have sought to articulate and defend the moral intuitions and social aspirations that animate American liberalism today. Given the institutionalization of intellectual life that has occurred over the course of American history, these figures of comparable intellectual stature now reside principally, though not exclusively, in the academy. Legally trained people who, like Jefferson and Lincoln, themselves both lawyers, are oriented toward larger issues of philosophy and politics are, for example, likely to be professors of law and jurisprudence, such as Ronald Dworkin, Bruce Ackerman, and Cass Sunstein.

My ideal type model of the animating beliefs of contemporary American liberalism, therefore, is derived principally from the writings of academic liberal theorists. Foremost among these theorists has to be the extraordinarily influential John Rawls. For Rawls has clearly functioned as the high priest or the court theologian of what some have referred to—in analogy with the "high medievalism" of a previous era—as today's "high liberalism."[1] "High liberals" believe that a broadly Rawlsian account of social justice provides "the most appropriate moral basis for a democratic society."[2] Rawls and his many followers argue, moreover, that this normative account of democratic ideals captures the moral intuitions at the heart of today's liberal democratic practices and institutions. As Rawls himself describes his enterprise, "It tries to draw solely upon basic intuitive ideas that are embedded in the political institutions of a constitutional democratic regime and the public traditions of their interpretations"; further, "it provides a reasonable way of shaping into one coherent view the deeper bases of agreement embedded in the public political culture of a constitutional regime and acceptable to its most firmly held considered convictions."[3] Rawls's claim, simultaneously self-effacing and politically aggrandizing, is that his account of democratic ideals represents a coherent synthesis of what he calls the "overlapping consensus" of "all the opposing philosophical and religious doctrines likely to persist and to gain adherents in a more or less just constitutional democratic society."[4] I'm not really doing anything particularly original, Rawls says: I am (merely!?) identifying, clarifying, and justifying the basic moral beliefs we all share, whether you recognize them or not, and the political implications of these beliefs, whether you accept them or not.

If this claim can be understood as an empirical account of the moral and political convictions of the American citizenry rather than as an anticipatory hope or a rhetorical ploy, then it seems clearly an inaccurate one. The current beliefs of today's American citizenry not only cannot be reconciled and incorporated into Rawls's characterization but also in some respects seem positively at odds with it.[5] But what Rawls has arguably instead done with extraordinary skill and perspicacity is to excavate the most fundamental and determinative moral intuitions of the mainstream left, to provide a theoretical justification for these intuitions, and to explain their implications for the goals and policies of contemporary democratic societies. Anyone who has attended carefully to Rawls's arguments emerges with a keener sense of both the measure and the implicit moral rationale for the invocations of fairness ubiquitous in today's liberal discourse. The same arguments likewise provide more specific content and justification for the redistribution of economic and political power widely promoted in the same quarters.

Rawls has his critics on the left, of course. Especially in light of the emergence of identity politics and the attendant concern for inclusiveness toward and empowerment of various cultural and ethnic minority groups, for example, some on the left have criticized Rawls for his alleged inattentiveness to these concerns and the social dynamics that generate them. Other liberal critics of Rawls worry that his distributive principles are insufficiently egalitarian because they allow room for social and economic inequalities they regard as morally illegitimate. These critiques, however, should be seen as internecine complaints that are not entirely compelling in a theoretical sense. It is understandable that liberal partisans of multicultural recognition and champions for the advancement of previously oppressed or marginalized minorities find insufficient attention to their critical social theory in Rawls. But it also seems fairly clear that Rawls's abstract norms and criteria are capable of incorporating most of the aspirations of the multicultural Left—at least in the domain of law and social policy: the parties to his version of a legitimate social contract embodying fair terms of social cooperation include representatives of all relevant social groups and positions, after all, and his account of the "primary social goods" subject to allocation in accord with norms of social justice include not simply economic goods but also things such as power, status, and respect. It may well be justified to complain, as does William Connolly, that Rawls is "rather tone deaf to the ethos of pluralization" and that he "underplays the contemporary ethical importance of the dense network of culturally defined discriminations" that pervade almost all social orders including those of contemporary pluralist democracies.[6] Yet Rawls is entitled to respond that providing such a critical concrete political sociology is beyond his purpose, however important and illuminating that task may be, and that his principles of justice do not because of his silence in this regard lose their force and legitimacy vis-à-vis all the participants in a democratic society. As for those who find his account of democratic legitimacy insufficiently egalitarian, Rawls is entitled to demand of them a clear and compelling account of why it would be morally mandatory or appropriate to insist upon an allocation of social resources that would diminish the absolute amount of these resources at the disposal of the most disadvantaged members of society in the name of greater relative equality.

It seems defensible, therefore, to see the core claims and tenets of the high liberalism of Rawls and his followers as the most representative and influential articulation of the public philosophy of contemporary liberalism available to us. The moral intuitions and political assumptions exhibited and defended there arguably provide the best approximation we have of the normative substratum of the kind of social analysis and policy prescriptions found in journals such as *The Nation* and *The American Prospect*. They also find expression in the dominant rhetorical tropes favored by liberal groups when they engage in public debate and importune political decisionmakers. My claim is certainly not that the prevalence of these moral intuitions within the mainstream left and the conception of democratic purposes these intuitions help to generate were produced by people reading Rawls and other academic

CHAPTER TWO

liberals. That would be an instance of those overly intellectualized accounts of ideology formation to which academics such as myself are attracted because they exaggerate the social impact of what we do. It may well be the case that, as John Maynard Keynes once famously said, the beliefs and actions of political leaders are often shaped by the writings of academic scribblers long dead. But the content of those scribblings—and the fact that they are the ones that receive a favorable reception in the face of competing alternatives—are profoundly determined by social circumstances and the problems, preoccupations, and desires created by these circumstances. Thus, social circumstances, social ideas, and social behavior all intertwine in a dialectical pattern of mutual influence. In the present instance, then, it is not that liberal academic social theorists conceived and concocted a new and distinctive public philosophy while sitting in a splendidly isolated ivory tower and that, mirabile dictu, they found ready followers in the real world simply because their ideas were so logically compelling. Instead, their ruminations and conclusions were themselves profoundly driven by the political setting in which they wrote, and they found a receptive audience because they served to clarify, consolidate, and ratify a somewhat inchoate but deeply felt and widely shared complex of moral beliefs and political attitudes that were already out there among significant portions of the public.

The core contentions of Rawlsian high liberalism, then—together with similar expressions of the same complex of moral beliefs and political ideals there on display—can serve as a helpful template for characterizing what can plausibly be seen as the operative public philosophy of contemporary American liberalism. In this respect, this complex of beliefs and ideals represents the contemporary heir and successor to the beliefs and ideals that informed and animated the populist and progressivist liberalism of an earlier time. The question then becomes: How do these public philosophies compare? Are there any notable changes that have occurred and are on display here? And if so, what are they and what are their implications and consequences?

FROM SELF-RULE AND DEVELOPMENT TO DISTRIBUTIVE JUSTICE

When contemporary American liberalism is contemplated from the standpoint of political philosophy and juxtaposed to what I have called the traditional American liberalism of the nineteenth and early twentieth centuries, one has to be struck by the contrast between their respective axial norms. By their axial norms, I mean what these social doctrines depict as the ultimate goals of a well-ordered society. What are the final and deepest purposes of political association? What is it the full attainment of which would lead us to say that a political society—or specifically, a democratic society—accomplished its core mission?

In the previous chapter, I argued that the answer to this question in the formulations of those political progressives who sought in an earlier era to explain America's democratic mission broadly corresponded with what Hegel meant when he said that the fundamental moral and political discovery of the modern world was that all were destined to be free. In Hegel's philosophical vocabulary this meant not that, in the new democratic world appearing on the horizon of a providential history, all people would be liberated from all social constraints or obligations, but that all people and not merely their aristocratic masters and superiors would have the social space and resources to become fully developed human beings. They could, each and every one, actualize their full human potentiality, could in that sense fulfill themselves as what Whitman called "separate and complete subjects for freedom." In effect, if not in name, the axial goal of traditional liberalism arguably was that all the people would be able to flourish in a broadly Aristotelian sense: even the common and average member of a fully democratized society could approach the form of life of Aristotle's *phronimoi* and could achieve *eudaemonia*.

For contemporary liberalism, in contrast, the fundamental moral aspiration of a democratic society is not so much the universalization of human flourishing as it is the attainment of social justice. As John Tomasi observes: "High liberalism is marked, more than anything else, by a tremendously expansive role within the normative domain of liberal theory for the concept justice.... In a high liberal society, when individuals consider how to respond to questions of fellow-treatment across a great variety of situations, it is justice that kicks in, demanding deliberative primacy for itself both institutionally and motivationally." The criteria and demands of justice dominate and even "supplant" the "great variety of other ways that well-meaning individuals think or might come to think of their relations with their fellow citizens."[7] The most fundamental moral intuition of contemporary liberalism is thus what Rawls refers to as "our conviction of the primacy of justice." The first substantive line of his *A Theory of Justice* is a stipulation of this primacy. "Justice is the first virtue of social institutions." *Justice* here refers to distributive justice or "social justice," the principles that determine what count as "proper distributive shares," and the "primary subject of justice" is therefore "the basic structure of society," since this set of political arrangements determines the "division of advantages" or the allocation of the benefits "produced by [social] collaboration."[8]

These bold assertions about the overriding status of distributive justice as the dominant moral aspiration for democratic society and as the dominant standard for evaluating social institutions and policies arguably represent rather faithfully one of the deepest and most important moral convictions of contemporary American liberalism. From the campaign rhetoric of Democratic candidates to articles in *The Nation*, one cannot help being struck by the ubiquity of invocations of justice and fairness. For good or ill, it seems a hallmark of contemporary American liberalism that its advocates ask first of any law, social institution, or public policy not whether or how much it is economically advantageous or promotes the general welfare or achieves broader social goals, but rather whether its distributive consequences will be fair or not. Whether or not they know who Rawls is and even if they have no idea what deontology in moral philosophy means, contemporary liberals seem instinctively to think and act deontologically rather than teleologically: they ask not what a political proposal can do for the country but whether it is fair to persons—and perhaps to groups. This is not to say that contemporary American liberals do not care about the general welfare. Of course they do. It is to say that for them, even the general welfare takes a backseat to distributive issues: first things first, and justice is the first virtue. For some among them, indeed, it could even be said that the concept of the general welfare is pretty much subsumed under the concept of social justice: the realm of res publica is coterminous with the bounds of social justice. The rest of human life is a private affair left to personal choice—so long as these choices do not impact the social allocation of resources in a way that violates the fair and publicly established terms of social cooperation.

THE SCOPE AND CONTENT OF LIBERAL JUSTICE

For today's high liberalism, then, distributive justice, aka social justice, is the first virtue of social institutions, and "first" here is taken to mean that it takes precedence over all other political purposes. The various other contenders for the status of first virtue/most important purpose of government are elbowed aside or demoted: the goal of universal personal development championed by Mill and that figures so prominently in the aspirations of earlier American progressivism; the peace and security Hume thought people valued as the first virtue of social institutions; the similar "peace, order, and good government" celebrated in the Canadian constitution; the civic friendship in pursuit of the human good that stands at the center of politics for Aristotle; and the individual liberty prioritized by advocates of a contract society. This priority accorded distributive justice is thus in itself a crucial moral postulate. But exactly how important it is, how pervasive and far-reaching its implications, depends upon the scope and content of social justice. How much of social behavior, what portion of the multiplicitous social interactions that occur in any society, is subject to regulation by the standards of justice? And how demanding are these standards themselves? Could their complete satisfaction be achieved by relatively parsimonious actions directed toward relatively modest alterations of outcome from those that likely would have occurred spontaneously in their absence? Or are the standards sufficiently divergent from the likely consequences of social relationships unconstrained by norms of justice that more extensive and even heroic legal intervention is required?

When James Madison wrote in the context of defending the proposed American constitution, for example, that "justice is the end of government," that "it is the end of civil society," he was saying something that sounds identical to Rawls's claim that justice is the first virtue. But what Madison means by injustice here is the "violence of the stronger" that does and would normally occur in a condition of "anarchy" or in "a state of nature."[9] Achieving social justice so conceived requires political artifice, but it is the relatively limited artifice of constitutionally protected rights and constitutionally contrived checks and balances. Justice has priority status, but its domain includes a relatively limited area of social life and its content is such that what it requires of the state is essentially defensive and protective in nature.

In contrast to the relatively limited purchase and rather low ceiling of justice in Madison's formulation, today's high liberalism accords to social justice a very wide latitude and sets forth an exceedingly demanding standard. The paramount status of justice as a social purpose assumes extraordinary practical significance because of the breadth of its scope and the height of its ambition.

For today's high liberalism, the jurisdiction of social justice effectively extends to all the resources of the society. Principles of justice should determine the allocation of any social good whose possession and control would be useful for the successful pursuit of a plan of life. These fungible assets Rawls calls "social primary goods," which include rights and liberties, opportunities and powers, wealth and income, and even the psychic asset of self-respect. In addition to these social resources conducive to one's life chances, of course, certain natural talents or attributes are conducive to success: health, beauty, intelligence, vigor, charm, and the like. Rawls calls these resources "natural primary goods," and as he notes—with a certain amount of regret, from the standpoint of justice—these attributes are not "directly under the control" of the society. But once these assets have been deployed to give rise to alienable resources that are not so inextricably connected to people's very bodies—into wealth and income, for example—then these fruits of people's natural talents may and must be reallocated if the criteria of social justice so mandate. We cannot redistribute Michael Jordan's athletic abilities more equitably, and it would be collectively irrational to seek to divest him of these abilities, perhaps in the fashion of Tonya Harding's minions taking a tire iron to the knee of her rival, Nancy Kerrigan. Instead, we can and should take the proceeds of his advertising endorsements and reallocate them in a just manner.

The proper reach of social justice for Rawls and other high liberals is, then, whatever society can get its hands on insofar as the standards of justice require a distribution that deviates from that which would otherwise prevail. What, then, are these standards in the view of contemporary liberalism? What does justice require, this sovereign virtue? To a certain extent, the response of contemporary liberals to that fundamental question is quite clear: justice requires "fairness," and fairness requires much greater equality of primary goods than currently is the case. The admonitions to this effect are ubiquitous among contemporary liberals—and, in light of the oftentimes grotesque and unseemly extremes of wealth and poverty produced by our current political economy, perfectly understandable and appropriate. What is less clear are the specific standard of and rationale for the conception of justice and fairness that informs these demands for "greater equality." How much more equality, and why?

It is Rawls's considerable achievement—and his usefulness in the context of our attempt to ascertain the public philosophy of contemporary American liberalism—to have provided specific and coherent answers to these questions. He provides an explicit criterion for the extent of morally permissible social inequality, he identifies the moral intuitions that support this criterion, and he explains the considerations that can be adduced as warrants for these intuitions. It is contestable, of course, whether Rawls's self-described attempt to excavate the moral imagination of contemporary liberalism represents a convincing hermeneutic exercise. But much evidence suggests that his rendering of this politicomoral persuasion is in its basic outline and core features quite an accurate one. Were it not so, the inordinate attention it has received from friend and foe alike would be very hard to explain.

All people may be created equal in Jefferson's meaning of that phrase: none of us are born endowed with the right to rule others, and none are born burdened with the obligation to obey others. But nature bestows very different levels of physical and intellectual talent upon its human progeny. The dynamics of almost all societies introduce distinctions and inequalities of status and social position. And market economics, especially in advanced industrial societies, generate a chasm between the wealth and income of those at the top and those at the bottom of the economic hierarchy. If Matthew Arnold is right that "a community having humane manners" must be "a community with the spirit of equality,"[10] the cumulative effect of these multiple inequalities must be morally troubling to all people of conscience. In the context of a public philosophy that makes social justice the first virtue, the question becomes more specific and insistent: What does justice demand? How much inequality is morally permissible? Is it the five-to-one ratio between top and bottom that Plato suggested in *The Laws* and that Ronald Beiner has more recently championed as an appropriate goal for social democracy?[11] Something more? Something less? Why?

To these queries the moral imagination of high liberalism provides a straightforward answer, at least in principle. Fairness demands equality in the distribution of all the resources at the disposal of society, excepting only those inequalities that function to improve the absolute standing of the least well-off members of the society. This important exception is clearly occasioned by the recognition that some incentives may need to be offered to the more talented in order to induce them to deploy their talents in an economically productive manner. In Rawls's words, the "general conception of justice" that should guide the distributive policies of a "well-ordered society" is this: "All social values—liberty and opportunity, income and wealth, and the bases of self-respect—are to be distributed equally unless an unequal distribution of any, or all, of these values is to everyone's advantage."[12] And the phrase "to everyone's advantage" is to be understood not as maximizing aggregate utility but as being "to the greatest benefit of the least advantaged."[13]

On this view, the only considerations that can legitimize departures from an equal distribution of social resources are entirely prudential. In a just society, some people may be permitted to have more than others, but these inequalities are allowable only to the extent that and only because they redound consequentially to the welfare of the least well-off members of the society. Social and economic inequality is either morally unacceptable or else a lamentable concession to unfortunate facts of life and to human frailty: the main unfortunate fact of life is that we do not inhabit a Garden of Eden, and someone must labor to generate the resources people need to pursue their plans of life; the main human frailty is that people may need some incentives beyond encouragements to altruism to motivate their efforts.

This conception of social justice represents an agreement that we, as democratic citizens committed by our sense of justice to accepting fair terms of social cooperation, will "share one another's fate."[14] But this kind of sharing does not mean that we are united in common quest of the humanly good life—as the classical understanding of the nature of a political association would have it. We are assumed to be too morally and religiously pluralistic for this to happen: we do not and cannot agree about the human good. What sharing one another's fate means is that our political association is governed by rules of justice that "regard the distribution of natural talents as a common asset."[15] People's abilities are properly to be viewed and treated by a democratic society "as a social asset to be used for the common advantage"[16]—this because justice requires the elimination of morally arbitrary inequalities and no one can credibly claim to have done anything to deserve their particular complement of natural assets.

Because no human agency is responsible for the unequal distribution of natural talents (i.e., the word *distribution* in this phrase designates merely a statistical pattern rather than an action—unless the allocation is attributed to a Divine will or to a personified Nature), it might seem logical to assume that this natural happenstance should be deemed irrelevant so far as *social* justice is concerned. Not being the product of human agency, it might seem incapable of serving as the basis for imposing obligations of justice (as contrasted with obligations of charity, decency, or humanity) upon particular persons or social institutions. That immunity against the imposition of a moral burden to rectify an ill one did not have any role in bringing about seems fundamental, for example, in the standard criteria of legal liability: I become subject to criminal sanction only if I did something and had mens rea, and I become subject to civil liability only if I committed a tort. The conflation of the notions of causality and answerability in the phrase "to be responsible for" reflects a similar moral logic and confers the same kind of moral immunity against demands in the name of justice to compensate for damages one did not inflict.

Rawls sees this issue differently, and his unwillingness to acquiesce in the granting of moral immunity for situations not of one's own creation is replicated by other high liberals and seems broadly representative of the moral imaginary of contemporary American liberalism. In this view, the norms of social justice and the rights and obligations consequent upon them do not extend merely to situations produced by human actions. Instead, they are to be construed as governing all the relationships of association and relative standing among the members of a democratic society, whether these relationships result from human agency or simply from natural contingencies. Democratic justice must be, in a sense, cosmic justice. It is not sufficient that all citizens must treat each other fairly and equitably. Instead, as Rawls expresses the scope of his ambition for social justice, it is "the arbitrariness *of the world*" that "must be corrected for."[17] The content of the social justice that has for him the status of the first virtue of social institutions incorporates at its heart a "principle of redress" that requires not simply that socially constructed and enforced hierarchies be dismantled but that even "inequalities of natural endowment," because undeserved, "are somehow to be compensated for."[18]

A striking and politically significant consequence and manifestation of this moral logic is the expansion/transformation under the aegis of contemporary liberalism of key morally inflected concepts of social criticism such as "exploitation," "domination," and "oppression." It is instructive in this context, for example, to contrast what can be called the traditional notion of exploitation with the expanded definition and deployment of that concept by Bruce Ackerman in his own account of liberal social justice. The traditional concept of exploitation, of which the Marxist account is the paradigmatic representation, denotes a situation in which the proceeds of one person's or one group's labor are appropriated by others for their own benefit without appropriate compensation or exchange. Classical economists and market enthusiasts would insist, of course, that exploitation is impossible in a market economy, since exchanges there are entirely voluntary and no one would consent to their own exploitation. But markets don't operate on the economists' blackboard: they operate within social and political structures that may have the result of constraining the field of consent in ways that undermine its prima facie morally validating power and permit one party to extract resources from others without providing proper compensation. The invocation of consent to accord moral validation to economic exchanges thus has force, but that force can be overridden by identifying social institutions that compromise consent and permit the siphoning off of the fruits of labor and by specifying a standard for measuring the extent of what is siphoned off. That is what Karl Marx's theory of class structure and his account of "surplus value" are designed to accomplish, and that is why Friedrich Engels designated the theory of surplus value as one of the two theoretical discoveries that created scientific socialism. The key point here is that in the traditional lexicon—and in the moral imagination that produces it—exploitation involves an act of (uncompensated or inadequately compensated) *appropriation* of someone else's justly attained resources. Conditions or situations of inequality, disadvantage, or misfortune do not in and of themselves suffice to sustain claims of exploitation. Exploitation must involve expropriation of the fruits of someone else's labor.

The standards for what counts as exploitation are different and far more encompassing within Ackerman's contemporary liberal moral imagination, predicated as it is upon his capacious and demanding account of liberal justice. Should I be born blind, Ackerman argues, I should not simply regard myself as having suffered a natural misfortune. Rather, I should consider myself to be "a victim of genetic domination." And as such, I am entitled to consider myself as suffering "exploitation" unless I receive some form of "compensation" from those with normal vision, who are "obliged to compensate the blind citizen by giving him advantages in other power domains." Hence, it follows that I, as a blind citizen, have "a right to insist that others make a greater sacrifice of their rights in nongenetic domains if overall equivalence [which is demanded by social justice] is to be achieved."[19] This moral claim embodies Ackerman's version of Rawls's "principle of redress," and in both cases, the result is the placing of a significant moral burden on those who are by some chance better off than some other citizens in some respect or other: every time an aspiring basketball player is born who can't dunk or drive left, Michael Jordan becomes ever more an "exploiter," and from him, compensation is required as moral redress.

A similar pattern of imposing compensatory obligations of justice upon those who might reasonably be seen as innocent bystanders, pursuing their own happiness without violating the rights or inflicting inquiry on anyone, is apparent in the moral imagination of contemporary liberals when it comes to what might be called social misfortunes. One example to illustrate this tendency is Iris Young's account of social "marginalization." Marginalized people she defines as those whom "the system of labor cannot or will not use." And this is a very large category, since "in the United States a shamefully large proportion of the population is marginal," including, inter alia, old people, young people who cannot find jobs, single mothers and their children, the unemployed, the disabled, and Native Americans. Marginalization is not simply an unfortunate situation, in Young's construction. It is "perhaps the most dangerous form of oppression. A whole category of people is expelled from useful participation in social life." To be marginalized is to be subject to "injustice."[20]

In terms of her own definition of what constitutes "oppression," Young's account is not illogical. For oppression on her rendering "consists in systematic institutional processes which prevent some people from learning and using satisfying and expansive skills in socially recognized settings, or institutionalized processes which inhibit people's ability to play and communicate with others or to express their feelings and perspectives on social life in contexts where others can listen."[21] In the context of such an encompassing construction of oppression, it is no wonder that oppression is depicted as running rampant. The issue here is the semantic propriety and—since the contestable definition is normatively loaded in a very profound way—the moral propriety of using the term *oppression* in this manner. For oppression conventionally refers to situations in which some people use force upon other people in an illegitimate manner in order to advance their own interests. It does not refer to any and every circumstance that impedes someone from flourishing.

Young seeks to lessen the semantic gap between her use of *oppression* and the traditional understanding of that term/

condemnation by the use of active verbs in construing relevant social situations, in conjunction with imputing agency to unnamed actors through the mediation of institutions and "structures." Thus, anyone who cannot find work is said to have been "expelled" from meaningful participation in the economy. If we assume that some party actually did the expelling and was exerting power illegitimately or maliciously, then the unsuccessful job seeker would have grounds to see himself or herself as suffering oppression in the conventional sense of that term. In a perfect world—one where all important goods such as gainful employment were unproblematically available for everyone—that would seem to be the case. The question is whether this moral construction is appropriate for our more imperfect world, in which not everyone who wishes to work has skills that are in demand.

I will not try here to adjudicate these complex and controversial issues. In the present context, my purpose is the more limited one of identifying the fundamental moral intuitions and perceptions of the world that give rise to the axial social goals of contemporary liberalism. What these examples demonstrate is that the moral imagination of contemporary liberalism not only accords social justice preeminence among the political virtues, but also understands its content in a most expansive way. As we have here seen displayed in Rawls's core contention that "the arbitrariness of the world must be corrected for,"[22] in Ackerman's expansion of the notion of exploitation to encompass the suffering of any inequality or misfortune not compensated by "equal sacrifice" on the part of the nondisadvantaged, and in Iris Young's expansion of the notion of oppression to incorporate any situational impedance to the flourishing of any subset of the populace, contemporary liberal justice is not only sovereign in status but virtually all-encompassing in its purchase and exceedingly stringent in its demands. When all the blanks are filled in, the paradigmatic moral claim of contemporary liberalism seems to be that it is the preeminent moral test of democratic governance to redress as far as possible all the morally arbitrary inequalities of human life.

THE PHILOSOPHICAL ANTHROPOLOGY OF CONTEMPORARY LIBERALISM: SHRINKING THE NOUMENAL REALM

Every political philosophy is to at least some degree predicated upon certain conceptions about human selfhood. These conceptions are partly empirical, involving an understanding of human powers and capabilities, and partly normative, involving an understanding of human satisfaction and perfection. In some political theories, the animating conception of human nature is front and center—a clearly articulated model explicitly used as a justificatory reference point for political prescriptions. Other political theories are often much less specific and forthcoming about the understanding of human nature that informs them. But even if tacit, these anthropological assumptions must be there and must be influential: any normative account of political order represents an attempt to specify the most appropriate form of social organization for a particular type of being characterized and constituted by a particular set or range of passions and capabilities. Plato's ideal republic is not the ideal home for aardvarks, and Rawls's well-ordered society is not the ideal home for zebras: each is the proper home for the particular kind of creatures that Plato and Rawls understand us humans to be.

Classical liberal theorists understood a necessary part of their task to be to provide a conception of human nature. That was why they sought to specify what human beings would have looked like in a "state of nature" devoid of any artificial social constraints. "As long as we are ignorant of the natural man," wrote Jean-Jacques Rousseau, in explaining the need to ascertain the constituent features of this natural condition, "it is in vain for us to attempt to determine either the law originally prescribed to him or that which is best adapted to his constitution."[23] Contemporary liberals generally do not undertake such inquiries. In part, this may represent a failure of philosophical reflection, but there are important principled considerations that lie beneath this apparent neglect. To the extent that human nature refers to empirical qualities that define the species, most contemporary liberals—and indeed most moderns—generally believe that there is here not much to specify: the content of our humanity is seen to depend almost entirely upon the social contingencies that shape us and almost not at all upon anything that is given and universal by nature. The empirical content of "human nature" is essentially the empty cupboard of a tabula rasa. To the extent that human nature refers to some normative notion of satisfaction, or perfection, or fulfillment, the characteristic moral fallibilism or skepticism of modern/postmodern philosophy seems to render any attempted specification of that sort to be unavailable or improper or both: we cannot really know or say what exactly human fulfillment consists in, and to the extent that it can be specified at all, it must be by individual human beings for themselves.

These philosophical considerations notwithstanding, it is nonetheless clear that for the norms and prescriptions of today's high liberalism to be compelling, we must be the kind of creatures for whom justice can properly be the primary virtue of our association and for whom the difference principle or something like it can be the proper measure of what is just. That recognition provided the basis for Michael Sandel's provocative attempt to tease out those assumptions about the self and its moral psychology that might seem logically necessary for Rawls to presuppose in order to sustain his account of liberal justice and its political role.[24] Although Rawls refused to accept Sandel's contention that his moral philosophy depended upon a metaphysical conception of the self, he nonetheless acknowledged that his account of justice and the moral foundations of democracy did involve acceptance of a particular "moral conception" of the person, "one that begins from our everyday conception of persons as the basic units of thought, deliberation, and responsibility." And although he maintained that "no particular metaphysical doctrine about the nature of persons, distinctive and opposed to other metaphysical doctrines, appears among [the] premises or seems required by" his presentation of justice as fairness, he conceded that this "everyday conception of persons . . . presupposes, or in some way involves, certain metaphysical theses about the nature of persons as moral or political agents."[25]

It is not my purpose here to recapitulate or to attempt to adjudicate this whole debate. For our purposes, it is instead sufficient to attend to certain core features of what Rawls considers "our everyday conception of persons" as moral agents to be. For this conception as he understands and presents it is by no means so generally accepted as he seems to imagine, and it plays a crucial role in justifying contemporary liberalism's insistence upon the primacy of distributive justice among democratic purposes and its account of what distributive justice consists in. It is, moreover, a conception of personhood and moral agency that departs in important ways from that found within traditional liberalism; therefore, it provides one important piece of the puzzle when it comes to understanding and explaining the transformation of American liberalism that is our central concern.

Traditional liberalism was, as the very name suggests, dedicated to the fundamental goal of expanding the range of human freedom and self-determination. That central aspiration was predicated, in turn, upon very deep and expansive conceptions of human agency and moral responsibility. Whitman's insistence that the ultimate purpose of a democratic society was to enable all its people to become "separate and complete subjects for freedom" captures this core aspiration quite nicely. It is also evident, of course, in the moral and political logic of Mill's *On Liberty*, cited by Whitman as his inspiration for penning "Democratic Vistas." And it is equally evident in the focus upon eliminating the personal and political dependency of some people and classes upon others that was so important to civic republicanism and also to people such as Condorcet, Adam Smith, and Thomas Jefferson. In a sense, traditional liberalism represented a political radicalization of moral traditionalism. What it sought to achieve was a political society where all people—as rational beings and/or

CHAPTER TWO

creatures created in God's image—could exercise their powers of transcendence over the realm of necessity instead of being submerged within that realm by political dominion.

Whether it be deemed a metaphysical doctrine of the self or, as Rawls preferred, a freestanding political conception of democratic persons, the understanding of human freedom and moral agency characteristic of contemporary American liberalism departs from the traditional liberal model in important respects. Specifically, contemporary liberalism adopts a considerably attenuated conception of human freedom and moral agency. Because Rawls depicts his theory of the moral foundations of democracy as updating and carrying to a higher level of abstraction the social contract tradition represented by Locke, Rousseau, and Kant, perhaps the best way to see what is distinctive and novel in contemporary liberalism here is to note the ways that Rawls departs from these liberal forebears in his moral anthropology.

Of these three philosophical forebears, it is Kant who provided the fullest doctrine of moral personhood and moral agency and the doctrine that maps most directly upon Rawls's anthropology. But Kant's account of the human moral powers represented a carrying to a higher level of abstraction the moral anthropology provided by Rousseau in his *Discourse on the Origins of Inequality*. So let us begin our account there.

Rousseau tells us in this *Discourse* that he sees "nothing in any animal but an ingenious machine, to which nature hath given senses to wind itself up." When it comes to human beings, then, he tells us that he perceives

> exactly the same things in the human machine, with this difference, that in the operations of the brute, nature is the sole agent, whereas man has some share in his own operations, in his character as a free agent. The one chooses and refuses by instinct, the other from an act of free will.... It is not so much the understanding that constitutes the specific difference between the man and the brute, as the human quality of free agency.

In addition to the power of free agency, "there is another very specific quality which distinguishes" humans from other animals, and "this is the faculty of self-improvement" or "perfectibility."[26]

Kant takes Rousseau's depiction of humans as spiritual beings with two moral powers inhabiting an instinct-driven machine, gives it greater metaphysical depth, and amends it slightly. Humans are uniquely subject to moral tension, Kant says, because we are uniquely creatures who inhabit both the world of intellect and the world of sense. The world of sense is the phenomenal world, and the world of intellect is the noumenal world. The phenomenal realm (and we human beings to the extent that we behave in accord with its laws) is governed by the mechanistic force of drives and instincts, inclinations and impulses. The noumenal world is the realm of the spirit, and it (and we insofar as we are spirit) acts freely and rationally. Kant's noumenal beings, like Rousseau's human beings, possess two moral powers. The first of these, as in Rousseau, is autonomy or the power of free agency, the capacity to govern one's own actions by laws one prescribes for oneself. The second, however, is not Rousseau's "perfectibility," which perhaps seems to Kant too deeply implicated in an outdated metaphysical biology and insufficiently deontological, but is instead the power of understanding that Rousseau had set aside—the *sapiens* part of *Homo sapiens*. Specifically, when it comes to the moral powers, it is the capacity to apprehend the moral law. This "moral law within one," as Kant puts it, is one of two things (the other is "the starred heaven above me") that "fill the mind with ever new and increasing awe and admiration the more frequently and continuously reflection is occupied with them"; it "raises my value infinitely . . . [and] reveals a life independent of animality and even of the entire world of sense."[27]

In his own conception of democratic personhood, Rawls also ascribes two moral powers to us: these are "a capacity for a sense of justice" and "a capacity for a conception of the good."[28] The first of these two powers formally maps very closely Kant's depiction of the human ability to apprehend the moral law. For Kant, to apprehend the moral law is to recognize the rational necessity of acting in accord with the categorical imperative to treat all persons as ends in themselves and to act only on the basis of precepts one could will to be universally applicable. For Rawls, our sense of justice is our apprehension of the imperative of reasonableness to interact with others on the basis of fair terms of social cooperation. Both of the accounts converge upon essentially the same moral obligation: to treat our fellow human beings/fellow citizens on the basis of what reason presents to us as valid norms of reciprocity.

Rawls's account of the second moral power, however, the capacity to choose a conception of the good, marks a significant departure from the account of moral free agency provided by both Kant and Rousseau. The crucial issue here concerns the range of the moral power to "choose," for the specification of what humans have the power to choose defines the scope of their free agency. (Rousseau makes this point by straightforward semantic identification: "the power of willing, or rather of choosing.")[29] For Rousseau, our moral power of free agency consists in our capacity—not shared by animals—to choose whether or not to act in conformity to natural impulse or instinct. When animals do something, "nature is the sole agent"; when human beings do something, they do it "from an act of free will" because we "know ourselves at liberty to acquiesce or resist" our impulses.[30] Kant's account is similar. He links the freedom of the human will more tightly than does Rousseau to the rationality of the human intellect. But just as much as Rousseau, he insists that human beings are not confined to the phenomenal world of mechanistic external causality but also inhabit as spiritual beings the noumenal world of freedom and self-determination—a world of which we are immediately and directly conscious. We have the ability to prescribe for ourselves the maxim of our own actions, and if we act solely by acquiescence to natural impulse, we do so by willfully foregoing the deployment of our capacity for self-determination. Either way, we are free agents, and we are rightly held responsible for our actions. Kant, indeed, imposes a very stringent standard of responsibility upon us—a standard well captured by Sartre in his own doctrine of "bad faith." For Kant and Sartre both insist that, as Rousseau said, we human beings do in fact possess the power to control our actions—either to acquiesce in or to overrule and resist the impulses and desires nature thrusts upon us—and we are conscious of having this power. We are therefore morally accountable for whatever transgressions we might commit, and any attempt to exculpate ourselves by denying our free agency is a lie that only compounds our guilt.

Rawls depicts our power of free agency as having a much more limited scope. We are free, Rawls says, "in three respects." First, we are free in the sense of "having the moral power to have a conception of the good." Second, we "view ourselves as free" in the sense that we regard ourselves "as self-authenticating sources of valid claims." Third, we are free in the sense that we "are viewed as capable of taking responsibility for [our] ends."[31] If we set aside the second of these three senses as fitting only rather oddly and imperfectly under the rubric of free agency,[32] we are left with the conclusion that the moral power of free agency in Rawls is confined to having the capacity to choose or affirm a particular conception of the good and, correlatively, because we have this power, to stand responsible for the "ends" or purposes we pursue as part of the conception of the good we have chosen.

What is most notable in Rawls's account of our human "moral powers"—especially against the backdrop of Rousseau's and Kant's parallel account—is the relative absence of any significant capacity to control our actions, what we actually do. We are credited, in Rawls's anthropology, with the powers of what was once called "right reason," that is, the possession of a moral conscience able to apprehend the reciprocity imperatives of justice. And we are credited with the power to have or to choose our conception of the good. But there is no mention of the moral capacity that Rousseau attributes to us to resist our natural impulses or the capacity Kant attributes to us to control our behavior, to determine the course of our own actions.

This omission of this core element of the traditional account of human moral agency is, moreover, no mere slip of mind—a failure to mention something important and taken for granted. Instead, the deletion of this "free will" aspect of the human moral powers from Rawls's moral anthropology is deliberate and in a sense necessary, given other parts of Rawls's moral theory. Not to delete this capacity of free action or self-control or self-determination from his account of our moral powers would produce a clash between Rawls's anthropology and the justificatory logic that sustains his principles of justice.

In Rawls's eyes, the moral agency we might suppose stands at the heart of making an effort is essentially illusory. Upon reflection, he argues, it can be seen to dissolve into a deeper network of causal forces. Any capacity and disposition I might have to put forward an effort may be said to be part of my character. But my character, in turn, is not itself something that I produced but is the result of "family and social circumstances for which [I] can claim no credit."[33] Putting forth an effort is thus not to be construed as an act of noumenal will, as Kant would put it. It is instead a dependent variable in a long chain of phenomenal causality.

This understanding of the nature and scope of human moral powers and agency has, of course, important political implications. There is a tight linkage, both conceptually and normatively, between causal agency and moral encumbrance. This intimate association between empirical attributions of causal efficacy and moral assignment of obligations is captured and reflected linguistically in the package of both of these elements into the phrase "to be responsible for." If I demand an answer to my query "Who is responsible for this mess?" I may be understood to be asking an empirical question: I want to know who did this, who brought about this state of affairs. But as any child knows when posed this question by a parent, the answer as to fact carries a direct moral corollary: if I was causally responsible for the mess in question, then I am on the hook to clean it up or to offer compensation to those I have hurt or inconvenienced. I become, as the linguistic stem of the term *responsible* (from the Latin *respondeo*) suggests, morally answerable for what I cause to happen.

It is only logical and appropriate, then, that when Rawls develops his conception of social responsibilities, it mirrors his theory of the moral powers. A well-ordered society, Rawls argues, would embody what he calls "a social division of responsibility." In this division, individual citizens have two responsibilities. As people capable of forming, revising, and pursuing "a conception of one's rational advantage or the good," citizens as individuals are expected "to assume responsibility for their ends" and to adjust these ends as necessary to comport with "the all-purpose means they can expect" to receive in light of the distributive principles of the society. As people with a capacity for a sense of justice, citizens are expected individually to choose, affirm, and live in accordance with distributive principles that are fair. But the responsibility for "providing a fair share of the primary goods for all" falls to "citizens as a collective body."[34] People do not bear responsibility as individuals for whatever productive efforts they may exert, for these are deemed to be a product of causal contingencies outside their control rather than a product of moral agency. Such a power of agency is not one of the human moral powers, and nothing of the sort can therefore have any bearing upon the moral responsibilities of individuals or upon the assignment of shares of primary goods.

When Rawls characterizes his core moral intuitions and philosophical aspirations at the outset of *A Theory of Justice*, he depicts himself as standing within the tradition of liberal social contract theory extending from Locke to Kant and wanting to refine and carry that theory to a higher level of abstraction. In the light of his account of human beings and their moral powers, this characterization turns out to be simultaneously justified and misleading. It is justified in that he builds his account of morally legitimate democratic society upon an understanding of what free and equal people would rationally consent to accept as the terms of their political association. It is, however, a misleading characterization in the way that it glosses over a striking departure from that tradition. The essence of this departure is the significant shrinkage of what Kant called the noumenal realm—the realm of human freedom and moral agency. For Locke, Rousseau, and Kant all construed the human capacity to exercise a willful affirmation of and control over one's actions as one of our most definitive and important moral powers. Rawls, however, provides a much more deterministic conception of human behavior, in which our actions are a product of the kind of outside causal forces Kant would have defined as part of the phenomenal realm—even though we retain the presumably distinctive human capacities to have a sense of justice and to choose a conception of the good.

This altered conception of human agency and moral powers, this shrinkage of the noumenal realm as it were, goes a long way toward subverting the moral imaginary and the central political aspirations of traditional liberalism. For what has to strike even the most cursory reader of people such as Whitman, Bancroft, and Jane Addams is their clear sense that the defining feature and the most important moral achievement of political democratization is the vast expansion of effective human agency that it unleashes and cultivates. That is precisely what becoming "complete subjects of freedom" and "full grown men and women" is all about. Although their philosophical vocabulary was a different one, traditional American liberals believed as much as Marx did that the animating telos of political advancement was the creation of a political world in which not just the few but the many could escape submersion in the realm of necessity and move into the realm of freedom. There seems little of this sense of exhilaration in the expressed hopes of contemporary liberal theorists. Perhaps it seems to them something of a romantic delusion fit for democracy's infancy but not for its maturity. In any case, the central aspiration of this form of liberal public philosophy is no longer so much the creation of a social world in which all can escape political subordination and social dependency and can grow into the full maturity of self-rule so much as it is the attainment of a kind of justice built for people who are seen as able to rise above the realm of necessity only in very specific and limited ways. The new conception of democratic persons generates a novel way in which we could aspire to *share* our fate, but in so doing, it changes and diminishes the way in which we can aspire to *shape* our fate.[35]

THE NORMATIVE SOCIOLOGY OF CONTEMPORARY LIBERALISM

Political philosophies aspiring to real world influence generally come packaged together with what can be termed normative sociologies—models of social structure that serve to identify and characterize the major component groups or classes or strata whose functions and interactions promote, incarnate, or frustrate the philosophy's favored social goals. These are not, therefore, evaluatively neutral descriptive sociologies. They are accounts of social dynamics seen through the prism of a moral point of view. The different functional groups take on hues of virtue and vice, heroism and villainy, productivity and incompetency, and they are assigned different roles—ranging from rule to destruction—accordingly. So, for example, Plato's model of the well-ordered society is not simply a polis where everyone is attuned to the cosmic forms of the good, the true, and the beautiful. Replicating the cosmic harmonies on earth is instead a task whose accomplishment must be mediated through the various kinds of people with various kinds of talents who populate the society. It is crucial to the way he constructs his idealized society in *The Republic*, then, that Plato believes in the existence of different character types governed by different component elements of the human psyche. Getting the polis right for him requires getting philosophic, spirited, and appetitive souls into the right places: "Each of the three orders in [a just state will be] doing its own proper work."[36] In similar fashion, Marxist political philosophy is not just a vision of an idealized future time of economic abundance where a new breed of "socialist men" will overcome all forms of psychic alienation;

live by the principle "from each according to his abilities, to each according to his needs"; and be free to farm in the morning, fish in the afternoon, and write poetry in the evening. That vision may provide the theory's horizon, but the guts of it involve understandings and depictions of the traits and behaviors of the bourgeoisie, the proletariat, the lumpen proletariat, and the vanguard.

The normative sociology of traditional American liberalism was fundamentally a civic republican one. It considered the middling classes as most likely to embody the civic virtues, and partly for that reason, it looked upon them as the key to the stability, the prosperity, and the liberty of the republic. Conversely, it looked upon both the rich and the poor with a certain degree of suspicion, even if it recognized the contribution that people of unusual talent and ambition—hence likely to be among the aristocrats—could make to the common weal. This republican belief in the practical advantages of a large and strong middle class has, of course, a long heritage in political sociology. Aristotle wrote in his *Politics* that "a state which is based on the middle class is bound to be the best constituted in respect of the elements of which, on our view, a state is naturally composed."[37] In support of this claim, Aristotle offered several reasons. First, he thought that a large middle class lessened the extent of "faction and dissension among the citizens." Second, he thought that the middle class was composed of equals and peers and hence could more easily become friends and associates, which in turn was conducive to what we today call social capital. He also argued that people in a middle condition "are the most ready to listen to reason." And finally, they were sufficiently secure not to covet the goods of others but not so wealthy as to be objects of envy; hence, "neither plotting against others, nor plotted against themselves, they live in freedom from danger." In contrast, both the rich and powerful, at the one end, and the mean and poor, at the other, presented problems for society. The former were inclined to excessive ambition for power, wealth, and glory, and they "are both unwilling to obey and ignorant how to obey." The latter "tend too much to roguery and petty offenses," and they "are ignorant how to rule." A society composed primarily of rich and poor, therefore, tends to become "a state, not of freemen, but only of slaves and masters."[38] Writing some 2,000 years later, Rousseau put the same point succinctly. A healthy republic, he said, should try to "allow neither rich men nor beggars" but rather to "bring the two extremes as near to each other as possible." This is because the two estates of rich and poor "are equally fatal to the common good. . . . It is always between them that public liberty is put up to auction; the one buys, and the other sells."[39]

Mediated by the republicanism of people such as Sydney and Harrington, by the bourgeois orientation of liberalism, by the anti-elitism of the Reformation, and by the predominantly middle-class background of émigrés to the New World, the normative sociology of traditional American liberalism followed a similar pattern. The principal difference was that, again in concert with the empirical demographics of the British colonies, the definition of the middling classes was broader and more latitudinarian than the Aristotelian one. Aristotle argued that mechanics, shopkeepers, and farmers could not really perform all the duties of citizenship because they had insufficient leisure to develop the necessary capacities of wisdom and virtue. Burke echoed this logic in his conservative complaints against democratization. But for traditional American liberalism, it was these kinds of folks they had in mind when they talked about the middle classes.

Melancton Smith gave voice to this American appropriation of classical republican sociology in his debate with Alexander Hamilton during the New York constitutional ratification convention. "The great," he complained, "consider themselves above the common people [and] they fancy themselves to have a right of pre-eminence in every thing. In short, they possess the same feelings, and are under the influence of the same motives, as a hereditary nobility." Therefore, "it has been the principal care of free governments to guard against the incroachments of the great." The best way to do this is to incorporate those he variously calls "the respectable yeomanry," "the substantial yeomanry," and "yeomen of sense and discernment" unto the ruling councils of government. That is because this class of "those in middling circumstances" is on the whole more imbued with civic virtues than either the great or the poor: "The substantial yeomanry of the country are more temperate, of better morals and less ambition than the great. . . . They are inclined by habit and the company with whom they associate to set bounds to their passions and appetites." Hence, "a representative body composed principally of the respectable yeomanry is the best possible security to liberty. When the interest of this part of the community is pursued, the public good is pursued, because the body of every nation consists of this class."[40]

Jefferson's policies and prescriptions were grounded in similar sociological perceptions and assessments. He also believed that the respectable yeomanry best embodied republican civic virtues, that their productive energies sustained the possibilities of democratic success, and that every effort of democratic statesmen should be devoted to increasing their number and fostering their welfare. His paradigmatic respectable yeomen, of course, were the independent farmers who were, he thought, "the chosen people of God, if ever he had a chosen people, whose breasts he has made his peculiar deposit for substantial and genuine virtue." The key to their superiority in the republican virtues was the way that their economic status and the mode of their livelihood made them self-reliant and independent, since as Jefferson opined—in line with traditional republican moral psychology—"dependence begets subservience and venality, suffocates the germ of virtue, and prepares fit tools for the designs of ambition."[41] Those who harbored such "designs of ambition" were a society's aristocrats. Jefferson's institutional proposals and legal reforms were directed, therefore, toward constraining the wealth and power of the great and linking their ambitions and values as closely as possible to the welfare of the independent freeholders. The cultivation of superior talent and its deployment into positions of leadership was desirable, he recognized. But he sought, especially by his proposals for a system of education open to all ranks from which a "natural aristocracy" would be drawn, to recruit such leaders from the broad mass of citizenry and keep it tied to their interests. At the other end of the sociological spectrum, Jefferson cast a wary eye upon the dangers presented to the body politic by a subservient, demoralized, and disenfranchised lower class of the sort he saw during his Parisian sojourn. "The mobs of great cities add just so much to the support of pure government," he wrote, "as sores do to the strength of the human body."[42] To prevent the growth of such "sores" on the political body, he proposed policies such as progressive taxation, the avoidance of an economy based upon wage labor, and the making available of uncultivated land at a nominal rent to any of the unemployed willing to put it to productive use. "The People" whom Walt Whitman looked upon as the foundation of his expansive democratic future were also, as we noted in the previous chapter, very much a respectable yeomanry. They were not the elite, whom he depicted as transplants from the courts and castles of the Old World, as the "merely educated," and as "genteel little creatures." They were in fact yeomen, the "average man" who "at last only is important." These average folk were not the poor or a rabble. They were respectable people despite their commonness, respectable in their economic self-sufficiency and in their aspirations for intellectual betterment.[43]

The normative sociology characteristic of contemporary American liberalism departs quite strikingly from this republican model. In contemporary liberal sociology, both the poor and the elite assume new prominence and legitimacy at the expense of those in middling condition: the interests of the poor now take priority over those of the respectable yeomanry, and the yeomen surrender their moral authority and entitlement to rule to a liberal meritocracy, aka "the best and brightest."

Under the aegis of today's high liberalism, the respectable yeomanry of the middle classes have lost the place of honor and special concern they occupied in the sociology of traditional progressivism because they have surrendered their claims to virtue

CHAPTER TWO

and competency—claims that provided the warrants for this pride of place. This crucial loss derives from changes both in moral intuitions and in empirical perceptions, the former of which undermine the claim to virtue and the latter of which challenge the claim of competency. These changes derive in turn from changes in the moral imagination of contemporary liberalism and from empirical and hermeneutic claims that emerge from contemporary social science. Taken in concert, these changes in effect dissolve the very concept or category of the "respectable yeomanry" because they subvert the grounds for their claim of respectability.

The moral criteria that served to define the respectability of those who qualified for inclusion in the "respectable yeomanry" of traditional American liberalism came from where the republican account of the virtues and vices overlapped and corresponded with the Protestant ethic. One prominent Revolutionary era account of the republican virtues alluded to people who were "industrious and frugal, simple in their manners, just and hardy, united and brave." Moral declension occurred when people succumbed to "pride and avarice, luxury and dissipation, idleness and sensuality, and too often . . . impiety."[44] The Protestant ethic concurred: self-restraint rather than dissipation, industry rather than idleness, responsibility rather than dependence, were all good both for society and for the soul. Displaying these virtues made people morally worthy and socially respectable, and these were virtues generally associated with the middle class.

This moral imaginary and its attendant category of respectability, however, cannot readily survive the impact of what Daniel Bell has called the cultural contradictions of capitalism. The move from early capitalism's need for production, saving, and accumulation to advanced capitalism's need for mass consumption turns what once were called avarice and sensuality into acceptable consumerist yuppiedom and turns adult self-restraint into irrational repressiveness. Perhaps even more devastatingly from the viewpoint of those aspiring to traditional yeoman respectability, the sociological determinism embraced by contemporary liberals turns a proud adherence to the work ethic into unseemly moral conceit. For to take pride in fulfilling the demands of the work ethic is to take pride in having what Rawls calls "the superior character that enables [one] to make the effort" to cultivate and deploy one's abilities, when in fact that character and the resultant effort are the product of "circumstances for which [one] can claim no credit."[45] Rather than being people of distinctive moral merit and particular social significance, the hardworking yeomen of middling condition metamorphose into a morally presumptuous social liability—a boring and repressed lot who have the temerity to think themselves better than their less advantaged peers.

The pivotal role of those of middling condition within the normative sociology of traditional American liberalism was also based upon imputing to them the capacity for reason and good judgment. They were—at least could be—people "of sense and discernment," to borrow a phrase from Melancton Smith. This claim too has undergone assault in the past several decades, and the resulting doubts about the knowledge and good sense of the average citizens of today's democratic societies have also been important in their loss of status within liberal scenarios of social progress. These developments and the social scientific findings and interpretive arguments that have powerfully contributed to them are a sufficiently important part of the story to merit a fuller review in the next chapter. For the moment, it must suffice to mention these doubts about the basic competency of the average democratic citizen here because they play a significant role in the loss of political purchase of the middle and lower middle classes within recent liberal thought: if "the people" are ignorant of politically essential realities and are insufficiently knowledgeable about fundamental democratic norms and values, how can they be trusted to rule?

In the sociological gaze of contemporary American liberalism, then, the respectable yeomanry lose the identity and status they held within traditional American liberalism. Instead of appearing as the "swarms of alert, turbulent, good-natured, independent citizens, mechanics, clerks" who filled Walt Whitman with "a singular awe,"[46] they appear in the guise of Archie Bunker—not coincidentally an archetype constructed from the contemporary liberal sensibility of Norman Lear—a character meant to fill the viewing audience with Menckenesque disdain.

As the erstwhile yeomanry become less respected, the lowest social ranks gain a new identity and a moral promotion. They are not simply the poor, much less the idle and dissolute. They are now conceptualized as "the least fortunate group," "the least favored," "those who have lost out," "the least advantaged," and "the most disadvantaged."[47] Two features of this benign reconceptualization are noteworthy here. First, all of the identifying terms refer to external circumstances or contingencies: "favor," "fortune," "advantage." None of the defining features reference either traits of character or levels of effort or achievement. Everything is in the passive voice. Second, there is no conceptual space or empirical distinction between starting points and outcomes, between being least advantaged in initial endowment and being in the end least well-off. It is not possible within Rawls's terminological repertoire to characterize people who began disadvantaged but became well-off or people who were similarly endowed but wound up quite differently: the status of disadvantage and the condition of being less well-off are definitionally conflated, as in the formulation that "all persons with less than half of the median income and wealth may be taken as the least advantaged segment."[48] The implicit claim here, definitionally embedded and terminologically enforced, is that advantage and outcome are the same thing. Anyone who succeeds in life is not (was not?) "disadvantaged" by definition. And anyone who does badly in life is (was?) among "the least advantaged."

All of the causal claims and moral appraisals implicit in this reconceptualization are, of course, logically quite appropriate within the context of Rawls's understanding of social causality and the limitations on personal agency canvassed above. Since not only someone's natural abilities and initial social standing but also his or her character traits and capacity for making an effort are deemed the product of external circumstance, to what else but "fortune," "favor," or degree of "advantage" could the level of well-being he or she attains be attributed? But the consequences of this reconstruction of the nature and causes of being among "the least favored" in society are more than merely academic and theoretical. This reconstruction brings with it, and quite deliberately so, the important moral and practical consequence of moving the poor from being objects of a certain wariness as potential threats to the health of a republican order to being objects of special concern and solicitude. Indeed, in the transformed normative sociology of contemporary liberalism, the yeomanry of middling condition not only lose the basis of their respectability; they also lose their status as what we might call the ideologically most favored class, in the sense of those whose interests and welfare are construed as most important to the purposes of a democratic society. In the Rawlsian moral and sociological universe it is no longer the case, as Melancton Smith averred, that "when the interest of [the respectable yeomanry] is pursued, the public good is pursued."[49] It is instead the welfare of the least advantaged that is to be maximized in accord with the most fundamental moral purpose of democratic society: to achieve social justice. Whereas in a democratic society understood as government of, by, and for the people, it was from the standpoint of the respectable yeomanry that the success and legitimacy of the social order were to be gauged, in the public philosophy of contemporary liberalism it instead is "from [the] position [of] the least advantaged representative man [that] the social system is to be judged."[50]

This displacement of the respectable yeomen of American republicanism from their pride of place in the shaping and assessment of a democratic society is graphically reflected in Rawls's argument regarding what he calls the "chain-connectedness" between the welfare of the least well-off and those another step or two above them on the socioeconomic scale. Chain connection is in effect the mirror opposite of trickle-down economics. Trickle-down theory seeks to justify policies favoring the wealthier investor classes in society on the grounds that they will use their resources in ways that will stoke the economic engines and cause benefits to filter down to the rest of us. Chain connection argues inversely that benefits directed to the least advantaged members of society will have the effect of improving the lot of those just above them. "Let us suppose," writes Rawls, "that inequalities in expectations are chain-connected: that is, if an advantage has the effect of raising the expectations of the lowest position, it raises the expectations of all positions in between. For example, if the greater expectations for entrepreneurs benefit the unskilled worker, they also benefit the semiskilled." Assuming that the world works like that, we can then reach the happy conclusion that "everyone benefits when the difference principle is satisfied." And what if this assumption proves counterfactual? What if everyone, including those formerly described as the respectable yeomanry, does not benefit from maximizing the welfare of the least well-off? Well, that really doesn't matter. As Rawls puts it, "Of course these conditions [i.e., chain connection] may not hold. But in this case those who are better off should not have a veto over the benefits available for the least favored. We are still to maximize the expectations of those most disadvantaged."[51] Traditional liberalism prioritized the welfare of the respectable yeomanry on the grounds of both public good and moral desert: the public good was fostered when they flourished because they were the archetypal (independent, self-supporting, law-abiding, nondominating) good citizens crucial to the health of the republic, and they deserved to flourish because of their industry and their other civic virtues. But on the moral scales of Rawlsian high liberalism, these claims are unavailing: justice trumps public good, and justice, as we have seen, is in its view flouted rather than served by conferring moral credit upon any particular traits of character, including those traits that had made the yeomen respectable.

Simultaneously with their loss of pride of place in the understanding of American liberalism about whose welfare and advancement should be of focal concern for a democratic society, the respectable yeomanry also lose their centrality when it comes to the question of who should rule in a democracy. They lose their pivotal status both in who democracy is deemed to be for and in who it is deemed to be by. Those who inherit the former role, as seen earlier, are the "least advantaged." Those who inherit the role of chief legitimate governing agent are the meritocratic elites who understand and are committed to what high liberals understand as democracy's constitutive values.

The transfer of authority from the people to elites in the reform scenarios of contemporary liberalism occurs for two principal reasons. The first of these is an altered perception of "the people" on the part of the relevant theorists, signaled terminologically in substantively unflattering characterizations: "the people" are now "the masses." As Christopher Lasch has observed,

> The new elites, the professional classes in particular, regard the masses with mingled scorn and apprehension. In the United States, "Middle America"—a term that has both geographical and social implications—has come to symbolize everything that stands in the way of progress: "family values," mindless patriotism, religious fundamentalism, racism, homophobia, retrograde views of women. Middle Americans, as they appear to the makers of educated opinion, are hopelessly shabby, unfashionable, and provincial. . . . They are at once absurd and vaguely menacing.[52]

They certainly, in any case, are not the kinds of folk you would want to have governing a democratic polity, however ironic it might be to counsel taking the demos out of democracy. As the political scientist Thomas Dye wrote in 1972 in a book entitled *The Irony of Democracy*:

> The masses are incompetent in the tasks of government. They have neither the time, intelligence, information, skills, nor knowledge to direct the course of a nation. . . . The masses

CHAPTER TWO

are anti-democratic and therefore cannot be relied upon to govern democratically. Despite a superficial commitment to the symbols of democracy, the people are not attached to the ideals of individual liberty, toleration of diversity, freedoms of expression and of dissent, or equality of opportunity. On the contrary, these are more likely to be the values of elites. Masses are authoritarian, intolerant, anti-intellectual, nativist, alienated, hateful, and violent. . . . Two hundred years ago Jefferson proposed universal free public education as a prescription for mass ignorance, incompetence, and alienation. Today the masses in America average twelve years of free public education, but, if anything, they appear less capable of governing in a wise and humane fashion than the masses of Jefferson's time.[53]

The second major reason that popular self-rule plays little role within contemporary high liberalism is that in its understanding of democracy, substance trumps process. "Democratic" does not refer so much to a mode of decisionmaking as it does to conformity with substantive criteria of distributive entitlement. It is outcomes that count. And the substantive standards for right outcomes are not themselves derived from or dependent upon the expressed will of the people so much as they are ascertained theoretically by what Rawls terms at one point a kind of "moral geometry" predicated upon axiomatic democratic principles. And clearly, the capacities of performing these feats of complex moral reasoning are more to be found among moral philosophers steeped in the fundamental verities of the liberal tradition or among judges habituated to the verities of liberal constitutional jurisprudence than among the democratic populace more generally.

This Rawlsian moral logic and its consequences for the high liberal theory of democratic governance are well captured in Amy Gutmann's account of the proper relationship between procedural and substantive norms of democratic legitimacy. It is, she writes, a "reasonable resolution" of tensions between procedural and substantive democratic norms to

> preclude the use of simple democratic procedures when we clearly know that x ought to be the resulting policy and y is to be greatly preferred on grounds of justice to any of its leading competitors. The most obvious policies in which we employ this "nondemocratic" alternative are those involving people's basic rights. In such cases, we rightly do not allow n to be determined by an imperfect democratic procedure once we know that the institution and perpetuation of x can be all but guaranteed by other means. Civil and political rights in liberal societies fall under this category of solutions [and] once a just society is instituted, welfare rights should also fall under this category of cases.[54]

In the context of our concern with the contemporary liberal theory of democratic governance, the most pertinent elements of this argument are the claim that "we clearly know" what is preferred "on grounds of justice," the reference to "other means," and the assertion that "welfare rights" are properly to be included among the "basic rights" exempt from determination by "imperfect democratic procedure."

The first significant claim here is that the specific content of "basic rights" and "justice" are "clearly known." Perhaps this claim should be construed as merely a flourish of political rhetoric, as in Jefferson's bold insistence upon self-evident truths. But the passage in question comes from an academic treatise rather than from a public political manifesto. Hence, this seems to be a straightforward characterization of the epistemic status of certain convictions regarding the content of social justice. These convictions, however, are not falsifiable truth claims that have been empirically validated. They are instead moral beliefs that, however deeply held and passionately affirmed, do not take as their subject matter features of the world we can be said to "know" in any standard sense of that term. The epistemic locution on display in this passage has to be seen, therefore, as a manifestation of contemporary liberalism's moral certitude about contestable rights claims and assertions about justice.

The second notable element of this argument is the indeterminate royal "we" on display in it. Who, specifically, are those of us to whom this putative moral knowledge is vouchsafed? Who are the knowers among us, and who are left out? The "we" in question cannot be all of us or even a majority of us, or else what Madison called "the republican principle" would suffice and there would be no need to look to some "non-democratic alternative." So the clear implication here is that there is some minority subset of the democratic citizenry who are entitled by their superior wisdom, virtue, and/or status to step outside of standard democratic procedures and put their convictions about rights and justice into law by "other means." Who exactly these people are and what exactly these other means may be are never specified. But in context, it seems hard to interpret this argument as anything other than an assertion of the right of a meritocratic liberal establishment to overturn or evade majority views and legislative outcomes by judicial or bureaucratic fiat. Moreover, this moral warrant is not limited to the protection of democratic rules of the game, which may in fact require judicial protection of insular minorities against tyrannical majorities who would disenfranchise them; to the protection of individuals threatened with the powers of the state; and to insistence upon equal protection of the laws: it extends also to the determination of substantive rules governing the allocation of social and economic resources among the citizenry. Thus, the Rawlsian moral imaginary of contemporary liberalism eventuates into a regime in which norms of democratic self-rule are subordinated to the instantiation of principles for the proper distribution of goods purportedly ascertainable by elites seeking to serve the interests of the least advantaged in the name of justice.

Recognizing perhaps that this formulation of the derivation

of definitive democratic principles might seem to evade the fundamental procedural requisite of democratic legitimacy—that governmental authority and hence the principles enforced by that authority must come from the consent of the governed—and also acknowledging that any moral geometry must take its leave from moral intuitions that function axiomatically and hence cannot themselves be products of philosophical deduction, Rawls in his later work modified and elaborated his account of the basis of the principles of justice. He was not a philosopher-king trying to force a democratic society to conform to "foundationalist" ideals he had stipulated a priori or found by noetic reasoning in some ivory tower. Instead, he argued, the moral intuitions from which the principles of justice were derived came from the jus gentium of contemporary democratic societies. That is, these moral intuitions represented the very basic and commonly accepted beliefs about liberty and equality shared by citizens—or at least by all "reasonable" citizens—of today's democratic societies.

This conventionalist account of the grounds or origins of the moral intuitions behind the principles of justice—sometimes called Rawls's hermeneutic or antifoundationalist turn—at least gives important lip service to the principles of democratic procedural legitimacy. The principles of justice are avowedly based upon popular consent in the form of an "overlapping consensus" that "includes all the opposing philosophical and religious doctrines likely to persist and to gain adherents in a more or less just constitutional democratic society."[55] Useful as this new formulation may be in illuminating Rawls's understanding of where the principles of democratic justice he champions ultimately come from, it does not succeed in lessening the tension between substantive and procedural legitimacy within his theory and within the public philosophy of contemporary liberalism. Nor does it ultimately suffice to change the priority of substance over procedure and the priority of moral philosophy over politics that de facto elevates liberal elites over the democratic populace. The problem here is that, as Rawls concedes and as contemporary survey research confirms, "the public political culture may be of two minds even at a very deep level" about the meaning of the norms of liberty and equality. And these disagreements are not then in Rawls's account to be adjudicated politically by the deliberation and voting of the democratic electorate but adjudicated theoretically by the liberal philosopher finding "a more fundamental intuitive idea within the complex structure of which the other familiar intuitive ideas are then systematically connected and related," thereby "shaping into one coherent view the deeper bases of agreement embedded in the political culture of a constitutional regime."[56] It also falls to the philosopher to define what counts as "reasonable" and hence which doctrines may or may not be included in the putative overlapping consensus that allegedly will accredit this "one coherent view." The "one coherent view," of course, is the theory of rights-based egalitarian social justice Rawls provides. And the preferred interpretation of "reasonableness"—which places beyond the pale of reason, inter alia, not only Nazis and racists but also libertarians and opponents of abortion rights—serves to insulate these principles of justice from challenge.[57]

When all of these facets of what I have termed the normative sociology of contemporary liberalism are brought together, the result is a striking departure from the paradigm of governance associated with that of traditional American liberalism. In the earlier conception, democratic governance meant the self-rule of the people on behalf of the self-realization of the people. And if "the people" meant all the citizenry, it was a category dominated both statistically and morally by those of middling condition, the respectable yeomanry, who best embodied the requisites of republican citizenship. To the extent that anything resembling an aristocracy was to survive and have legitimate functions, it had to be a "natural" aristocracy in Jefferson's sense—one that emerged from the ranks of the people by virtue of achievement and was kept on a reasonably short leash, answerable to the people it served. At the other end of the spectrum, those unable to achieve the competency and independence of the respectable yeomanry were not to be oppressed, but they were seen mostly as something of a management problem, and they certainly held no particular moral purchase.

By removing from the middling orders the moral grounds for their claims to the status of respectability, by giving to the "least advantaged" occupancy of the vantage point from which a democratic society is to be judged, and by conceding to a contemporary natural aristocracy/meritocracy a special role in governance, the moral imagination of contemporary liberalism arrives at a novel model of good democratic governance. That model is one captured succinctly and paradigmatically in the words of Donna Shalala, then president of the University of Wisconsin, who commended to the audience for her 1989 David Dodds Henry Lecture at the University of Illinois "the ideal of a disinterested technocratic elite . . . , society's best and brightest in service to its most needy" through "the miracles of social science."[58]

CONCLUSION: A NEW LIBERAL POLITICS?

Our exposition has proceeded for the most part in the context of academic theories of liberalism and democracy. It would not be difficult, however, to identify many of these core beliefs and moral commitments of academic high liberalism out there in the world of everyday politics doing a lot of work in shaping the rhetoric, the policies, the strategies, and the moral judgments of contemporary liberalism. No doubt, these academic ideas reflect as much as they shape the evolving moral and political sensibilities in society as a whole. But the relevant claim here is that the content and implications of the ideas of liberal theorists are not of "merely academic" interest in the pejorative and dismissive sense of that phrase. These are ideas deeply implicated in the changing face of what passes for liberal politics in contemporary America. Manifestations of the practical embodiment and influence of the moral priorities, the moral psychology, and the normative sociology of high liberal philosophy arguably include familiar features of contemporary liberal politics, such as the ubiquity of reference in liberal rhetoric to fairness, social justice, and entitlement rights; the ubiquity of tropes of victimhood and the terminology of "disadvantage" in characterizations of those on the lowest rungs of the socioeconomic hierarchy; the iconography of passivity and pathos rather than of energy and competency when it comes to "the people"—as seen in the FDR Memorial or in what could be called the parade of pathos at the center of the 1996 Democratic Convention; the derogation of the work ethic and the disregard when it comes to social policy of whether individual resources derive from labor or from social reallocation; the widespread condescension toward and neglect of the interests and values of the working and lower middle classes on the part of liberal elites; the tendency of socially reformist students to aspire to become "movement lawyers" or administrators rather than electoral politicians; the comfort of liberal reformers with strategies that bypass public opinion and coalition building in favor of gaining desired outcomes through judicial rulings or bureaucratic directives; and the tendency of many liberal groups, such as the American Civil Liberties Union (ACLU), to absolutize and prioritize individual rights claims even where these claims are made at the expense of the functioning of public spaces and institutions. In contrast, the rhetoric, social goals, and strategies of self-realization and self-rule characteristic of traditional American liberalism have over the past several decades seemed notable mostly by their relative absence.

3   Why Did It Happen?

The purpose of my argument so far has been to sketch two contrasting ideal type models of American reform liberalism that have exerted great influence over American political life. The first of these, what I have termed traditional liberalism, is a conception of democratic aspirations representing the American embodiment of what Jürgen Habermas has characterized as the "revolutionary consciousness" that inspired the democratic upsurge of the late eighteenth and nineteenth centuries. This drive toward the democratization of political power embodied, in Habermas's words, "a new mentality, which was shaped by a new time consciousness, a new concept of political practice, and a new notion of legitimation." This new mentality, he wrote, centered on "the understanding of political practice in terms of self-determination and self-realization,"[1] the same political goals that Walt Whitman embraced under the rubrics "by the people" and "for the people." The second model, that of contemporary rights-based egalitarianism, turns, in contrast, about the pursuit of distributive justice understood as maximizing the social and economic welfare of the least well-off. This latter and more recent conception of democracy is one in which the norm and significance of popular sovereignty are considerably less salient, elbowed aside by Donna Shalala's vision of "the best and brightest in service to the most needy" through whatever political or legal contrivances can conduce most effectively toward the attainment of social justice.

CHAPTER THREE

It is important to every part of my argument—analytical, empirical, critical, and prescriptive—to emphasize that the displacement of the more venerable populist and republican version of American liberalism by a rights-based egalitarianism focused upon social justice represents a change in public philosophy of sufficient depth and extent to require a term such as *transformation* to characterize it. This change cannot properly be styled as an *adaptation*, a term that in this context invites serious misunderstanding. This terminological insistence is not simply a rhetorical one. It instead is a substantive claim grounded upon the logical structure of moral and political philosophical arguments.

The nature and significance of the difference between what I am calling a transformation and an adaptation can be clarified by invoking Ronald Dworkin's distinction between what he has termed "constitutive" and "derivative" components of political theories. As Dworkin argues,

> For any full political theory [and] in any coherent political program . . . we may distinguish between constitutive and derivative political positions. A constitutive position is a political position valued for its own sake: a political position such that any failure fully to secure that position, or any decline in the degree to which it is secured, is *pro tanto* a loss in the value of the overall political arrangement. A derivative political position is a position that is not, within the theory in question, constitutive. . . . [Derivative positions] are valued as strategies, as means of achieving the constitutive positions.[2]

Given this analytical distinction between core and subsidiary components of a political theory, then, we can define a change of public philosophy in which derivative positions are altered but constitutive positions or goals remain constant as an adaptation. By contrast, a case in which the original constitutive positions are displaced by other ultimate goals can be labeled a transformation.

WHY DID IT HAPPEN?

John Dewey provides us with a paradigmatic example of an adaptation of liberal public philosophy in his *Liberalism and Social Action*. He wrote there of liberalism: "If we strip its creed from adventitious elements, there are . . . enduring values for which earlier liberalism stood. These values are liberty, the development of the inherent capacities of individuals made possible through liberty, and the central role of free intelligence in inquiry, discussion and expression." What many people of his day failed to understand, he complained, was that important doctrines associated with liberal politics were but what he called "adventitious elements." Specifically, the sociology of "rugged individualism" and the economic mechanisms of laissez-faire needed to be seen as, to use Dworkin's terminology, derivative positions that did not possess the intrinsic value of constitutive or enduring purposes. They may have been defensible earlier on as plausible means of producing the axial goods of liberty, development, and free inquiry, but they were merely strategic doctrines "relevant only to their own time" and now obsolete because the "contemporary scene" was "radically altered." The new political economy of corporate industrial capitalism demanded, then, a change that would take the form of an adaptation in our technical sense: the "enduring" constitutive value regarding "the necessity of liberty for individuals" could not be achieved by the previously touted derivative measures of laissez-faire but instead would "require social control of economic forces in the interest of the great mass of individuals."³

By contrast, the shift from the public philosophy of what I have called traditional liberalism to the public philosophy of contemporary high liberalism cannot accurately be described as an adaptation in this technical and structural sense. For this change was not one in which strategic or derivative positions were changed as a result of altered conditions in order to attain enduring purposes taken largely intact from the earlier theory. In the transformation we have described, the older constitutive ends of self-rule and self-realization were set aside or subordinated, and the goal of social justice of a particular sort took over their central place. What

CHAPTER THREE

this means in the context of any attempt at causal explanation, then, is that it will not suffice to identify changes in social and economic circumstances that might require the adoption of novel strategies in the service of established goals. Instead, the relevant causal factors have to include developments that could change the historical situation or change the understanding of that situation in such a way and to such an extent as to give impetus to an abandonment or demotion of some very fundamental social aspirations in favor of new and different ones. For the same logical reasons, in the context of justification it will not suffice for those seeking to defend a transformation of public philosophy to rest their case simply upon the invocation of new circumstances that might necessitate the deployment of different strategies or new institutions in order to get to a previously established destination. Instead, an adequate justification for a change in the ultimate destination itself will have to involve arguments of greater depth.

The purpose of this chapter is to venture something in the way of explanation of the transformation in the public philosophy of American liberalism canvassed in the previous chapters. Although this task may not be essential to the core concerns of this book, which are philosophical and normative rather than historical and explanatory, the significant changes in moral sensibility and political aspirations that I claim have occurred beg some kind of explanation. Such changes do not occur adventitiously or in a vacuum, and trying to answer the "why" question presents an interesting intellectual puzzle in its own right. Beyond the intrinsic intellectual tug of the explanatory challenge, moreover, addressing it contributes something to our normative and philosophical project as well. That is because identification of some of the underlying forces, both ideational and material, that have provided impetus for these changes helps to flesh out and illuminate the content of the contemporary liberal moral imagination by contextualizing it. Public philosophies are neither disembodied pieces of abstract speculation nor freestanding intellectual constructs. They develop from and depend for their substance upon the complex of motivations, social perceptions, and associated philosophical assumptions—be these anthropological, metaphysical, or epistemological—that shape and inform them. When it comes to political theories, the causal forces leading to their emergence are not purely external and prior to them but are part of their larger substance and simultaneous with them in the sense that they are absorbed and incorporated into them.

I entertain here no quixotic hope to achieve anything remotely resembling explanatory completeness about the causes of the changes in the theoretical orientation of American liberalism. Indeed, it is hard even to imagine what a truly "complete" explanation would look like in this context. Profound changes in political worldviews of the sort under consideration here always result from complex and reciprocal interaction among changing historical circumstances and forces, social problems and concerns generated by these new situations, and the cupboard of ideas available to those who seek to address these problems and concerns theoretically. It is hard to do much more in explanatory terms in these cases than to identify some of the more important strands of historical contingencies, ideas, and moral preoccupations that go into this mix and to suggest their bearing on the theoretical developments at issue.

One final disclaimer should perhaps be entered before proceeding to this task. The two conceptions of liberalism in question include one that developed in the nineteenth century and another that appeared or was consolidated during the latter half of the twentieth century. The causal issue here is: why is the latter so different from the former, and why does it differ in the ways it does? A second possible question then becomes: What about the intervening period? How does the first half of the twentieth century and its most characteristic forms of liberal politics fit into the picture? Specifically, how do Progressivism and the New Deal comport with the two ideal type models? Do they fit under one or the other model, or do they represent yet another distinct model or two? Or, alternatively, are they best understood as transitional hybrids of lesser status in theoretical terms—rather like Auguste Comte's conception of what he styled as "negative" and "critical" models intervening between successive "positive" and "organic" ones? Apart from offering a very cryptic response to this last question, I plan largely to evade or gloss over it here. I do so for two reasons, one practical and the other theoretical. As a practical matter, it would not be particularly helpful to attend to this question because it would take us far afield and would admit of only very inconclusive answers in any case. What we call Progressivism was a very complex, multifarious, and loosely integrated social movement with many strands and many protagonists.[4] It would take another volume to survey and catalog all these strands, and after that task was accomplished, it would still not be possible to reconcile and integrate them all into a single, coherent theoretical model.

If it is practically inadvisable to try in any extensive and precise way to identify the location of Progressivism with respect to the two ideal type models of American reform liberalism constructed in the previous chapters, it also seems permissible on theoretical grounds to sidestep this task. Such a sidestep is theoretically unproblematic because the central hermeneutic and prescriptive issues that concern us here turn around the distinctiveness of contemporary high liberalism and its adequacy or inadequacy as a resource for dealing with the challenges of progressive politics in the twenty-first century. Even my deployment, with a good bit of hermeneutic license, of my model of traditional liberalism is geared to that concern. Remembering the dominant philosophical preconceptions, moral values, and political goals of an earlier form of democratic idealism accomplishes three things in this regard: first, it serves as a contrasting frame to bring into relief the novelty and distinctiveness of the philosophical/ideological orientation of contemporary high liberalism; second, it makes it clear that this orientation is not part of a continuous and doctrinally stable tradition of American progressive politics; and third, it gets onto the table an alternative version of progressive goals and beliefs that might have worthwhile contributions to make to our sense of what twenty-first-century liberalism should look like.

For whatever value it may have in filling in the gap in my schematic "rational reconstruction" of American liberalism or in the service of full disclosure, however, my very cryptic answer to the query about where Progressivism and New Deal liberalism fit into this picture would be that both of them remain in my view for the most part within the theoretical orbit of what I have called traditional or populist liberalism. In both cases, however, the question is hard to answer with any great confidence because each of these reform movements was focused not so much upon fundamental theoretical debates about core moral norms and political purposes as it was upon a consuming set of practical social problems—problems that threatened to undermine traditional liberal goals and that therefore required sustained attention and work at the tactical more than the theoretical level.

Progressivism's continuity with traditional liberalism is manifest, I would argue, in Dewey's specific designation of "the development of the inherent capacities of individuals" as one of the core "enduring values for which earlier liberalism stood"—a value he wants to highlight and endorse.[5] Dewey's claim here coincides both normatively and hermeneutically with what Whitman meant by government "for the people." In both Whitman and Dewey, moreover, this feature of their thought represents their common appropriation of Mill's understanding of the ultimate purpose of a free society and their common quasi-Hegelian understanding of the deeper meaning of democracy as a way of life rather than as merely a set of political institutions. This theoretical appropriation and endorsement of Wilhelm von Humboldt's norm of personal development cited by Mill in his epigram for *On Liberty* is also clearly reflected in some of the defining practical projects of Progressive reformers, such as Jane Addams's enterprises in Chicago and the remarkable popularity and scope of the Chatauqua movement. The continuity of Progressivism with its precursors is also manifest in its attempt to promote and institutionalize the norm of popular self-rule. This dedication to government "by the people," for example, clearly animated the implementation of procedural innovations such as referendum, initiative, and recall under the aegis of Progressive reformers such as Hiram Johnson. And it is also apparent in Jane Addams's insistence that a welfare state should not be created "unless the power of direct legislation is placed in the hands of the people, in order that these changes may come, not as the centralized government [gives] them, from above down, but may come from the people up; that the people shall be the directing and controlling factors in the legislation."[6]

If Progressivism exhibited these important strands of continuity with what I have called traditional liberalism, it also contrasted with contemporary liberalism in equally fundamental ways. Especially significant in this respect is what Eldon Eisenach has characterized as the Progressives' "direct opposition to an abstract rights-based discourse, whether expressed as individual rights, state rights, or as constitutional formalism." Contemporary liberalism is famously and properly characterized precisely as "rights-based liberalism," whether Rawlsian or Nozickean in content. But the Progressives explicitly rejected this deontological account of the moral foundations and axial purposes of liberalism. Instead, they resembled Whitman in what Eisenach calls their emphasis on "the collective responsibilities to achieve a common future" and their "liberating call to a larger life, an escape from an illusory individualism trapped in a polity that thwarts civic capacity and democratic purposes."[7]

The evidentiary base for attempting to characterize "the political philosophy of the New Deal," if there can be said to be such a thing at more than a very pragmatic and theoretically superficial level, is more limited than in the case of Progressivism, and any generalizations made in this respect are necessarily highly suspect. Hubert Humphrey's master's thesis was devoted to this topic, and it was in content as pragmatic in orientation and as hortatory in tone as one might suspect. Henry Steele Commager once called Lester Frank Ward "the philosophical architect of the welfare state" and "the prophet and protagonist" of the New Deal.[8] If that be so, then New Deal liberalism would have to be seen as technocratic at a pretty deep level, given Ward's Comtean inspiration and his endorsement of "sociocracy." But Commager's claims on Ward's behalf are based much more on what he sees as the content of Ward's argument for active government than on his actual influence upon the shape of the New Deal or upon the conduct of its creators; and evidence for the latter is slim at best. Michael Sandel, moreover, is almost surely correct to depict the New Deal as "beset by conflicting ideologies" and therefore very difficult to categorize.[9] My own sense is that the public philosophy of the New Deal, to the extent there can be said to be such a thing, did not depart greatly from that provided by Dewey in *Liberalism and Social Action*: the purposes of a democratic society were still liberty and personal development within the context of deliberative and communal self-governance, but an active government was ever more urgently needed in the Depression era to foster economic production and to countervail concentrations of private power. It also is worth noting in this context Franklin Roosevelt's explicit condemnation of dependence on government relief as inducing "a spiritual and moral disintegration fundamentally destructive to the national fibre." "To dole out relief in this way," he continued, "is to administer a narcotic, a subtle destroyer of the human spirit. . . . I am not willing that the vitality of our people be further sapped by the giving of cash. . . . We must preserve not only the bodies of the unemployed from destitution but also their self-respect, their self-reliance and courage and determination."[10] That express concern corroborates the insistence of Harry Boyte and Nancy Kari that the New Deal, as represented in its art and iconography, retained the traditional liberal conception of human agency/responsibility and the traditional republican preoccupation with the avoidance of dependency.[11]

Where technocratic strands appear within Progressivism and the New Deal, these do not constitute a new philosophy of democratic governance, much less a new conception of democratic

CHAPTER THREE

purposes. Instead, they appear as tactical expedients of constrained scope directed toward combating what Progressivism and the New Dealers saw with good reason as the overriding threat of their time to democratic self-rule and self-realization. For Progressive thinkers and reformers, this threat was the colonization of public power by private and factional interests in the form of economic corporations and political machines. In that context, innovations on behalf of popular control of political institutions—such as the initiative and referendum—were not seen as standing in tension with attempts to create "neutral" expert governance mechanisms such as a politically insulated civil service or commissions composed of cost-benefit-guided experts. Although on their face these two reform strategies embody sharply divergent models of governance and authority, the Progressives could and did see them as alternative tactics that worked in tandem on behalf of a common goal: to wit, to protect and promote the general welfare or public interest against the depredations of what Rousseau called "partial associations," what Bentham called "sinister interests," and what Madison called "factions." That battle could be fought both by mobilizing the larger public to override the organized private colonizers of government power and, in some contexts, by circumventing the influence of these private groups by authorizing politically buffered boards or commissions to determine policies in accord with a utilitarian calculus. In similar fashion, the New Deal reliance upon its "brain trust" was a tactic logically appropriate to the specific crisis of its day. That economic crisis resulted not from any breakdowns at the level of individual agency or even at the level of institutions of democratic governance. It resulted from a breakdown in the regulative mechanisms of a market economy, and as such, it required what only technocrats could offer: more astute strategies of macroeconomic management.

Finally, in neither Progressivism nor the New Deal can one find any systematic or influential call for changes in our understanding of the central purposes of democracy. In his preface to

A Theory of Justice, Rawls does make this kind of claim, arguing that the conception of social justice he is going to defend should be seen as constituting a novel account of "the most appropriate moral basis for a democratic society."¹² I don't believe that a logically comparable claim—that is, a claim to have established a new and different "moral basis" for the democratic enterprise—can be found in the accounts that adherents of Progressivism or the New Deal provided to explain what they were up to. Instead, these accounts generally referenced and endorsed quite specifically some version of what Dewey referred to as the traditional "enduring values" of democracy in the process of arguing for changes in important but nonetheless "derivative" (in Dworkin's sense) practices, strategies, and institutions. This kind of argument from silence can also be applied to the content as well as to the logical structure of these arguments. With the possible exception of Lester Frank Ward's somewhat ambiguous accounts of his hopes for an emerging "sociocracy"—accounts that do bear resemblance to Donna Shalala's expressed hopes for a "disinterested technocratic elite" serving the public through "miracles of social science"—there are few if any of the distinctive features of contemporary high liberalism discernible in Progressive or New Deal writings. These latter doctrines seem first to appear in any clear, coherent, and explicit form only in the sixties and after. There were, of course, many exhortations regarding the social imperative to improve the lot of segments of society suffering from want and poverty. Indeed, these exhortations are a constant within the long history of political progressivism in this country. But arguments against economic exploitation or on behalf of assistance to those who lack the economic wherewithal to benefit from the promises of democracy need not be and were generally not represented as appeals to imperatives of distributive justice in the Rawlsian sense. Nor can one readily find within Progressivism or the New Deal operative conceptions of human nature or social structure resembling the philosophical anthropology and the normative sociology of high liberalism we examined in the previous chapter.

CHAPTER THREE

Most of the events, developments, and trends that I suggest may have played some causal role in bringing about the transformation of American liberalism, therefore, took place during the last half of the twentieth century. The partial exception to that pattern occurs in the realm of underlying changes in philosophical predispositions. That is unsurprising, I think, since deep alterations in fundamental intellectual presuppositions tend to take a longer time to develop and to have an impact on culture and politics.

The potentially contributing causes surveyed here fall under four headings. Two of these involve changes in ideas and beliefs, and two reference important historical events. These ideational and empirical causal elements are mutually related and have no doubt shaped each other in complex and dialectical ways. I will not be so foolish as to try to specify which is chicken and which is egg. The changes in ideas and beliefs include changes in what I shall call the "metaphysic of morals" and changes in perceptions/hermeneutic constructions of the attributes and capacities of the "common man"/average citizen in contemporary American society. The historical events I examine are crucial political conflicts and issues that have powerfully driven changes in political values and alignments over the past several decades, which in turn have shaped the transformation of American liberalism.

THE CHANGING METAPHYSIC OF MORALS: NATURALISM AND DECISIONISM

In terms of the freestanding intellectual factors—to the extent any ideas can be said to be freestanding—that have influenced the emergence and shape of today's transformed version of American liberalism, the most general and fundamental ones can be characterized as parts of a changing "metaphysic of morals." By a metaphysic of morals, I refer to those deep, underlying presuppositions about the world and the place of human beings within it that provide the setting within which our understanding of the moral and political world and its tasks is configured. The most pertinent developments in this regard have been the emergence of what have been called naturalism and decisionism. Naturalist presuppositions exert their most important influence when it comes to our understanding of human agency, and the presuppositions underlying decisionism exert their most important influence when it comes to our understanding of the nature and ontological status of the human good. Some elements of these conceptions were touched on in our look at John Rawls's philosophical anthropology in the previous chapter. The point here is that Rawls did not suddenly awake one morning and create these features of his conception of democratic persons out of whole cloth. Instead, he was able to reach out and appropriate these notions from the surrounding intellectual landscape, use them to help shape his convictions, and deploy them to support his moral and political purposes.

The underlying metaphysic of morals that informed and sustained traditional liberalism came from three principal sources: civic republicanism, Enlightenment rationalism, and Protestant Christianity. It would be hard to find a major theorist of liberal democracy between Locke and Lincoln who did not situate his political ideas within some combination of these three philosophical orientations. That list would include European liberals such as Adam Smith, Condorcet and the French philosophers, James and John Stuart Mill, Rousseau, and Kant. The same generalization would apply to Americans such as Tom Paine, James Madison, John Adams, Thomas Jefferson, and the Progressives. What is important here is that all of these traditions incorporated within them both a strong conception of human moral agency and some kind of teleological or universal conception of human fulfillment. These conceptions therefore provided in turn a strong basis for the axial goals of traditional liberalism: the affirmation of moral agency confirmed the possibility and the point of self-rule, and the axiological understanding of the human good provided both the content of and a strong warrant for the goal of self-realization.

CHAPTER THREE

Important intellectual developments and discoveries around the turn of the twentieth century, however, presented serious challenges to these traditional beliefs about human action and motivation. The result was a philosophical landscape decreasingly congenial to traditional liberalism's metaphysic of morals. The major figures in this process were not philosophers so much as scientists whose discoveries and theories seemed to carry implications for our understanding of the human world, people such as Charles Darwin and Sigmund Freud. That was because of the way in which their ideas worked toward transforming and undermining the understanding of human beings as rational animals. In the traditional conception of us as rational animals, we were seen as members of a metaphysically essentialist biological species. That meant that we, like all species, had certain definitive motivating ends. Unlike other species, moreover—this is the *sapiens* part—we possessed cognitive powers that allowed us a meaningful degree of transcendence over the causal determinacy of blind brute nature. We could, unlike the beasts, reflect and deliberate, and by so doing, we could achieve meaningful and important powers of self-control and self-determination.

Aristotle's account of practical reason and those who are fully capable of exercising its powers—the *phronimoi*—is paradigmatic here. Some of the political implications he drew from this conception grate upon modern ears. Only those competent at *phronesis* (practical reasoning) are capable of political rule, he argued. Absent that capability, human beings are devoid of self-control and deliberative self-direction and therefore can function only under the control of others: they are slaves to nature and hence slaves by nature. In parallel but in contrast, Kant provided a version of human beings as rational animals that was ontologically Cartesian and more democratic. He assigned reason and animality to separate realms, essentially distinct modes of existence. Human beings thus became in his rendering noble schizophrenics, both free and determined and therefore uniquely subject to the moral tension created by their simultaneous residence within dual ontological domains. We were spiritual ghosts somehow resident within natural machines—an unfortunate model that works better as a myth akin to Plato's myth of the metals than as literal anthropology or cosmology. However fantastical and philosophically precarious Kant's version of the conjunction of rationality and animality may have been, however, his account was politically less hierarchical and hence more democratic in its implications than Aristotle's. Guided by what he deemed to be Rousseau's proper recognition of the moral and spiritual powers of this average run of humankind, Kant attributed noumenal capacities to us all. Our moral powers were for him not a function of intellectual superiority but a common aptitude, and his "kingdom of ends" or community of mutually respectful rational beings served him as a model of the political republic.

The findings and arguments of Darwin and Freud proved deeply subversive of some of the most important features of this whole rational animal motif and especially of its understanding of human freedom and the human good. The Darwinian account of evolution was not limited in its purchase to biology in the specific sense of that term but instead carried unavoidable implications for philosophical cosmology and anthropology. This larger philosophical impact had three major components to it. First, the idea that species are not permanent but instead change and mutate over time undercut the cosmological model of the world as composed of a finite panoply of eternal fixed substances. Second, the specific genealogy of human origins broke the ontological dike between humans and other animals. Finally, the claim that the creative engine in the whole process of evolution was random mutation introduced an unsettling element of deep and radical contingency or accident to the whole universe and to the particular forms of life found therein, including human life.

Logically speaking, a Darwinian universe is not incompatible with meaningful conceptions of human freedom and self-realization. We can still be animals of a peculiarly highly developed sort, endowed by virtue of our unique biological capacities with the power to reflect, to deliberate, and thereby to exercise a significant degree of control over our actions. It is still perfectly coherent, moreover, to speak of mature oak trees as distinguished from saplings, of normal calves as contrasted with two-headed ones, and of healthy dogs as compared to sickly ones. Pari passu, then, it is still entirely possible and logically coherent to speak of human beings who attain self-realization in the sense of achieving the full development and enjoying the felicitous deployment of their human faculties. Nevertheless, the effect of Darwin's theory was to knock the deep and venerable philosophical moorings of the ideas of human free agency and self-realization out from under them. Moreover, it created a push toward an alternative understanding of human behavior as less free because more beastlike, and it also suggested that the human good should be reconceived as subjective and variable rather than grounded in objective reality and universal.

The intimation that human beings behave more like other beasts and hence are not the responsible free agents of our moral conceit is what, following Samuel Scheffler, I am calling naturalism here.[13] These suspicions were clearly bolstered by Freud's so-called discovery of the irrational—that is, his insistence that human behavior is driven by the brutish id rather than governed by the conscious ego and his psychoanalytically based claim that the reasons we give for our actions are often mere glosses in the service of desires we neither recognize nor understand. These naturalistic conceptions of human behavior were given literary voice by "realist" American novelists such as Jack London and Frank Norris. In his book *McTeague*, for example, Norris depicted his title figure as an impulsive animal covered by a thin veneer of civilized inhibitions that would break down under the slightest pressure. "The brute that in McTeague lay so close to the surface," he wrote, "leaped instantly to life, monstrous, not to be resisted. . . . It was something no longer human; it was rather an echo from the jungle."[14] Norris also went on to draw the implication that McTeague and his lover, Trina—not being rational and free agents—could not really be held responsible for what they did. "I can't help it. It ain't my fault, is it?" asks McTeague at one point. And Norris later answers: "Yet neither of them was to blame. . . . Chance had brought them face to face, and mysterious instincts as ungovernable as the winds of heaven were at work knitting their lives together. . . . [They were] the sport of chance."[15]

In more recent years, broadly naturalistic assumptions such as these have seemed to enlarge the range of human behavior seen as driven by natural forces and diminished the scope of those seen as subject to determination by responsible free agency. As William Connolly has observed, "It is clear that a sea change has been under way during the last few decades. Areas of conduct in which judgments of self-responsibility, merit, and blameworthiness were prominent have been evacuated or converted into fields of contestation. . . . In some cases, what was once the responsibility of the individual is now treated as a genetic or contingent predisposition resistant to rectification through individual will."[16] And Samuel Scheffler similarly alludes to "the growing tendency in our culture to reinterpret what were previously viewed as vices—excessive drinking or gambling, for example—as diseases or addictions, thus relocating them outside the ambit of personal responsibility."[17] Connolly considers this "sea change" as a generally healthy development that embodies valid psychological insights and leads toward the amelioration of harsh punitiveness and socially corrosive resentments. Others have seen it as a retreat from moral adulthood that has given rise to a deplorable epidemic of self-exculpation. I will not try to adjudicate these complex and controversial issues here. Instead, I want simply to chart one feature of a changing metaphysic of morals that I—in agreement with Scheffler—believe has contributed to the shaping of contemporary American liberalism.

The second element in this changing metaphysic is the shift toward conceiving the human good as subjective and plural rather than in some sense objectively grounded and applicable to all people. This is a change again invited by abandoning Aristotelian and Newtonian fixity and universality in favor of Darwinian flux. It is a shift consolidated and given paradigmatic display in the thought of Max Weber, specifically in what his commentators have termed his "decisionism." As what Elie Halevy has called a "moral Newtonian," Kant depicted all human beings as partakers in a uniform rational will that was the moral/practical reason counterpart to scientific/theoretical reason. A second-generation neo-Kantian in a post-Newtonian world, Weber transformed this common rational will into a plurality of particular "demonic"—that is, radically free to the point of arbitrariness—wills. On this account, each human being creates his or her own moral meaning and confers this purely subjective purposefulness upon a world that itself is devoid of any purpose or meaning. The objective world, Weber tells us, is an "irrational reality," a "vast chaotic stream of events, which flows away through time," including human history and culture, which he characterizes as "a finite segment of the meaningless infinity of the world process."[18] There is, then, no such thing as the human good. Instead, to the extent there is such a thing it is a multiplicity of very particular constructs created by "a series of ultimate decisions through which the soul . . . chooses its own fate, i.e., the meaning of its activity and existence."[19] Whether or not it is true, as Alasdair MacIntyre has argued, that "the contemporary vision of the world is predominantly, though not perhaps in every detail, Weberian,"[20] this represents a twentieth-century conceptualization of the human good that has been profoundly influential. It has, moreover, a neo-Benthamite counterpart in the widely deployed notion of "preference maximization," which also represents the human good not as the object of rational desire but as variable sets of subjective wants immune to rational assessment or moral critique. So whereas traditional liberals could assume that the axial goals of their political faith—self-rule and self-realization—were real and meaningful notions comfortably grounded within the moral universe that we as human beings inhabit, contemporary liberal theorists have become more reticent about or outright skeptical of those goals because they are more dubious about that moral universe. Naturalistic doubts about the scope of human agency undermine the power of self-rule as a central democratic goal, whereas subjectivist doubts about the meaningfulness of conceptions of human fulfillment or perfectibility undermine the propriety of human development—Mill's "mental and moral progress"—as a defining democratic purpose. The dominant tendency within contemporary liberal public philosophy instead becomes—in concert with naturalism—to incorporate a more deterministic account of human behavior and—in concert with decisionism or what Rawls terms "moral constructivism"—to bracket conceptions of the human good (now seen as irremediably plural, nonrational, and morally on a par because ontologically akin to contingent features of personal identity among moral equals) from serving as a basis for democratic ends. The combined result of these changes in the metaphysic of morals, moreover, is to create a "value slope" that greases the skids toward centering liberalism on an egalitarian conception of distributive justice:[21] once the human good is morally neutralized by decisionism/constructivism, only justice can provide any moral reference point for a liberalism that is more than a prudential modus vivendi; and a deterministic conception of human behavior leaves everyone by default as claimants of equal standing when allocations of social goods are at issue.

THE WAR OF SOCIAL SCIENCE ON THE RESPECTABLE YEOMANRY

A second significant theoretical causal factor in the decline of traditional liberalism in this country and the ascension of a new liberal public philosophy centered on social justice is what can be characterized, for rhetorical effect, as a war of American social science on the respectable yeomanry. That characterization is, of course, a deliberately provocative one. Most American intellectuals, including most professional social scientists, tend toward the left side of the current political spectrum. They incline, as a result, to sympathize with people toward the lower end of the socioeconomic hierarchy. They would, therefore, likely be both startled and chagrined to encounter the claim that the findings and interpretations of social scientific studies of political attitudes and behavior over the last several decades have played a role in what someone of populist sympathies would consider a decline in both the substance and the political appeal of liberalism as a public philosophy. I want to argue here, nonetheless, that this has in fact happened and has been inadequately noted and remarked.

The construction of the contemporary American respectable yeomanry emanating from the quarters of academic social science that concerns me here has been aptly captured by John DiIulio in a recent review essay. DiIulio is himself a prominent political scientist who grew up in a working-class area of Philadelphia. He recalls the neighborhood of his youth as

> Irish, Italian, and Polish, in that order. Nearly everybody prayed Catholic and voted Democratic. Dads were cops, firemen, bricklayers, or truck drivers . . . white-collar professionals and bums (we did not quite see a difference) were few. Adult drunks, but not young punks, were tolerated. Weekends were for fun and occasional forbidden pleasures, but, come Monday morning, everyone was expected to "answer the bell" (go to work and live responsibly). Big families in one-bathroom rowhouses managed okay from paycheck to paycheck. Parish schools performed miracles: With one nun for every 90 kids, they still taught us to read, pay attention, and behave. Nobody talked about "race," but most people revered black sports stars, respected black co-workers, welcomed working-class black neighbors, and avoided high-crime black neighborhoods. . . . Nobody bowled alone, and you couldn't walk three blocks in any direction without somebody waving or calling your name. Hardly anybody went to college, and most who did stayed local.

DiIulio himself went to the University of Pennsylvania and then to Harvard for graduate school. As he reports, the social science corpus he encountered in his studies there seemed to cast a disturbing and condescending eye upon his friends, family, neighborhood, and culture:

> From my days at Penn, through graduate study at Harvard in the mid 1980s, I read much of the voluminous literature on America's white working class, and learned that many intellectuals had it in for us. We thought that, warts and all, we were pretty patriotic, loving, and law-abiding, but beneath it all was our "authoritarian personality." We knew more Ralph Kramdens than Archie Bunkers, but that was a figment of our "de-racialized consciousness" (you know, the sort of thing that subtly feeds "white hegemony"). We felt that most employers gave our working class parents a fair shake, and that we would do as well or better if we worked as hard. But that was just our "false consciousness" talking white trailer trash. In sum, we thought that we were basically good, godly people and solid citizens pursuing the American dream. But the intellectuals taught that we were wage-slave racists and churchgoing crypto-fascists, which, of course, also explained why we became Reagan Democrats, stopped joining unions, moved to the suburbs, and started investing in mutual funds.[22]

To some extent, the condescension and unflattering depiction of the white working class sardonically referenced by DiIulio are just the recent manifestation of a standing social phenomenon Walt Whitman remarked upon over a century ago: "The people," he wrote, "viewed in the lump, displeases, and is a constant puzzle and affront to the merely educated classes."[23] But in the latter half of the twentieth century, a number of lines of research on public opinion and political attitudes seemed to provide specific grounds for this displeasure and affront. It was not simply that "the mass . . . suffers from an incurable incompetence," as Roberto Michels put it.[24] Nor was it simply that "the People are ungrammatical, untidy, and their sins gaunt and ill-bred," as Walt Whitman said.[25] The evidence gleaned from sociological research seemed to suggest that the American lower middle and working classes, considered in the mass, were disconcertingly ill informed, intolerant, only weakly supportive of civil liberties, racist, and authoritarian in their psychic disposition.

In the years following World War II, political scientists and sociologists began to avail themselves of new techniques of survey research to seek better understanding of why it was that people voted as they did. To anyone who entered upon these investigations looking for democratic citizens who investigated the issues, assessed them rationally and judiciously, and then voted accordingly—preferably in line with their considered views on the public interest—the findings of these studies quickly proved disillusioning. The American electorate—taken as a whole and considered on average—was revealed by these empirical studies to be remarkably underinformed or positively misinformed about important political matters. Vast percentages of the voting public could not identify the names of their representatives, the content of basic constitutional principles, the geographic location of countries relevant to issues of the day, or, at times, even the relevant issue positions of leading candidates for public office. Against the backdrop of this very weak grasp of important political facts relevant to anything resembling informed and rational voting decisions, the principal causal factor in determining how people voted—at least statistically—seemed to be the voters' prerational "party identification," a component of people's personal self-image that they seemed (again on the basis of compelling high levels of statistical correlation) to have absorbed from their parents or their surrounding environment. Strike one on the image of "the people" as it emerged from the explorations of modern social science. The people were a dull and irrational crowd apparently unequipped or disinclined to play the role of democratic sovereign. Small wonder that some of the principals in these studies were driven to ponder openly whether it might make sense to appreciate rather than decry the significant levels of apathy among this uninformed public.[26] Some of these social scientists suggested for similar reasons that our basic understanding of the nature and requisites of democracy should be revised to incorporate a greater emphasis on the role of elites and correspondingly to reduce expectations regarding the role of the people as a whole. Properly understood, a democratic "system demands much less from the political beliefs and behavior of the mass of citizens than from the elites. . . . [The] low level of attention and control by the mass of the public leaves a wide latitude to the elected elite for creative leadership."[27]

Sober doubts about the desirability of widespread political participation on the part of such an uninformed citizenry gained greater impetus from another line of public opinion inquiry that discovered what seemed to be widespread lack of understanding of and commitment to democratic values—among them basic civil liberties and political rights for unpopular groups. Two paradigmatic and influential journal articles from the early 1960s convey the substance and the potential implications for democratic theory quite well.

In the first of these studies, James Prothro and Charles Grigg interviewed a 1 percent random sample of registered voters in Ann Arbor, Michigan, and Tallahassee, Florida, to see whether this random subset of the voting public understood and supported the core democratic norms of majority rule and minority rights. They found that their interviewees endorsed these principles in overwhelming numbers when they were presented to them "in abstract terms." But when they were queried about their acceptance of more specific practices that arguably followed logically from those principles, the unanimity evaporated: "When these broad principles are translated into more specific propositions, . . . consensus breaks down completely." Despite endorsing the propositions that "every citizen should have an equal chance to influence government policy" and that "public officials should be chosen by majority vote," half the respondents agreed with the proposition that "only people who are well informed" about a referendum issue "should be allowed to vote." And almost 80 percent of those responding agreed that "in a city referendum deciding on tax-supported undertakings, only taxpayers should be allowed to vote." About a third of the sample disagreed that someone who wished to "make a speech in this city against churches and religion . . . should be allowed to speak." Half of the respondents would have barred a communist from running for mayor of their city, and a quarter (more in Tallahassee, less in Ann Arbor) would likewise have barred an African American candidacy. Although the article began as an attempt to test the claim that a significant degree of consensus on basic principles was a sociological prerequisite of democratic governance, the findings (1) that large percentages of interviewees gave "undemocratic" responses to questions, and (2) that respondents with more than a high school education consistently gave more "democratic" responses led the authors to conclude, first, that the more educated members of the voting public could justifiably be seen as "the carriers of the [democratic] creed" and, second, that we should not "overlook the functional nature of apathy for the democratic system"—because "many people express undemocratic principles . . . but are too apathetic to act" on them, and "fortunately, . . . those with the most undemocratic principles are also those who are least likely to act."[28]

Writing in 1964, Herbert McClosky reported on findings from his own similar research that seemed to ratify the basic claims of Prothro and Grigg. His respondents came from two sample groups, the first of these drawn from political "actives" who had served as delegates or alternates to either the Republican or Democratic national conventions in 1956, the second of these a representative national sample of 1,500 adults in the population at large. McClosky asked more and different questions of his interviewees, but many dealt with democratic "rules of the game," including general principles and specific applications regarding free speech and procedural rights. Like Prothro and Grigg, Mc-Closky concluded that "a large proportion of the electorate has failed to grasp certain of the underlying ideas and principles on which the American political system rests." Both the elite and the mass sample groups responded with approval to abstract statements about free speech, but the general electorate sample was less supportive of these general principles in their application to specific cases and also less consistently supportive of democratic procedural rules. "The average citizen," McClosky wrote, "has greater difficulty appreciating the importance of certain procedural or juridical rights, especially when he believes the country's internal security is at stake." Hence, again like Prothro and Grigg, McClosky concluded that the real hope for the maintenance of democratic procedures and liberties lies with the elites and that the people at large are not trustworthy in this regard: "The evidence suggests that it is the articulate classes rather than the public who serve as the major repositories of the public conscience and as the carriers of the Creed. Responsibility for keeping the system going, hence, falls most heavily on them."[29]

Woefully uninformed politically and shaky in their commitment to democratic norms and civil liberties, the American populace also came across in public opinion studies as having their political positions contaminated by racist attitudes. During the earlier postwar years of this research, of course, such findings were basically no-brainers. Overt racism was on display in prime time in the 1960s, from Selma to Little Rock to Cicero. And, as noted earlier, in 1960, fully 42 percent of the sample survey of voters in Tallahassee agreed with the proposition that "a Negro should not be allowed to run for mayor of this city." Even after the passage of the major civil rights legislation of the later 1960s and the striking and encouraging decline of express "old-fashioned" racist sentiments and attitudes reflected in survey research data, many social scientists have argued that racial prejudice among whites—and especially among whites with less education—is still pervasive in a somewhat more subtle or perhaps simply less candid form. "Old-fashioned" racism was in this account defined by agreement with propositions to the effect that blacks are less intelligent than whites, that full racial integration is not a good thing, and that the respondent would have objections to a family member's close relationship with someone black. "Modern" racism, or "symbolic racism," was defined, in contrast, by agreement with more perceptual propositions about the situation of blacks in American society and normative/perceptual propositions about whether blacks had "gotten more than they deserve" from recent public policy. A representative article employing this modified definition of racism argued, for example, that the widespread opposition to court-ordered busing to achieve racial balance in schools in Louisville, Kentucky, was motivated principally by this kind of racism rather than by self-interest. The author concluded, then, by endorsing the contention of the NAACP Legal Defense and Educational Fund and of other busing proponents that opposition to busing policies was basically a function of racist attitudes: "In short, it is not the buses, but the blacks that arouse the ire of so many whites—parents and non-parents—in Louisville and across the nation."[30]

In recent years, the depiction of racial attitudes and their bearing on political affiliation and policy preferences has evolved into a complex and contested area of research and interpretation. Some researchers have argued, for example, that widespread white opposition to racially preferential admissions and hiring practices and to government programs specifically targeted toward blacks are motivated to a considerable extent by principled beliefs about individualism, equal protection of the law, and to a lesser extent, racial animus.[31] Other researchers, however, tend to discount today's near-universal endorsement of norms of racial equality and nondiscrimination as largely lip service to prevailing standards of social propriety. They argue that white opposition to policies such as busing and affirmative action is driven primarily by the desire to maintain political and social dominance over blacks.[32] Or they argue that white racism of one form or other remains an important factor in motivating opposition to policies specifically directed toward black advancement.[33] These issues are complex ones to adjudicate in any definitive way and continue to be subject to controversy.[34] But it is safe to say that the social science literature in this area, taken as a whole, has functioned to discredit many of the concerns and policy positions of (especially) working- and middle-class whites by depicting them as driven more by racial bigotry than by either legitimate self-interest (e.g., for public safety or quality education for their children) or moral principle (e.g., the equal protection clause or the work ethic).

A last line of research that has played a significant part in a cumulative negative construction of the not-so-respectable yeomanry by social scientists over the past several decades is that devoted to "working-class authoritarianism." The underlying theoretical notion of the "authoritarian personality" originated in the famous book of that title, written by the German émigré and Frankfurt School social theorist Theodor Adorno together with his colleagues Else Frenkel-Brunswik, Daniel Levinson, and R. Nevitt Sanford.[35] This book was part of a series, Studies in Prejudice, sponsored by the American Jewish Committee. Understandably aghast at the apparent complicity of such large numbers of ordinary Germans in the racist atrocities of the Nazis, the contributors and sponsors of this study sought insight into the causal dynamics of such complicity in hopes of preventing the recurrence of such horrors. The originating intuition of *The Authoritarian Personality* was that there must be some psychological traits or syndromes that predisposed their bearers to intolerance, prejudice, and aggressiveness against other ethnic, religious, or cultural groups.

The actual data and attempts at theorizing about them in this very unwieldy book of nearly a thousand pages are so diffuse and ambiguous that its enormous influence is a bit surprising. Notwithstanding these difficulties, however, the authors claimed that patterns of response to sets of propositions they posed to their experimental subjects indicated that there was such a thing as a

CHAPTER THREE

"prejudiced" or "antidemocratic" syndrome of certain psychic traits and predispositions that could be styled as an "authoritarian" personality type. This personality syndrome revealed itself by positive responses to propositions praising "obedience and respect for authority" as "the most important virtues children should learn," to propositions praising "strict discipline . . . and the will to work and fight for family and country," to propositions expressing hostility to homosexuals, and so on.[36] The authors argued in their conclusion that the "over-all fascist potential" of this personality syndrome was "great."[37] And they also argued, on the basis of rather limited statistical evidence, that members of the working class were particularly susceptible to this dangerous personality syndrome: "Those attitudes centering around authoritarianism . . . are more pronounced in this group than in most others."[38]

Other researchers soon picked up this line of inquiry, and in 1960, Seymour Martin Lipset summarized some of their findings and arguments in a chapter in his influential book *Political Man: The Social Bases of Politics*.[39] "Both evidence and theory suggest," he wrote, "that the lower strata are relatively more authoritarian, that (again, other things being equal) they will be more attracted to an extremist movement than to a moderate and democratic one, and that, once recruited, they will not be alienated by its lack of democracy."[40] Members of the lower social strata are also "the least tolerant." They have a tendency to see the world "in black and white terms" and to have a "desire for immediate action." Hence, they are ready to follow leaders who "offer a demonological interpretation of the evil forces (either religious or political) which are conspiring against them."[41]

Several factors, Lipset argued, "predispose the lower classes toward authoritarianism." One of these is the insecurity and tension produced by their relative economic instability. A second cause is the working-class pattern of child-rearing, which is characterized by a greater likelihood of punishment by ridicule or infliction of physical pain and by parents teaching their children "to strike out with fists or knives and to be certain to hit first." A third factor is the lesser educational attainment of these lower classes, which leaves them with "an unsophisticated perspective" on the world. "All of these qualities [of working-class life and culture] are part of the complex psychological basis of authoritarianism," concludes Lipset: "To sum up, the lower-class individual is likely to have been exposed to punishment, lack of love and a general atmosphere of tension and aggression since early childhood—all experiences which tend to produce deep-rooted hostilities expressed by ethnic prejudice, political authoritarianism, and chiliastic transvaluational religion."[42]

Taken all together, these several lines of research into political attitudes and behavior from the decades following World War II added up to a pretty devastating portrait of the twentieth-century American "common man." He was more or less a real-world version of Archie Bunker: racially prejudiced and unsympathetic to the plight of disadvantaged minorities, suspicious and intolerant of "others" and outsiders, ready to sacrifice civil liberties whenever challenges to conventional mores or threats to public security appeared on the horizon, woefully ignorant of fundamental political facts, mentally befogged by religious credulity, and highly susceptible to quasi-fascist syndromes of social aggression and submission. This was, to invoke John DiIulio's words once more, "America's ostensibly socio-pathological, economically failing, politically duped white working class (we are also supremely anti-intellectual and devalue education)."[43]

This depiction of the white American working class tacitly exerted a crippling impact on the democratic vistas of a Walt Whitman, the hopeful democratic faith of a John Dewey, and any other scenario of political progress that assigned an important role to an enlightened democratic populace. Those accounts of benign democratic self-rule had to appear naive, sentimental, and even somewhat dangerous. Instead of hoping to give fuller expression and reality to the democratic boast of "here the people rule," it logically if somewhat ironically made more sense to acknowledge the prudence of letting sleeping dogs lie. It might not seem very democratic in a traditional and procedural sense, but if the desire were to defend liberal freedoms and achieve greater social equality, perhaps it was best to rely upon the more educated elites who were the "carriers of the creed."

If this depiction of the working-class yeomen seemed to make touting the virtues and promise of self-rule delusionary and inadvisable, the possibilities of self-realization for a democratic populace so understood might seem rather modest, as well. Forget the paeans of a John Stuart Mill to "the absolute and essential importance of human development in its richest diversity" as the "grand leading principle" of democratic aspiration. Archie Bunker can "develop" to his fullest extent, and he'll still be Archie Bunker. After all these years of democratic freedoms, what you see there is likely to be all you can get. There is no great reason to see much larger potential. When it comes to women and minorities, it is a different story because they have been subjected to social oppression. But otherwise, we are pretty much a meritocracy these days, with the Scholastic Assessment Tests (SATs) and all; so those who don't fall under the heading of one or another of these oppressed groups have presumably pretty much arrived at their level of achievement and reward. As William Connolly puts it: "By implying that professional and corporate males have earned their position while asserting that women and minorities are victimized by discrimination, liberals imply that only one group deserves to be stuck in the crummy jobs available to it: white working-class males."[44]

If the changing metaphysic of morals, then, undermined the ideals and hopes of traditional American liberalism by challenging its assumptions about moral cosmology and philosophical anthropology, the unflattering construction of the American common folk produced by the data and the interpretations placed upon those data by students of public opinion in the decades after World War II undermined the credibility of the populist and Progressive traditions' embrace of popular sovereignty and their hopes for what Mill had styled as the ultimate measure of political achievement: the mental and moral progress of the people.[45] For traditional American liberalism, the advancement and flourishing of the respectable yeomanry were its focal concern. For contemporary liberalism, in contrast, the focus is the proper distribution of primary goods, mostly material ones, rather than the promotion of virtue and intelligence. The respectable yeomanry are at best the accidental collateral beneficiaries of the preferred distribution. And given the way they have been depicted in recent decades by a lot of social scientists, it is easy to see how this drastic loss of their political status might be seen as prudent revisionism rather than as apostasy from the deepest animating principles of democracy.

FRACTURING THE PROGRESSIVE COALITION: THE REACTION TO McCARTHYISM

The developments canvassed so far in this chapter have been largely ideational ones: changes in philosophical assumptions about morality and human identity and changes in beliefs about the predispositions and capacities of the democratic populace. Both of these intellectual sea changes, as we have argued, exacted a toll on the intelligibility and credibility of traditional liberal values and aspirations. Ideas don't appear and convictions don't change in a vacuum, however. Political ideas in particular are given impetus and inspiration by defining events, problems, and conflicts in their historical setting. The transformation of American liberalism is no exception to this general pattern of synergy between ideas and events. It took the shape it did and gained its appeal in significant measure from several of the most salient political issues and battles that occupied Americans during the latter half of the twentieth century. The most fateful of these major contretemps from the standpoint of their effects upon the public philosophy of reform liberalism in America were the strains and fears

CHAPTER THREE

engendered by Senator Joseph McCarthy's assault on the liberal intelligentsia at the outset of the Cold War and the social divisions and strategic choices produced by the civil rights revolution. The shifts in political affiliation, sociological coalitions, and attitudes toward democratic governance driven by these critical movements were then compounded by divisions over Vietnam and by deeper cultural pluralism within American society.

It is hard for those of us who did not live through the early fifties to appreciate the remarkable influence that the junior senator from Wisconsin—"Tail-gunner" Joe McCarthy—had upon the politics of that time. Equally hard to appreciate is the impact that the phenomenon of what quickly came to be called McCarthyism had upon the political sensibility of liberal elites and intellectuals of that time. But his influence was both huge and malignant, and the impact exerted by the specter he posed upon the public philosophy of American liberalism was fateful.

McCarthy appeared on the national political scene in 1946, when he was elected to the Senate. In what turned out to be a kind of prescient irony, he had defeated the great legatee and practitioner of populist Progressivism, Senator Robert La Follette Jr., in the Republican primary by 5,400 votes out of 410,000 cast. La Follette had previously been elected as a candidate of the Progressive Party of Wisconsin, but that party disbanded earlier in that election year; it—and La Follette—had opted to return to the Republican fold for its party home. In the 1940s, a poll of political correspondents and political scientists had voted La Follette to be the best senator. The same poll a decade later designated McCarthy to be the worst.

The mood of the American electorate during Harry Truman's second term in office was marked by anxiety and insecurity—of an unexpected and highly unwelcome sort. Only a few years before, the country had felt exhilaration and relief at the successful conclusion of an exhausting and enormously destructive world war. It thought it could now celebrate, relax, and enjoy a return to peace, prosperity, and freedom from outside threat. Instead, it found itself suddenly and frighteningly confronted by an erstwhile ally turned implacable foe in the form of the Soviet Union. And another set of allies, the Chinese nationalists, were pushed out of power by another version of totalitarian Marxist-Leninism, led by Mao Tse-tung. In a sense, a very hard-won victory had seemed to turn to ashes, as the savagery of worldwide military conflict gave way not to calm and security but rather to an ominous Cold War against a new and powerful adversary that seemed to be gaining ground at an alarming pace. Little wonder that an anxious and dismayed populace grasped for explanation and felt a profound sense of betrayal.

For the first several years of his term, Joseph McCarthy was an inconspicuous and unnoteworthy figure in the Senate. He bounced around from one petty cause to another in search of a way to make himself a role and a name. And he occupied much of his legislative energies fronting for corporate groups such as soft-drink companies and makers of manufactured homes who rewarded his services by lining his pockets. This relative anonymity evaporated, however, early in 1950 when he stumbled almost by chance into the occupation that would bring him notoriety and henceforth define him indelibly: that of exposing and rooting out communists, former communists, communist sympathizers, and alleged fellow travelers from the government and from other positions of influence in society. In a speech to a Women's Republican Club in Wheeling, West Virginia, McCarthy alleged that "I have here in my hand a list of 205 that were known to the Secretary of State as being members of the Communist Party and who nevertheless are still working and shaping the policy of the State Department." He had in fact nothing of the sort. He had only an old letter written by Truman's secretary of state, James F. Byrnes, in response to a query four years before from a member of the House Appropriations Committee. In that letter, Byrnes reported that political loyalty screening of State Department employees pursuant to an executive order had resulted in a recommendation by the screening committee to deny permanent employment in

CHAPTER THREE

284 cases and that 79 of these employees had, upon further review, actually been terminated.

This utterly speculative—and in its specificity, simply false—assertion created a great sensation, one that McCarthy, with his mixture of cynical opportunism and demagogic genius, was able to exploit to the hilt. In the almost five-year period between this speech and his eventual censure by the Senate in December 1954, McCarthy's menacing visage exacted an enormous toll on American government and society in terms of lives and reputations ruined, policies skewed by the intimidation of vulnerable policymakers, enormous waste of time and energy by governing institutions with more and better to do, and alarm and conflict among an anxious public whose fears and susceptibility to scapegoating McCarthy played upon with dark virtuosity. He managed to cow President Dwight Eisenhower, drive George Marshall from office, and—it was believed by his Senate colleagues—play a key role in the defeat or resignation of as many as eight senators in the 1950 and 1952 elections. (Interestingly, McCarthy himself was the low performer on the Republican ticket in his home state, running over 100,000 votes behind Eisenhower. He faced more opposition among his own constituents than some realized or remember. But he still won, and that—together with his ability to exert power on a wider stage—was what really mattered at the time.)

The main features of this whole sorry and sobering episode in American politics are common knowledge and the stuff of legend. For our purposes here, the most important part of the story is the response of important sectors of the liberal intelligentsia to these events. And for the part of that response that contributes to our story line regarding the forces that pushed along the transformation of the dominant public philosophy of American reform liberalism, the historical and political revisionism of the eminent American historian Richard Hofstadter provides an exemplary case in point.

The alarming spectacle and threat to liberal values posed by McCarthyism drove Hofstadter and others like him toward the conviction that the standard depiction by historians of the reform tradition in America was naive and misleading, badly in need of a reassessment, which he undertook to provide in several celebrated works. In the standard telling, the liberalism of Hofstadter's day was generally represented as standing directly in the lineage of nineteenth-century populism and early twentieth-century Progressivism. New Deal economic liberalism and the social reform liberalism of the day were heir to these earlier reform movements in that all of them embodied a championing of the political interests of the middle and lower classes against the depredations of the "aristocracy of manufactures" whose incipient threat to a democratic society Tocqueville had warned against well before its ascendance to power after the Civil War. All of these political movements, moreover, shared a commitment to egalitarian aspirations and to the civic republican ideals of a self-governing, independent, morally virtuous middle class.

With the glowering visage of McCarthy looming over the politics of his day, Hofstadter decided that this picture of continuity and isomorphy among the various forms of reformism in America was a mistake. It was mistaken principally because it rested upon a selective and overly benign construal of nineteenth-century populism. The disturbing possibility suggested itself that the politically reactionary truculence, irrationality, and destructiveness of Joe McCarthy were, if not the authentic face of American populism in contemporary form, at least an authentic manifestation of both the style and content of populist politics. McCarthy was elected, after all, by the same voters (or at least the same electorate) who had put the La Follettes onto the national political stage. And there was clear evidence that the crucial and unexpected votes that gave McCarthy his very narrow victory over Bob La Follette Jr. in the 1946 primary came from working-class wards in Milwaukee. (Ironically, the communists, who had a strong influence within important union organizations in Milwaukee, disliked the anticommunist liberal La Follette and did nothing to fend off McCarthy. The *Daily Worker* said after that election that "the people will not mourn La Follette.")⁴⁶ Hofstadter was well acquainted, as a Columbia colleague of Seymour Martin Lipset, with the "working-class authoritarianism" thesis, and this ability of McCarthy to do better in working-class areas than did most Republicans seemed to vindicate that thesis about "the people's" unreliability regarding liberal values, as well.

Upon further review, then, Hofstadter argued that the populist tradition in this country had received far too favorable a press—and an inaccurate one, at that—from historians of liberal sympathies. Instead of being fundamentally liberal and progressive in their social goals and political values, the American populists had been social reactionaries, seeking nostalgically to preserve or more accurately to re-create an idealized past of agrarian romanticism—against the inevitable and largely beneficial development of a more advanced and urban society. Rather than being liberal in the sense of protecting individual freedoms and welcoming social diversity, moreover, the populists were largely nativists of a racist disposition who sought to perpetuate and enforce the hegemony of their white Anglo-Saxon Protestant (WASP) culture over American society as a whole. The populists were also scientifically backward (think here of William Jennings Bryan and the Scopes trial), hostile both to ideas in general and to intellectuals in particular. Indeed, in their parochialism, rigidity, moralism, hostility to change and to outsiders, and status anxieties, the populists, in Hofstadter's account (again indebted here to the psychologizing social diagnostics of the Frankfurt School, Harold Lasswell, and others), bordered upon exhibiting the characteristic traits of clinical paranoia.⁴⁷

Hofstadter's revisionist account of American history and its political reform tradition was immensely influential. "Thirty years after its publication," wrote historian Alan Brinkley, "even its critics recognized *Age of Reform* as the most influential book ever published on the history of the twentieth century in America."⁴⁸ Both *The Age of Reform* and *Anti-Intellectualism in American Life* won Pulitzer Prizes. But these two books, along with "The

Paranoid Style in American Politics," did a lot more than establish Hofstadter's academic reputation: they reflected developments in American political and intellectual life that went far beyond changes in academic historiography. Two of these developments figured directly in the transformation of American liberalism, the essence of which was the abandonment of a focus upon popular self-rule in the service of universal self-realization in favor of a program of technocratic reformism in the service of civil rights and social and economic equality.

The first of these significant developments was a nascent divorce or at least estrangement between midwestern progressivism and eastern liberalism, which Hofstadter's unflattering take on what populism was all about both reflected and accelerated. In the first half of the twentieth century, the affinity and alliance between these two political orientations/public philosophies were arguably the foundation of reform politics in this country. Given a bit of rhetorical license, one could even have referred to a Wisconsin–New York City progressive axis. Along with Eugene Debs, the most prominent figures in American socialism, for example, were Victor Berger, leader of the Wisconsin socialists, and Morris Hillquist, of the New York garment workers' union. And two of the most important and prominent Progressive officeholders were Wisconsin's La Follette and New York's Fiorello La Guardia. Hofstadter's depiction of midwestern populism/progressivism as backward, socially reactionary, and illiberal exposed and contributed to a fateful rift in this axis. As one recent commentator observed, "It is difficult to imagine the intellectual communities in Progressive bastions such as Madison or Berkeley providing warm support for *The Age of Reform* or *Anti-Intellectualism in American Life*."[49] Hofstadter's old mentor, Merle Curti, who held the Frederick Jackson Turner Chair at the University of Wisconsin and was a personal friend of Charles Beard, did indeed greatly regret what he saw as his former student's retreat from political progressivism, and he expressed that disappointment in his correspondence with him. Curti and his fellow Progressive historians at Madison and elsewhere not only thought that Hofstadter's attack on the progressive bona fides of populism was misleadingly one-sided, but sensed that this rejection of the legacy of midwestern reformism on the part of a major figure in the eastern liberal intellectual establishment did not augur well for the future success of progressive politics in this country.

The Madison historians also discerned—and worried about—what they saw as the "neoconservative" content and implications of the democratic theory that furnished the implicit backdrop of Hofstadter's historical hermeneutics. And this deeper normative perspective on democracy was in fact the second significant development reflected in Hofstadter's work that bears upon the transformation of American liberalism. For Hofstadter's account was not merely critical of the specific and particular historical phenomenon of American populism: it was also dubious about the possibilities and propriety of democratic self-rule. One part of this skepticism was Hofstadter's clear sympathy for the argument—explicit in the theological neoconservatism of a Reinhold Niebuhr and implicit in social scientific theories about the psychopathological dimensions of populist political enthusiasms—that liberalism was afflicted by a naive and romantic belief in the natural goodness of human beings. This unwarranted optimism, he thought, resulted in a misguided and delusionary "sentimentalization of the folk." And that liberal weakness led in turn, he thought, to a dangerous and improper understanding of democratic authority: it led to "the idea that anything done in the name of the people is *ipso facto* legitimate."[50]

The phenomenon of McCarthyism was again paradigmatic for Hofstadter. He not only saw McCarthy as, in some respects, a genuine representative of American populism. He also, as he rose valiantly to the defense of the American university against the McCarthyite assault on the professoriat, saw that assault as a manifestation of this faulty conception of democratic authority: that is, that the people or the majority is always right, always entitled to rule democratic institutions, and therefore entitled to determine and censor the content of instruction in the American university. In his book entitled *The Development and Scope of Higher Education in the United States*, in fact, Hofstadter offered a thesis about the derangement of American higher education that was eerily similar to that of Allan Bloom in *The Closing of the American Mind*. Bloom was a conservative intellectual exercised by attempts, from both within and without, to bend the academy to the political and social purposes of the left. Hofstadter was a liberal intellectual alarmed by the McCarthyite attempt to purge the academy of leftist influence. For both of them, however, despite this difference in political coloration, the basic complaint was the same: populist democracy, or what Hofstadter called "democracy with a vengeance,"[51] was not good for higher education, for the social status of the professoriat, or therefore for the health of the society in general. Hofstadter actually seemed wistful for more socially hierarchical times past, observing that the university's "greatest periods" seemed to come "in societies that were not notably democratic" and in ages "of political and economic oligarchy."[52] More democratic times and societies, however, were inclined to be hostile to the life of the mind and correspondingly bad for the health of the university.

Such neo-Platonic ruminations about the perils of democracy are, of course, quite fitting for a Straussian political theorist such as Allan Bloom. But apparent nostalgia for past times of greater social hierarchy and the corollary gestures toward what Ian Shapiro has called a "vanguardist" approach to politics were more striking and arguably anomalous for an intellectual doyen of the American Left intelligentsia. Hofstadter's argument certainly was seen as worrisome by his fellow historians who retained more traditional progressive sympathies, with Merle Curti, for example, pronouncing himself "somehow a bit disappointed" with Hofstadter's argument. He told Hofstadter that he thought he seemed to have been overly "influenced by the neo-conservatism that is now so pervasive in academic and non-academic circles alike."[53]

CHAPTER THREE

The allusion here to political neo-Platonism is not purely rhetorical. For the political dynamics and the consequences of the McCarthy episode in American history were strikingly foreshadowed in the events surrounding the trial and execution of Socrates as these were portrayed in Plato's *Apology*. The story line and dramatis personae in both cases are pretty much the same. An anxious and insecure democratic populace worries about its safety and the threat of powerful enemies. Some of its golden boys (Alcibiades / Alger Hiss) are seen as having fraternized with the threatening forces. A somewhat crude demagogue (Meletus / McCarthy) attempts to promote his career by seeking out and persecuting subversives allegedly responsible for having encouraged such treasonous activities. In his efforts, he is aided and abetted by somewhat more able and "respectable" political leaders (Anytus / Robert Taft, William Buckley, John Bricker) who see him as somewhat crude and distasteful but as nevertheless an effective instrument for crippling their political opponents.[54] These alleged "subversives" (Socrates / American liberal officeholders and members of the intelligentsia) are hauled in front of public tribunals for intimidation and condemnation. And a sensitive and influential observer properly appalled by the spectacle (Plato / Hofstadter) develops grave doubts about democratic politics, takes refuge in an academy devoted to elite education, and ponders strategies for "the professionalization of reform."

FRACTURING THE NEW DEAL COALITION: CIVIL RIGHTS AND VIETNAM

If McCarthyism pushed influential sectors of the liberal intelligentsia (especially eastern urban sectors) away from populist and participatory democratic ideals while it simultaneously and correlatively encouraged more elitist and technocratic strategies of political reform, the successes and political dynamics of the civil rights revolution—and the interpretation placed upon them—led many liberal theorists and activists to move toward what Ben Barber has called a "juridical democracy," one directed toward putative rights and social justice to the detriment of more populist and civic republican social goals and strategies. The politics and policies of civil rights also created new fissures between liberals and the white working class.

The major events and achievements of the civil rights revolution are sufficiently common knowledge to need little rehearsal here. Ever since the Supreme Court had in effect ratified the retreat from the social agenda of Reconstruction through its decisions in the *Slaughterhouse* cases and *Plessy v. Ferguson,* the consolidation of a racial caste system, enforced by Jim Crow laws and social mores, eventuated into what Gunnar Myrdal famously styled as the American dilemma. Here was the world's longest-lasting continuous democratic polity—conceived in liberty and dedicated to the proposition, as Lincoln put it, that all are created equal—which seemed utterly incapable of dismantling a deeply entrenched system of racial oppression and apartheid. In 1954, however, those who had fought a long campaign against this ugly anomaly achieved the huge legal breakthrough of the Supreme Court decision in *Brown v. Board of Education,* outlawing segregation in public schools. After a decade marked by marches, protests, sit-ins, riots, and a number of racially motivated killings, there followed the landmark national legislation of the '60s that guaranteed voting rights and outlawed racial discriminatory practices in housing, hiring, and public accommodations. And during the next decade, executive orders and judicial rulings pursuant to these laws mandated remedies such as affirmative action and busing.

Although this legal and social revolution was disgracefully tardy and although progress toward the full social inclusion and equality that were its ultimate goal remains frustratingly slow, it has been, from a comparative and long-run viewpoint on social change, a stunning achievement. Arguably, indeed, it has been the definitive political achievement of post–World War II liberalism. For that reason—and because accomplishing the full goals of

CHAPTER THREE

this social movement remains a work in progress—the events and the presumed lessons of the civil rights revolution have achieved a paradigmatic role in the self-understanding of contemporary liberalism. It has become a kind of template that exerts a profound influence upon the way that most contemporary liberals conceive their moral purposes and their political strategies. That influence has helped to motivate and reinforce the changes in the public philosophy of American liberalism that are our principal concern here. It has done this, I believe, in at least three ways.

First, the very term *civil rights revolution* has functioned to promote the core assumption of deontological liberalism that the primary goal of progressive politics is to protect rights and attain social justice. That was seen as being, as the phrase *civil rights* denotes, what the destruction of Jim Crow was all about; by implication, the ultimate social goals of liberal reform are, in their essence and in their justification, simply the extension of the rights and justice agenda throughout the entire social order. Those whose political sensibilities were formed and whose social conscience was fired by the civil rights movement, in short, could accept almost reflexively the stipulation of a John Rawls and his deontological compatriots that justice is the first virtue of social institutions. They knew that already from their socialization and were predisposed to believe it in the same way that John Stuart Mill was predisposed by his own programmed socialization to receive Bentham's happiness principle as the revelation of an obvious truth.

The success of the civil rights movement also pushed many contemporary liberals toward some important practical inferences about what political strategies and modes of governance were most effective in the service of social progress. And these putative lessons drawn from this paradigmatic chapter of liberal reform in their turn had ramifications for contemporary liberalism's normative priorities.

It has become standard to represent the civil rights revolution as a political campaign that was successfully waged by a resolute minority in the face of determined opposition from the majority of the populace. As such, it was waged outside the standard venues of majoritarian democratic campaigning—building electoral and legislative coalitions—through constitutional and sometimes extraconstitutional channels available to activist minorities: by obtaining judicial mandates; by fashioning bureaucratic rules; and by engaging in protests, boycotts, and civil disobedience. In point of fact, this rendering of the politics of civil rights is a misleading half-truth. It is, of course, quite true that the crucial breakthrough of the *Brown v. Board of Education* ruling was the result of a long-term campaign of constitutional litigation pursued by attorneys for the NAACP Legal Defense Fund and their allies. The impetus for further successes came from extraconstitutional pressure and suasion exerted by the Freedom Riders, by marchers across the bridge at Selma, by college students who sat in at segregated lunch counters, and by participants in the Montgomery bus boycott. And the desegregation strategies of busing and affirmative action came from courts and bureaucratic agencies, not from legislatures. What this telling of the story forgets, however, is the truth in the old adage about the Supreme Court following the election returns. That was not literally the case in the *Brown v. Board Education* decision, perhaps, or in the decisions that led up to it, but the Court clearly calculated that public support for the principles embodied in their decision and for the changes necessitated by it was sufficiently widespread for their ruling to be accepted and enforced. This telling of the story also seems to forget that the most definitive legal mandates that consolidated and extended the civil rights revolution from its initial beachhead in public schooling into voting rights, housing, hiring, and public accommodations were enacted by national legislative majorities.

Despite being at best a partial truth about the mechanisms of this paradigmatic liberal success story, this story has encouraged among contemporary liberals the belief that their social goals can be achieved and perhaps can only be achieved by bypassing the normal political channels for building democratic majorities.

CHAPTER THREE

Instead of focusing on the slow boring of hard boards required of those who try to win elections and build legislative support for their policies, it is better to convince judges and strategically placed people in executive agencies to do your work for you. And this tactical orientation both presupposes and reinforces a very important judgment about democratic values, priorities, and legitimacy: it embodies and depends upon an insistence that substantive democratic outcomes (i.e., civil rights and social justice/equality) possess the requisite certainty and moral weight to override and subordinate the norms and sustaining values of procedural democracy whenever these come into conflict or whenever the latter are deemed insufficiently expeditious. Contemporary liberalism in both its academic and real-world forms seems, for the most part, to have endorsed that moral judgment and accepted its political implications: rights are trump, procedures are only instrumentally significant, democracy is a set of outcomes rather than a way of life, social justice is what really matters, and self-rule carries moral weight only when it conduces to that end.

The third contribution and shaping influence of the civil rights revolution upon the public philosophy of contemporary liberalism has been this: it has served as a tacit narrative that has given both power and concrete meaning to the abstract imperatives of deontological social theory. The life of public philosophy, like that of the law, is not logic but experience. Or perhaps it would be better and more precise to say that people are able to understand and give meaning to the abstract principles and categories of law and political theory only by fleshing them out with concrete reference points and cases from their own lives and experiences.

In the latter half of the twentieth century, the issues and personae of the civil rights revolution were at the foreground of the nation's political imagination, and they functioned accordingly as these concrete reference points for understanding and assessing the claims of liberal theory. When I first taught Rawls to college students, it was quite obvious from our discussions that they based their conceptions of the situation of the "least advantaged" upon their concrete recognition of the plight of African Americans as they struggled to overcome the effects of systematic and institutionalized racial discrimination. That identification helped lend credibility to the claim that maximizing the welfare of the most disadvantaged was the essence of social justice and an overriding moral imperative. The recognition that it was a self-serving presumption of those further up the social hierarchy—who were arguably complicit in this pattern of enforced social subordination—to demand that the victims of oppression lift themselves up by their bootstraps also was important: it made more persuasive the insistence of Rawls and others like him that people's very ability to make an effort was a product of their social circumstances and therefore should not be used as a basis for norms of proportional justice grounded in preinstitutional desert. The fact that the white working class—in places such as Cicero, South Boston, and Detroit—seemed a locus of opposition to black advancement, moreover, helped suppress reservations that might have arisen about the delegitimation of work as a basis of social status and economic reward and the correlative marginalization of the working class in the specification of the criteria for social justice.

Finally, populating Rawls's abstractions with the concrete historical figures of the civil rights drama gave a great deal of added force to what Rawls called the "principle of redress" that lay at the heart of the difference principle. Within the abstract confines of Rawls's theoretical model, *redress* means the attempt to eliminate, to the greatest possible extent, all purely adventitious social inequalities. Requiring redress in this sense depends upon acceptance of the moral intuition that different levels of well-being produced by sheer accident, being "morally arbitrary," demand evening up because they are not fair. When the historical facts of racial domination are mapped onto this abstract argument, however, redress takes on a different meaning that carries additional moral weight. It then invokes and trades upon the fact of historical oppression rather than referencing all forms of fortuitous inequalities per se, thereby gaining added credence by becoming parasitic upon the logic of rectification (righting past wrongs), which is something quite different.[55]

If teaching Rawls when civil rights was the overriding issue of the day provided evidence on behalf of this somewhat speculative account of the importance of the civil rights revolution as an interpretive template for contemporary liberalism's account of social justice, my experience teaching Rawls today gives confirmation of a different kind. For students today, for whom Jim Crow is something encountered in history books instead of in real life and who experience a more complex and morally ambiguous racial situation, clearly respond both differently and more skeptically to Rawls's core argument. They are much less likely spontaneously to map the lived facts of discrimination and oppression onto Rawls's categories. Hence, for them, the "least well-off" are conceived as exactly and only that: people who are not as well-off as others, possibly by pure circumstance rather than as a consequence of oppression by those who are better-off. Their less hermeneutically infused reading of the text in fact conforms more accurately to the unadorned logic of Rawls's account of justice as fairness. And that less experientially prejudicial encounter with the argument makes it a considerably harder sell to them.

The additional fissures produced within the New Deal liberal coalition by the politics and policies of civil rights stemmed from a clash between the reform aspirations of suburban and upper-class liberals, on the one hand, and the interests and values of white and ethnic working-class whites, on the other. Members of the former group were understandably and admirably anxious to attain what they saw as the ultimate goal of the civil rights revolution as quickly as possible. This ultimate goal was not merely legal and formal nondiscrimination—the end of Jim Crow laws—but the attainment of full racial social equality. In the real world of geographic specificities and finite resources, however, the reform policies devised in the service of this altogether admirable goal came mostly at the expense of those demographic groups that stood closest to previously disenfranchised African Americans, both in physical space and on the socioeconomic scale. The unfortunate concrete result was that open-housing laws threatened cohesive white working-class neighborhoods, school busing disrupted the lives largely of working-class children and their families, and affirmative action narrowed the vocational paths traditionally available to working-class ethnics. As resistance flared against these measures, so deepened the distrust and derogation felt by upper-class and academic liberals toward the putative Archie Bunkers of the world—now to be met in return by resentment against the imperious condescension of alleged limousine liberals from people keenly aware that it was schools such as Southie in Boston rather than schools like New Trier in Winnetka that were disrupted by busing and that the urban crime supposedly a figment of their racist imaginations afflicted places such as Hamtramck a lot more than places such as Scarsdale.

The conflicts and controversies surrounding the Vietnam War also played a part in this story, deepening the alienation between liberal elites and the working class. Some of these fissures would have made any orthodox Marxist queasy, as the sons and daughters of the upper bourgeoisie marched in the streets of our major cities bearing signs telling the government in graphic terms what it could do with its war while construction workers looking down upon them from steel girders waved flags and signs that read "God bless the Establishment." And forty years later, these odd cleavages fracturing the New Deal coalition and impacting the political sensibility of its various elements were still in evidence in remarkable and seemingly irrational ways, as a Democratic presidential candidate with a Bronze Star was subjected to a systematic campaign of vituperation by middle- and working-class veterans who had long memories and still bore grudges from his opposition to that war.

This chapter has been an unavoidably speculative venture in causal explanation. So it seems useful at this point to say a few words of clarification about the several variables involved here and the suppositions about their relationship informing this

CHAPTER THREE

venture. The book's title mentions transformation and decline, and it is the first of these two terms that has been the dependent variable here—the "it" in the chapter title. The question of decline will be broached in the next chapter, where I will argue that the transformation in the public philosophy of American liberalism I have described represents in some important respects a theoretical and moral misstep while simultaneously and partly for that reason playing a role as one important variable among others in the electoral decline of liberalism over the past several decades. To repeat for emphasis, then, the question addressed in this chapter has been: what are some of the more important independent variables—intellectual developments and historical events and the reaction to them—that drove and shaped the changes in liberal public philosophy on display in the first two chapters? Despite some overlap, then, it has certainly not been my claim here—or elsewhere—that I have canvassed all the causal forces behind changes in liberalism's electoral fortunes.

With these intentions in mind, we can recapitulate briefly the several variables canvassed in the preceding pages, together with the specific component features of the contemporary social justice–centered liberalism they helped shape.

The first contributory causal variable cited was what I called a changing metaphysic of morals that appeared in stages around the turn of the twentieth century. This metaphysic was in turn composed of two main elements: naturalism and decisionism. The first of these involved cosmological anthropology—that is, the understanding of human nature as it fit into the basic structure of the created universe. The second involved moral ontology—that is, the understanding of the nature of the human good and its relationship to the shape of Being.

Naturalism here means the expansion of the realm of phenomenal causality at the expense of a shrinking noumenal realm of freedom and rationality in the understanding of human behavior: the degree to which we act like animals driven by internal impulse and instinct, on the one hand, and external contingencies, on the other, is seen as larger than previously thought. Naturalism thus diminishes our sense of the power and scope of moral agency, thereby problematizing the assumption that we humans have the capability of determining our actions and, pari passu, compromising attributions of moral responsibility. In the context of liberal theory, these trends functioned to undermine the meaning and force of the traditional "constitutive" (in Dworkin's sense) goal of self-rule. They also functioned to undermine the logical basis for norms of preinstitutional moral desert, thereby compromising traditional moral distinctions between deserving and undeserving poor and between the proletariat and the lumpen proletariat. In the context of what I have called the normative sociology of liberal public philosophy, these changes in turn undermined the warrants for the commendatory adjective in the appellation "respectable yeomanry."

Decisionism refers to the construction of Being in such a way that the human good loses its footing within it. The human good is thereby simultaneously de-objectified and de-cognitivized. That is to say, the human good is not construed to be a component of the objective reality of the world, and it therefore is not something that can meaningfully be understood as an object of knowledge. On this account, we live in the world of Weber and moral aestheticism—a world where values are chosen "demonically" and where goods are matters of taste. In the context of liberal public philosophy, the most important consequence of decisionism is that it knocked the traditional base out from under the constitutive traditional goal of universal self-realization or what Mill and others called human "development." It undermined the traditional grounds for considering some human purposes or goods to be better or "higher" than some others: its value slope conforms much more readily to Bentham's admonition that "push-pin is as good as poetry" than to Mill's riposte that there are qualitative distinctions to be made among pleasures and that it is "better to be Socrates dissatisfied than a fool satisfied." Correlatively, the logical conception of the moral powers imputable to democratic

CHAPTER THREE

citizens was altered and diminished: these democratic persons may need to have a sense of justice, but when it comes to the good, they need possess only the capability to choose a plan a life and not the kind of moral judgment, definitive of Aristotle's phronimoi, required to ascertain what is rationally desirable.

The other ideational independent variable contributing to the transformation of liberal public philosophy was social scientific in provenance: namely, the disparaging depiction of the mind and heart of the democratic populace that emanated from public opinion research in the decades after World War II. This literature, as we saw, cumulatively gave credence to a Menckenesque view of the average American *Homo civicus* as depressingly ignorant and worrisomely authoritarian, intolerant, and racially prejudiced. Nineteenth-century champions of democratization and universal suffrage were, of course, by no means oblivious to the political dangers created by the political empowerment of the uncouth and illiterate, but they hoped that these dangers would diminish with the advances of public education. To see in what seemed to be hard numbers how far from appropriately enlightened the democratic public remained a full century later was sobering enough to produce revisionist reflections about what a democratic polity looked like and could ever hope to be.

This democratic revisionism contributed to the transformation of American liberalism in multiple ways. First and perhaps foremost, it worked to sap the constitutive traditional liberal goal of self-rule of its normativity and desirability. Given the visage of the all-too-common people glowering from the survey data, why indeed would it seem all that rational or morally imperative to prioritize the political rule of such a crowd? As a practical corollary of this disenchantment with democratic self-rule, the devotion to enhancing institutional mechanisms to give force to popular voice and will—something quite prominent in the Progressive era—lost ground. Improvements in democratic process, thus diminished in their normativity, could be subordinated to the urgency of attaining the substantive goals of social and economic equality—through whatever means seemed most expedient. The unflattering depiction of the average citizen also exerted an important influence upon what I have referred to as the normative sociology of liberal public philosophy. It had the effect of eroding the moral credentials of the "average man" of traditional liberalism, thus depriving him of the pride of place he enjoyed in the social goals and policy imperative of that persuasion. The role of common men as the principal agents of democratic advance was more or less assumed instead by the political elites who functioned as the new "carriers of the creed"; the status of common men as the principal object of concern in democratic social policy in turn more or less devolved upon the "disadvantaged"—a different subset of the populace. Finally, the negative portrayal of the democratic common man, at this point in time well down the road from the onset of democratic governance, leached some of the persuasiveness from all those traditional hopes for the universal self-realization of the democratic citizenry. If that citizenry seemed not to have progressed any further along the curve to developing into something resembling Mill's ideal democratic citizens or Whitman's "first-class men," then maybe those hopes stood revealed as romantic fantasies. What you see is all we are likely to get: the democratic people have maxed out at a relatively low level. Whitman's "grand experiment of development" appeared to have turned into a disappointing case study of arrested development, and the traditional liberal goal of self-realization could be placed upon the back burner for empirical as well as theoretical reasons.

The two major historical events cited here as contributing factors to the transformation in liberal public philosophy—McCarthyism and the civil rights revolution—worked in tandem with these philosophical and social scientific developments to reinforce the distancing of American liberalism from its traditional populist commitments and perfectionist aspirations, while giving added impetus to components of the new public philosophy. The chilling phenomenon of McCarthyism made popular self-rule look menacing and dangerous. It inspired the thought that liberal intellectuals needed to work to buffer and constrain democratic self-governance more than to encourage and facilitate it. The historical revisionism it fostered opened up a fateful rift between the coastal and midwestern axes of the Progressive and New Deal coalitions. That rift in turn encouraged the siphoning off of the populist and communitarian elements of the political sensibility of traditional American liberalism, giving a more eastern, urban, and individualistic cast to the new face of liberalism. And all of these aspects of the revulsion against McCarthyism helped provide both impetus and part of the rationale for the movement toward the professionalization of reform.

Finally, the civil rights revolution that belatedly began the dismantling of the moral scandal of America's legalized racial caste system exerted its own influence on the transformation of liberalism in several ways. It gave a strong boost to making rights and justice the axial goals of liberal reform, in the process expanding their purchase by encompassing but subordinating within them the larger social aspirations to inclusion, civic friendship, and universal flourishing that were powerfully invoked in the speeches of Martin Luther King Jr. It gave concrete embodiment to the revisionist normative sociology of contemporary liberalism, putting the faces of historically oppressed people onto the abstract category of the "least advantaged" and providing thereby the implicit rationale for according moral priority to their welfare. And it had the collateral consequence of deepening the alienation between liberal elites and members of the white working class, who felt with some justification that they often bore the brunt of social policies intended to remediate black social and economic disenfranchisement while finding themselves condemned for their racism—real and imagined—in the bargain.

There were, no doubt, many other causal elements that played some part in the movement away from the axial goals and moral imaginary of traditional liberalism toward a rights-based liberalism devoted to the achievement of social distributive justice. But taken all together, the several trends and events canvassed here surely go a long way toward accounting for the important changes in the public philosophy of American liberalism during the latter half of the twentieth century. These changes were not the inexplicable product of some mysterious kind of spontaneous generation. Nor were they created out of the blue in a sudden flash of inspiration by some academic in an ivory tower. Instead, like all significant ideological innovations, the transformation of American liberalism grew from the reflective responses of thoughtful and engaged people to problematic contingencies of their lives and times. Whether those responses were the best ones to make becomes another question.

4   The Deontology Trap

The argument to this point has largely been analytical and explanatory. With a generous helping of hermeneutic license, I have sketched two ideal type models: "traditional" American liberal progressivism, on the one hand, and contemporary American liberalism, on the other. The central strands woven into the first model were taken from people such as Jefferson, Walt Whitman, George Bancroft, John Dewey, and Jane Addams. The second model is based upon what has been termed the high liberalism of deontological moral philosophers and egalitarian social theorists such as John Rawls and Ronald Dworkin. I have argued that these philosophical conceptions are not merely academic curiosities but that they broadly mirror the dominant moral intuitions and social goals both of populist and Progressive politics and of post-1960 social justice liberalism. I have argued that the philosophical differences between these two public philosophies run deep: they involve a change in axial principles and not merely changes in tactics or secondary principles. And in the previous chapter, I sought to explain some of the philosophical developments and political events that helped shape and motivate this transformation of American liberalism.

It is time now to shift into normative gear. The questions occupying us from here on are critical and constructive ones. Were these developments desirable and beneficial? Did they represent a morally proper and politically prudent change of orientation and strategy? Or should this change instead be seen as an unfortunate turn of events from the standpoint of those who seek to advance a progressive social agenda for this country? Was the shift from a devotion to popular self-rule and universal self-realization to a fixation upon distributive justice—together with its attendant philosophical and political implications—on balance more costly than advantageous? In short, should American liberals at the outset of the twenty-first century consider this transformation of their public philosophy from a politically populist form of philosophical perfectionism into an egalitarian form of a philosophy of rights as setting its best course? Or should they instead view this shift as representing a zeitgeist of temporary relevance—a detour from the main highway rather than their best path for the future? The answer I offer here is presaged by the title of this chapter. I believe that this late twentieth-century recasting of liberal public philosophy has been on balance unwise and imprudent. It may have served a valuable role in providing voice and moral support to very important liberal reforms over the past several decades. For the long run, however, it has placed American liberalism on problematic theoretical foundations while not coincidentally contributing to its political decline and electoral misfortunes over the same time period.

As seen in chapter 3, much of the impetus toward the transformation of liberal public philosophy came from changing ideas and findings in philosophy and social science in conjunction with salient and paradigmatic political events that worked in tandem to undermine the central animating goals and normative sociology of traditional liberalism. In addition, however, there were important constructive hopes and needs that drove the turn away from a democratic teleology of self-governance and personal development toward a deontologically grounded version of social egalitarian reform liberalism. The wholly understandable preoccupation with rights and social justice engendered by the civil rights revolution and its attendant liberation movements prompted the idea that this social justice agenda was in effect what liberalism was all about in its entirety—that its consummating goals could be encompassed within the ambit of norms of justice without any reliance on democratic teleology.

This hopeful prospect was especially enticing because if it could be successfully attained, it would bring with it two hugely attractive corollary benefits. The first of these ancillary achievements would be a practical yet principled solution to the problems of legitimacy and stability presented by the increasingly morally and religiously pluralistic composition of American society. The coexistence within our society of many different persuasions about the content of the humanly good and proper life—persuasions that in some respects seem at least competitive, if not outright incompatible and even incommensurable—presented a serious stumbling block to the venerable notion that what held a political society together was a common devotion among its members to achieving the good life together. If there was in fact no conception of the good held and pursued in common, the moral foundations and the social bonds of such a society seemed in great jeopardy. One logical fallback position was to see the democratic state as a pact of convenience entered into as a bargain based in self-interest. But that basically Hobbesian "solution" to the seeming untenability of the Aristotelian account of the social bond—one carried over into many canonical liberal theories—seemed to sap the democratic state of its moral status and thereby simultaneously weaken its legitimacy in the Weberian sense of that term. Equally alarming to those of progressive/egalitarian sympathies, building a democratic society upon a panoply of self-interested contractual agreements among its individual members provided neither grounds nor legitimate institutions for ameliorating the profound inequalities generated over time by advanced corporate capitalist political economies. It was enormously appealing, therefore, to imagine that a neo-Kantian egalitarianism could fill the vast void between Aristotelian obsolescence and Hobbesian dangers. A democratic state built upon common fealty to justice might provide contemporary societies with the moral weight and social glue—and therefore the legitimacy and stability—

not found in a modus vivendi and no longer attainable through a classical polis.

The second profoundly enticing ancillary attraction of grounding democratic society on deontological foundations was the hope that doing so would provide a morally compelling and substantively determinate rationale and justification for traditional liberal aspirations for greater social and economic equality. The appealing prospect here was the creation of a principled philosophical vehicle for these egalitarian aspirations that would suffice to persuade the American populace that the civil rights agenda of breaking up the prevailing racial caste system and bringing hitherto excluded and oppressed African Americans into full and equal membership in the American polity was just one paradigmatic aspect of a larger moral imperative on behalf of social and economic equality across the board—that is, "social justice." The key to these aspirations, then, was a compelling and expansive understanding of social justice whose scope and content incorporated and validated the goals and ideals of social democracy. Widespread acceptance of this kind of moral imaginary could then provide the basis and impetus for the triumph of an ambitiously egalitarian form of liberalism over its traditional ideological competition—all without having to rely upon the more protean goals and potentially controversial assumptions informing traditional democratic teleology.

Social justice liberals, then, were not engaged merely in generalizing and carrying to a higher level of abstraction the social contract tradition that Kant, among others, exemplified, as Rawls wrote in his preface to *A Theory of Justice*. At a deeper level, they were adopting the fundamental philosophical strategy and moral intuitions Kant had deployed in his central mission—saving morality from the serious threat posed to it, in Kant's reckoning, by David Hume's empiricist reduction of the good to the "useful and agreeable." The only way to protect morality from succumbing to what he called this "lax and low" hedonism, Kant argued, was to identify the true content of morality—that is, imperatives of duty—and explain how these imperatives were solidly based on reason alone and not upon the vagaries of human desire, including the desire for happiness.

Social justice liberals in effect took Kant's moral strategy and enlarged its ambit. They undertook to extend the sovereignty of right/justice/duty from morality to public philosophy. By believing, as Rawls did, that a theory of justice can establish the moral foundations of democratic society, they sought to use deontology not simply to establish the nature of moral rectitude as goodwill—meaning fidelity to the logical imperatives of pure practical reason. They sought more ambitiously to use deontology to provide the moral criteria for determining the basic structure of a well-ordered society and the proper allocation of the benefits and burdens of social cooperation within that society.[1] And to sustain that enlarged purchase of deontology, the scope of moral reasonableness had logically to be expanded, pari passu, from requiring fidelity to universalizable maxims of action and respect for all rational beings to also establishing compelling standards of distributive justice.

The parallel strategies of Kant in moral theory and social justice liberalism in political philosophy each embodied a very large and bold wager. Kant's gamble took the form of an insistence that his account of morality represented the sole viable alternative to Humean hedonism: either accept my conception of morality, he told his readers, or you must accept Hume's account. You face an either/or, all-or-nothing kind of choice because there is no coherent middle ground and no viable moral alternative. And the principal reason there is no viable alternative is that the only apparent claimants for that role purport to derive moral imperatives from some species of human desirability—which is impossible because all human desires are merely "phenomenal" and therefore lack moral content.

Kant's bold gamble was at best a mixed success. On the positive side of the ledger, his moral paradigm of the "kingdom of ends" has served as a model for understanding the logic and the force of human rights and also for depicting the moral relationship among citizens of political republics. Both can be understood and legitimated as incarnations of the logically proper rights and reciprocities among persons qua rational beings. Kant's larger ambitions for deontology, however, have widely been rejected as unpersuasive and emptily formalistic. Moreover, the enemies Kant sought to dispatch—utilitarian hedonism and moral aestheticism—survived his assault upon them. Emotivism and decisionism seem alive and well. Indeed, the latter arguably was one of his own progeny: Weber was a second-generation neo-Kantian. Moreover, one signal destructive side effect of the either/or choice he posed was the derogation of eudaemonistic ethics: for in reducing all human desire to moral insignificance, Kant was consigning not only hedonism but also a lot of classical ethics to the scrap heap. (In effect, Kant agreed with Bentham that push-pin was as good as poetry. It's just that Bentham gave them equal moral significance as sources of happiness/pleasure, whereas Kant considered them both equally devoid of moral significance because they were both "phenomenal" in content.)

Contemporary American social justice liberalism followed a similar strategy and took a similar bold gamble. Like Kant, social justice liberalism presented itself as the only viable alternative to modus vivendi and libertarian conceptions of a democratic society. Utilitarian justifications of the democratic general welfare as the greatest good for the greatest number were rejected as unacceptable, both because the utilitarian calculus would give weight to morally inappropriate desires/pleasures/preferences and because it was a purely aggregative standard that violated justice by not taking the separateness and hence the inviolable integrity of persons seriously. Other teleological conceptions of democracy were likewise dismissed as unnecessarily indeterminate (because "intuitionist" or "pluralist" in the Isaiah Berlin sense) and/or because they were held to entail a commitment to comprehensive conceptions of the human good, which violated acceptance of what Rawls called "the burdens of judgment" (i.e., due recognition of our epistemic limitations in the moral domain) and

CHAPTER FOUR

thereby violated principles of legitimate power in a society of free and equal people. Casting aside in this way the animating teleological purposes relied upon by traditional liberalism to inform and justify its political and socially egalitarian aspirations forced social justice liberalism into taking its own big gamble. This gamble was, in fact, a double wager. In placing its political and moral bets entirely upon the reach and power of deontology, social justice liberalism had to wager, first, that the concept of justice could be convincingly construed in a way sufficiently capacious to encompass the broader range of democratic social ideals. And it also had to make a second wager that this capacious conception of the concrete imperatives of social justice would prove sufficiently attractive and compelling to win a decisive victory over any and all alternative and competitive versions of political deontology—in particular and most importantly over the strongly individualistic conception of rights championed by self-styled "classical liberals" and libertarians.

My fundamental claim in this chapter is that the contemporary liberal attempt to replace the democratic teleology of self-rule and self-realization with a reliance on an expansive ideal of social justice has suffered a fate similar to that of Kant's moral philosophy. It may have succeeded in highlighting the importance of reciprocity among equal and reasonable people as a core element of democratic morality and practice. But the larger and more ambitious hopes of this deontological strategy have proved chimerical and in some respects self-defeating. The competing conceptions of liberal rights and ideals the advocates of the new rights-based liberalism sought to displace have retained a potent appeal, and the traditional moral and philosophical grounds for an inspiring conception of democratic vistas have unwisely been shunted aside by adherents of the very political persuasion most in need of them.

This noble (in terms of its aspirations and intentions) failure has been both theoretical and practical, both philosophical and political. Upon critical reflection, the philosophical logic has proved to suffer from a number of intractable problems. The normative principles its advocates wanted most to promote seem ineluctably to require adherence to assumptions that are unpersuasive or unattractive. And in the meantime, the attempt to sell the goals of reform liberalism as imperatives of distributive justice has played a contributory role in the erosion of reform liberalism's ideological appeal and electoral strength. This is the dual decline referenced in the title of this book. My claim here is that the logical and causal dynamics of this decline are a product of contemporary American liberalism's falling into what can be called a "deontology trap."

THE DEONTOLOGY TRAP AND THEORETICAL DECLINE

The basic goal of the attempt to squeeze the hopes and ideals of American liberalism onto a deontological base—that is, to make distributive justice the moral foundation of a democratic society—was to strengthen them in two ways: first, to give them a determinate content, and second, to provide them with greater imperative force. This goal of added clarity and strength was captured by phrases such as "moral geometry" and "rights as trumps." In both respects, an invidious contrast was made with what was seen as the comparative vagueness of traditional liberal goals and the softness of traditional liberalism's teleological norms. But pursuing this strategy has weakened rather than strengthened liberal public philosophy because the attempt to complete the deontological project—to present democratic purposes as justice writ large—runs into several serious problems.

These problems involve the scope of liberal justice, the content of liberal justice, and the social functions of liberal justice. The problem of scope is that in order to stretch justice far enough to cover reform liberalism's aspirations for democracy, it becomes overextended. It is expanded beyond its legitimate purchase and competency, thus losing its persuasiveness. Call this the hypertrophy of justice. The problems of the content of liberal justice are ones of coherence and credibility. The problem of coherence refers to the way that the content deontological reform liberals want to accord to justice seems to dictate acceptance of presuppositions at war with other important liberal values and beliefs. The problem of credibility is that some of these necessary presuppositions seem quite implausible in and of themselves. The problem of functionality refers to the difficulty of using the sense of justice as the motivational force for liberal politics. Call this the fragility of justice. The several problems are also interrelated: the attempt to push justice beyond its competency contributes to distortions in the content of liberal justice, and these together add greatly to the fragility of justice as a motivator. Some of these critical observations are not entirely novel ones; I therefore do not claim to be the first to have identified all of the problems I shall discuss. My purpose here is to gather and explain these difficulties with the intent of displaying how they cumulatively undermine the theoretical case for jettisoning the democratic teleology at the heart of traditional American liberalism and trying to fill the void thus created with claims about social justice.

Consider first under this heading the problems regarding the scope of demands of liberal justice. The central difficulty here is that in order to reach their desired outcome, social justice liberals are driven into making excessive claims about the purchase of justice. If the imperatives of justice are to produce the degree of social and economic equality to which contemporary American liberalism aspires, the claims of justice must embody demands for redressing the multifarious and profound inequalities found in our—and all—human society. This is why Rawls aptly characterizes his principles of justice as embodying the principle of redress. But to be effective, this redress cannot be limited to socially created inequities because the origins of so many of the morally arbitrary inequalities we see about us are not the result of human actions or institutions: they stem instead from the many serendipitous disparities placed upon us by natural forces that—were they to be personified—would be deemed callous and irrational. Actually to produce a social situation that could truly seem "fair" in a full and complete sense—that is, to be free of morally arbitrary inequalities—would require redressing these natural inequalities and not only socially created ones. That is why, as Rawls acknowledges in a remarkably blithe admission/demand, it is "the arbitrariness of the world" that "must be corrected for."[2] This is the insistence upon what I referred to as "cosmic justice" in chapter 2, and it is an insistence to which social justice liberalism is logically driven if it wishes to base its hopes for social equality upon demands of justice alone.

But these demands for cosmic justice take justice beyond its realm of competency. In a sense, this misstep represents a normative version of what Wittgenstein termed the confusion that occurs when language "goes on holiday." The grammar of justice is simply out of place when it comes to dealing with the massive arbitrariness of nature. However much we might wish to inhabit a world that is perfectly fair, the pervasive and profound inequalities of natural endowment make that morally admirable wish a fantasy. And trying to impose obligations of justice on particular people—or the abstraction of "society," which only linguistically buffers the same reality—in this context leads to the making of morally questionable demands. Thus, the hypertrophy of justice creates problems of both feasibility and moral propriety.

Edmund Burke thought that going to war with nature constituted a great impiety. I think that is not a real problem. We go to war with nature whenever we build dams or take antibiotics, and such interventions seem morally unobjectionable—even though Christian Scientists, for example, might disagree in the case of medical interventions. But going to war with nature in the name of justice certainly raises enormous feasibility questions. And because "ought implies can," serious problems of feasibility tend to generate moral dilemmas, as well. Rawls says that his core conception of justice that is embodied in the difference principle "is not the same as that of redress,"[3] but "it does achieve some of the same intent."[4] And one fundamental mandate of this principle of redress is that "since inequalities of birth and natural endowment are undeserved, these inequalities are somehow to be compensated for."[5] The same moral intuition and resulting mandate appear in Bruce Ackerman's "principle of equal sacrifice," which requires, inter alia, providing compensatory advantages to the "genetically disadvantaged." It follows from this principle, Ackerman writes, that "a blind citizen has a right to insist that others make a greater sacrifice of their rights in nongenetic domains" in order to achieve the "overall equivalence" demanded by justice.[6] The questions here concern the issues that surround the word *somehow* in Rawls's principle and the alleged "right to insist that others make a greater sacrifice" conferred by Ackerman upon those who suffer from natural disabilities.

It is certainly true, of course, that deep and arbitrary inequalities can be extraordinarily unfair. Contemplating them, as Edmund Cahn has observed, is one of the primary occasions for arousing what he calls our "sense of injustice"—a moral revulsion against fundamental failures of fairness and moral propriety.[7] When such capricious inequalities are imposed by human acts or authorities, we are offended and insist they be corrected. When they are imposed by nature or by blind fate, we suffer a kind of moral distress. Morally sensitive individuals favored by the luck of the draw are often afflicted by a sense of guilt for their undeserved relative good fortune and are moved to engage in remedial sacrifice where possible. Sometimes, the guilt occasioned by this recognition that one is on the upside of a great and wholly irrational inequity can even be crippling—as in the case of soldiers who survive battles in which comrades at their side are killed. A Rawls or an Ackerman could invoke such deeply felt sentiments as constituting testimony on behalf of the propriety of their demands for redress of natural inequalities. Other moral intuitions run in a different direction, however, suggesting that imposing such demands in the name of justice may be morally improper. Contemplation of the costs, limitations, and difficulties of accomplishing such redress, moreover, makes it hard to avoid the conclusion that serious efforts to achieve meaningful "redress" of this magnitude are bound to be quixotic.

Demands based on principles of justice confer rights and impose obligations. Arbitrary inequity is unfair. Robert Redford clearly has been favored over me in looks, Michael Jordan clearly has been favored over me in athletic ability, Eric Clapton's musical gifts put my paltry talents to shame, and Bill Gates has more technological genius in his little finger than I do in my entire body. Does that mean they all owe me something? Do I have the right to demand that they compensate me for my being less favored than they by nature? Why? What gives me that right? Granted, life is always unfair—sometimes indeed with consummate brutality. But when I am battered by some of life's contingencies, do their irrationality, arbitrariness, and inequity give me moral purchase to impose suffering or loss upon someone else as compensation? Or should such demands be seen instead as a piece of moral effrontery—as a failure to recognize that all our talents are undeserved gifts of God or nature and that I have then no right to those I have, much less to more—or perhaps even as a churlish attempt to gratify my instinctive wish that my misery have company?

Isn't it, moreover, quixotic to suppose that differences in natural capacity or incidence of gratuitous suffering can really be "redressed" or compensated for? Rawls assures us that "it does not follow" from the fact that "no one deserves his greater natural capacity" that we "should eliminate these distinctions" because "there is another way to deal with them": that is, to arrange the basic structure of society so that the superior talents of the more favored "work for the good of the least fortunate" by giving them "compensating advantages."[8] But isn't it delusionary to suppose that such attempts could ever be truly and pertinently compensatory? If you have wealthy parents who can send you to Harvard, providing me financial aid for my tuition may do the job. But a few shekels tossed my way by taxing Robert Redford, Michael Jordan, and Eric Clapton are pitifully irrelevant and fruitless in terms of compensating me for the lack of what I want and what they have. What I want is the rush of slamming home a spectacular dunk to win a big championship, the power to turn the ladies' heads with my countenance, the rush of having the adulation of an adoring crowd as I cavort around the stage. And you want to pretend that you or society can really "compensate" me in any meaningful way for the sad fact that I lack the natural talents to achieve those satisfactions? Even worse, once we recognize the futility of the pretense that there is "another way to deal with" the deprivations produced by the arbitrary and inequitable distribution of "natural assets," are we not propelled by the "principles of redress" or the "principles of equivalent sacrifice" toward the Handicapper General in Kurt Vonnegut's mordant fable of egalitarianism gone berserk?[9]

Or consider in this context another pertinent example, one that points toward the deeper dilemma embedded in cases like these. In *Frontiers of Justice*, Martha Nussbaum reflects upon the life of a profoundly disabled young woman named Sesha. "Sesha's life," she writes, "is in many ways a dignified and fruitful human life: but that is because of the work of her parents and other caregivers. Her success depends to some extent on the fact that her parents are highly educated and relatively well-off. A just society would not permit such crucial matters to depend on chance in this way."[10] She then follows this passage with a speculative account of ways that some fairly heroic public policies and allocations might help people such as Sesha "have some of these functionings [i.e., those on Nussbaum's list of 'basic human capabilities'] available to her" and concludes that such interventions are mandatory on grounds of justice so that people with mental impairments and disabilities may be "fully equal as citizens."[11]

Nussbaum's deep moral concern for people such as Sesha is entirely proper and admirable. Moreover, it seems also entirely proper that a decent society undertake to do some of the things she suggests for its members who are born or who wind up with such serious disabilities. But even relatively cursory reflection reveals how the pitfalls produced by what I have called the hypertrophy of justice—that is, quixotic claims and problematically categorical demands—arise when we try to handle such difficult situations entirely by reference to standards of justice. Let us first observe that the demands of justice invoked here skate lightly over or around some of the potentially tragic choices and trade-offs presented in this context by what Rawls—following Hume—termed the objective "circumstances of justice" themselves: moderate resource scarcity. What Nussbaum would require of "a just society" in these cases would obviously be highly expensive. Even if we concede without protest the great desirability of these beneficent interventions and agree that any decent society would provide them were its resources unlimited, we can wonder how these alleged imperatives compare with other similarly expensive but valuable provisions that might develop the capabilities of other disadvantaged people. A decent society of unlimited resources would also, for example, provide personal tutors for every struggling student at all levels of education—from elementary students of limited intelligence to Harvard students who can't deal with calculus. And at least the former of these would qualify on the basis of Nussbaum's list of basic capabilities. Enormous improvements in the availability of health care can be demanded on similar grounds. What are the proper trade-offs here?

In similar fashion, is it not both quixotic and misleading to expect, much less demand as a matter of justice, that a society could do things that would truly make profoundly disabled people "fully equal as citizens," much as we would like to do that? Nussbaum says of Sesha in this context, for example, that "we could allow her to vote through a guardian as a sign of her full political equality."[12] But wouldn't that really be instead a manifestation of her lack of full political equality and of our inability to deliver that good to her, to fully make good the arbitrary inequity visited upon her by nature? Wouldn't this resemble allowing me to take a trampoline on court to make me "fully competitive" with Michael Jordan?

CHAPTER FOUR

And, finally, isn't it similarly quixotic and misleading to make such ringing pronouncements as the one that "a just society would not permit such crucial matters [the quality of care given to disabled people] to depend on chance in this way," when the "chance" in question is the quality of one's parents? How would a society go about nullifying the disadvantage relative to Sesha suffered by similarly disabled youth who had parents less competent and less caring? Presumably, Nussbaum would not advocate trying to handicap and impede the effectiveness of Sesha's parental care in the mode of Vonnegut's dystopic fable. But even the most just society we can imagine does not have the power somehow to make all parents as loving and able as Sesha's, and even the best institutional care it could provide could never fully replicate or replace parental love, which is to some degree sui generis. So the hard fact is that, contrary to the fine principled pronouncement that a just society "would not permit such crucial matters to depend on chance," even the most just society imaginable would be unable to prevent having the fortuitous contingency of luck of the draw when it comes to one's parents profoundly affect one's life chances. Moreover, this obdurate and problematic—from the standpoint of justice—fact of life is hardly an issue relevant solely to the disabled. All of us are born "nonable" and hence deeply dependent upon the care and competence of those adults who nurture and support—or fail to nurture and support—us for the extended and crucial period of our immaturity. There is nothing other than health so important to our lives as the arbitrary fortune we have when it comes to the quality of our parents. Some of us draw bright and attentive parents who socialize and educate us in ways anyone would hope for, and others draw abusive or neglectful incompetents and alcoholics. And the extraordinary inequity driven by these facts of natality, nurture, and human variance are beyond the competence of social policy—hence beyond the competence of liberal justice—except in very indirect ways.

At a general level, the excessive expectations and demands imposed upon justice by deontological social democratic liberals represent a failure to recognize and account for the inability of any conception of social justice to provide a satisfactory answer to the problem of gratuitous suffering. The injustice visited upon those whom Rawls characterizes as the disadvantaged is that they suffer a paucity of social and/or natural assets that is both inequitable and undeserved. Precepts and practices of liberal social justice can handle the inequity part of the problem, but they can do so only by imposing compensatory costs or sacrifices upon the "more favored" members of society: Ackerman's "principle of equal sacrifice" captures this logical necessity quite nicely. But unless one believes that all inequality is a result of theft or exploitation[13]—a claim hard to countenance in terms of social assets and obviously untenable in terms of natural assets—this is solving only one part of the unfairness problem. It eliminates the undeserved inequality faced by those who have less only by spreading around the undeserved sufferings involved. Perhaps it is morally appropriate to do this, but it is not truly appropriate in these circumstances to say that justice has been done or fairness achieved.

The problem is that in common parlance, fairness is measured in two ways. It is measured not only in relation to what others receive but also in relation to what one can reasonably be said to deserve. When people who lead exemplary lives are visited by devastating tragedy, we exclaim that this is a terribly unfair turn of events—and we would say and believe that this is so utterly without regard to the incidence of tragedy on other people. Job's lament to God is not about some kind of disproportion between the miseries visited upon him and those suffered by others: it is about the seemingly morally irrational disproportion between these miseries and the upright life he had endeavored to live. For the same reason, people required by a society implementing Rawls's difference principle or Ackerman's principle of equal sacrifice to hand over to someone else goods they can reasonably claim to have earned are not likely to be impressed or mollified by being assured that this taking represents justice or fairness. They might instead feel like a child who is told by a parent: "I have discovered that I punished your brother twice for something he did not do; so the next time he does something wrong I will punish you instead. That way I will have achieved fairness because you will each have suffered the same number of times for something you did not do."

So far, what I have criticized as the hypertrophy of justice within the moral economy of contemporary American liberalism has consisted of the excessive claims made on behalf of the competence or range of justice and similarly excessive claims made on behalf of its determinacy. The first problem grows out of the ambition to create what I called "cosmic justice," that is, the noble but hubristic aspiration to redress the moral arbitrariness of the world. The second problem grows out of the unwarranted belief that the antinomies of justice produced by gratuitous—hence morally arbitrary—suffering can somehow be overcome by "moral geometry."[14] The third and final strand of the hypertrophy of justice relates to the excessively high status accorded to it by deontological liberalism. This problem grows out of giving justice the role of "first virtue of social institutions."

To understand this problem, it is necessary to recognize that this latter claim has (at least) two importantly different meanings. One of these meanings is not problematic, but the second is. Deontological liberals, certainly including Rawls, fail to distinguish these meanings clearly, and they seem to suppose that arguments on behalf of the unproblematic meaning of "first virtue" serve to justify the second meaning, which they do not. The first signification of giving justice the status of first virtue is to insist, quite properly, that "each person possesses an inviolability founded on justice that even the welfare of society as a whole cannot [i.e., with moral propriety] override."[15] This formulation essentially identifies the first virtue claim with the formulation of the categorical imperative, which says that human persons as rational beings are not to be treated as mere means to other ends. But Rawls then proceeds in the paragraph immediately following this formulation to speak of principles of justice as rules that determine and govern "proper distributive shares," and this is to give a different meaning to what justice is than that in the first formulation. (Indeed, it is not even clear that the phrase "founded in justice" is appropriate in the first formulation. Arguably, this gets the relationships of justice and human inviolability backward: it is the dignity of human beings that makes them properly inviolable, and the demands of justice are "founded on" this inviolability rather than the other way around.) By eliding these different meanings of justice—respect for human inviolability, on the one hand, and rules governing distributive shares, on the other—Rawls implies that the grounds for the former suffice to confer inviolability upon the latter. But given the different meanings of "justice," this is a non sequitur. And this non sequitur is then taken in turn as justification for the claim that "the most appropriate moral basis for a democratic society" is provided by distributive principles.

This dubious argument—that the categorical imperative entails according principles of distributive justice the status of first virtue of social institutions and correlatively the role of the moral basis of a democratic society—leads, in short, to the third component of the hypertrophy of justice: according distributive justice a higher status than it deserves in the human moral economy. The difficulty here is that according this status to justice results in giving what Hume properly characterized as a "remedial virtue" moral priority over other "nobler virtues." Hume's point here is this: the function of rules of justice is to prevent people from being predatory upon each other. We need such rules principally to deter inappropriate actions produced by deficiencies of human virtue and the presence of human vice—to wit, by the absence of benevolence and the power of selfishness. "If every one had the same affection and tender regard for every one as for himself," Hume wrote, "justice and injustice would be equally unknown."[16]

The costs and dangers of attributing the status of moral priority in human affairs to the remedial virtue of distributive justice have been nicely limned by Michael Sandel in his *Liberalism and the Limits of Justice*, so I will not try to improve upon his critical observations here. As he notes, insistence on the moral priority of justice over other norms and patterns of human interaction seems to imply that "an increase in justice is associated with overall moral improvement," but that may or may not be so. "Where justice replaces injustice, other things being equal, the overall moral improvement is clear." However, "when fraternity [or benevolence] fades, more justice may be done, but even more may be required to restore the moral status quo. . . . The breakdown of certain personal and civic attachments may represent a moral loss that even a full measure of justice cannot redeem." Unqualified insistence upon the priority of justice seems to concede too readily the absence or powerlessness of friendship and benevolence. And it occludes the recognition that a sense of justice may be "misplaced": when norms of justice are invoked where the "nobler virtues" are called for, the consequence is that "questions of what I get and what I am due . . . loom [too] large" in the relationship, thereby changing and diminishing the nature of the association.[17]

The hegemony accorded social justice in the moral geography of contemporary American liberalism not only has the result of squeezing out important "nobler" political virtues. It also has the effect of neglecting the essential place of certain important teleological goods when it comes to the definition of a "well-ordered" democratic society. Particularly relevant in this context are the goods of democratic community and personal self-realization/ development/ cultivation that were central to earlier understandings of constitutive democratic purposes. It is not that all these goods are explicitly denied any relevance or value by deontological liberals. To take one important example, Rawls suggests a role for self-realization in a well-ordered democratic society when he invokes what he calls "the Aristotelian principle." This is not in fact for Rawls a moral claim but an empirical claim about human motivation. Although justice requires that we "avoid any assessment of the relative value of one another's way of life,"[18] Rawls finds satisfaction in the thought that "human beings enjoy the exercise of their realized capacities";[19] we can thus suppose that, when given the opportunity, a person will act so as to flourish in the Aristotelian sense and "to exercise his realized abilities as much as he can."[20] Despite this happy thought and gesture toward the value of human self-realization, however, three problematic claims—both in their content and in their consequences—are packed into this account. The first is that—in effect following Kant's lead—these goods are depicted as merely prudential goods that lack real moral status.[21] Second, there is embedded here a rather utopian supposition about the spontaneous quality of self-realization: create justice and all this will automatically be added unto you.[22] Third, it is not only supposed but actively insisted upon that the dynamics of democratic community are impossible and morally problematic in the context of today's large and pluralistic societies. All of these claims are questionable. A better conception of democratic ideals would accord moral significance and a constitutive role to teleological goods such as self-rule, self-realization, and moral association. A more realistic empirical sociology and psychology would suggest that democratic norms need to address the ways in which the moral associations of civil society and the cultivation of human capacities receive institutional support rather than imagining that these occur automatically in the context of a just state. And both could work in tandem to suggest the legitimate and plausible ways that civic friendship and cooperative association on behalf of common goods can play a valuable role in well-ordered democratic societies.[23]

To summarize the argument thus far, the first problematic consequence of liberalism's falling into the deontology trap is the expansion of justice beyond its proper domain. This is the hypertrophy of distributive justice. This overreaching includes excessive claims about the reach of justice, excessive claims about the certainty and determinacy of justice, and excessive claims about the moral hegemony of justice. These excessive claims produce in turn the levying of improper moral demands; the creation of misleading expectations about what justice can accomplish; and the neglect, subordination, or political sidelining of moral virtues and human goods central to democratic purposes.

We turn now to a second set of theoretical and moral difficulties created by the insistence upon identifying the moral foundations of democratic society with adherence to principles of distributive justice. This problematic consequence of being lured into the deontology trap is that liberalism finds itself logically driven into committing itself to claims about the powers and attributes of moral persons and of democratic citizens that lack plausibility or do not cohere with other core moral intuitions and goals of democratic liberalism. The theoretical site of the unfolding of these difficulties is the conception of "democratic persons" that develops from the logic and core commitments of social justice–centered liberalism's public philosophy. And, once again, it is Rawls who exemplifies this pattern most clearly because of his analytical diligence in following the implications of this philosophy's core claims and commitments.

The understanding of democratic personhood at work within the moral imaginary of deontological reform liberalism, Rawls insists, is not grounded upon or prompted by a commitment to some specific and particular metaphysical conception of the self—as Michael Sandel had suggested in *Liberalism and the Limits of Justice*, in his "transcendental" argument about the "unsituated selves existing prior to their ends" that could be seen as presupposed by the claims in *A Theory of Justice*.[24] Nor, Rawls says, does the conception of democratic persons represent some kind of empirical or scientific account of human nature. His "moral psychology of the person," he writes, "is not a psychology originating in the science of human nature but rather a scheme of concepts and principles for expressing a certain political conception of the person and an ideal of citizenship."[25] The conception of democratic persons operative as a "fundamental idea" within the public philosophy of deontological liberalism is instead a freestanding normative construction. It is a political and moral conception, "one that begins

THE DEONTOLOGY TRAP

from our everyday conception of persons . . . and adapted to a political conception and not to a comprehensive doctrine."[26]

What this means is that what I presented as the "philosophical anthropology of contemporary liberalism" in chapter 2 is not properly understood, at least in Rawls's view, as having logically preceded the normative claims and commitments of social justice liberalism and as therefore something that serves as the philosophical foundation or premises from which these normative imperatives are derived—however logically proper that might seem. Instead, the relation of premises and conclusions works the other way around. We begin with and take our bearings from what Rawls takes to be our moral intuitions about what is morally arbitrary and what is just and also from our understanding of the proper attributes of democratic citizens, and we then construct a conception of democratic persons to fit these intuitions about justice. Rawls makes this direction of the causal/logical relationship between democratic justice and democratic persons explicit when he writes: "Since our account of justice as fairness begins with the idea that society is to be conceived as a fair system of cooperation over time between generations, we adopt a conception of the person to go with this idea."[27]

This means that my students are in a sense quite correct when some of them maintain that Rawls does not reach his conclusions on the basis of facts about human beings but instead creates "facts" about human beings in order to justify his preordained conclusions. They are somewhat indignant about this, seeing it as presumptively illicit as argument and fundamentally deceptive as persuasion—a form of rationalization rather than reasoning, as it were. Although I am sympathetic with their discovery and consequent indignation, I point out that his is not really a case of rationalization in the presumptively illicit sense of constructing fanciful explanations post hoc to justify satisfying one's desires. Given the real but nondeductive relationship obtaining between his moral claims about justice and his normative conception of democratic citizens, Rawls can make the argument that the

CHAPTER FOUR

requisite relation between them is not one of derivation but one of coherence.

That response, however, may suffice to justify constructing a model of persons to fit with preexisting moral intuitions, but it cannot justify giving carte blanche to the content of this construction. For a conception of persons, however normative, is not simply some empty fantasy. It is created to perform several significant explanatory and normative functions of its own. It has to answer the question: For what kind of people/beings are the principles of justice both proper and feasible? It has to sustain these principles of justice dialectically and reciprocally even if it does not provide them with an independent metaphysical or empirical basis. And it has to perform the important regulative role of specifying the moral powers and requisite political virtues of democratic citizens.

An acceptable conception of democratic persons, therefore, has to be able to perform these functions. And in order to be able to do that, such a conception of personhood has to satisfy both moral and empirical tests. It has to be a morally acceptable and attractive conception in its own right, cohering not simply with the particular moral intuitions that helped produce it but also with other moral intuitions and democratic norms we do not wish to relinquish. And it has to have a significant degree of empirical plausibility or credibility. That is to say, although it need not conform wholly and directly to a scientific and empirical depiction of "human nature" in its current or universal form, it cannot be purely fictive and it cannot be inconsistent with the fundamental properties and possibilities of human beings. If a normative theory of democracy could be made to square only with a conception of democratic persons who appeared to have the properties and powers of unicorns, angels, or pigs, for example, that normative conception of democracy would clearly not be defensible.

My central claims in this section of the argument are that some of the most striking and distinctive features of the conception of democratic persons that Rawls derives from the moral intuitions packed into his central "device of representation"—the original position—are in fact ineluctably dictated by the fundamental defining beliefs of contemporary social justice–based liberalism but that these features of his conception of persons fail to satisfy the moral and empirical tests described in the preceding paragraph. This represents a second manifestation of the dynamics of the deontology trap, paralleling those that produced the hypertrophy of justice previously discussed. In both instances, a democratic philosophy dedicated to a demanding standard of social and economic equality and determined to justify that standard on grounds of right and justice finds itself logically driven into having to defend important claims that seem upon examination to be morally problematic, empirically implausible, or both.

The logical unfolding of this particular pathway into the deontology trap proceeds in the following way. Its starting point is the conjunction of a fundamental moral belief and attendant commitment with a fundamental theoretical belief and attendant strategy. The moral belief is to the proposition that people in a democratic society should be as equal as reasonably possible socially and economically. The attendant commitment is to making that the fundamental imperative of democratic practices and institutions. The theoretical belief is to the proposition that this commitment to social equality can be demonstrated to be an imperative of justice. And the attendant political strategy consists in demonstrating to the relevant public that this is so and then relying upon their sense of justice to fuel the actions needed to bring this social ideal to life.

To make this happen, it becomes necessary to achieve a decisive defeat over any arguments on behalf of proportional justice. Aristotle, it may be recalled, maintained that the contestation between claims of egalitarian justice and proportional justice were irresolvable and hence perpetual—and that the antagonism between these competing conceptions and their adherents was a principal cause of violent regime change. For the social ideals of social justice–based liberalism to triumph in the real world,

CHAPTER FOUR

this alleged perennial and irresolvable standoff would have to be overcome, and the only way to do that would be successfully to deprive the case for the moral propriety of unequal distributions of its credibility. And the only way to accomplish this feat in a truly definitive way—or at least the most powerful way to do this—would be through developing a successful undermining argument instead of relying upon weaker overriding arguments. Overriding arguments are less decisive because they are "yes, but" kinds of arguments. They begin by conceding the truth of the opposing argument ceteris paribus but then go on to explain that relevant other things are not in fact equal and that these considerations provide adequate reasons for overriding the conclusions that otherwise would follow from the initial argumentative claim. Whether this kind of argument works or not, of course, depends upon one's judgment about the relevant weight of the initial argument as compared with the cumulative weight of the considerations invoked to override it. Undermining criticisms of an opponent's argument, in contrast, concede nothing and if successful are therefore final and definitive. In these arguments, the fundamental opposing proposition is held to be false and unpersuasive per se because its validity is dependent upon untenable premises.

When it comes to distributive justice, arguments for instantiating some form of proportional distributive shares in a society all take the same basic form. Different people deserve to receive different shares because they make different levels of contribution to their societies, and to receive what they are due—what justice demands—means that they should receive in proportion to these contributions. It is either presumed or expressly contended in these arguments that people have some form of entitlement to the two component elements that go into the making of social contributions—namely, their talents and their efforts. Both one's talents and one's efforts are part or a product of one's own body, and the assumption is that each of us has legitimate ownership rights in our own body—at least vis-à-vis other people if not vis-à-vis God, who in some versions of the argument maintains a lien upon the bodies he created. In the present context of distributive justice with respect to one's proper share of social resources, Locke's argument on behalf of private property rights represents a paradigmatic and pertinent example of this form of argument. A just society, he argued, must recognize and respect people's preinstitutionally established entitlement to private material possessions because the value of these goods was produced by their sweat equity. To keep his case from being compromised, Locke goes to great lengths in this claim. He first claims that it is a "modest computation" to attribute nine-tenths of the value of "the products of the earth" to the "effects of labor." And he then redoubles the claim to say that a reasonable estimate of the relative contributions of nature and human labor to the value of useful goods would "find that in most of them ninety-nine hundredths are wholly to be put on the account of labor."[28]

This line of argument could be countered in part by attributing a greater portion of the value of goods to "Nature"—that is, to the things of the earth, which even Locke concedes are given to all in common and to no one in particular—and then by insisting that the Lockean proviso (that those who take from the commons leave "enough and as good" for others) is rarely satisfied. But even were this criticism to be granted, clearly a lot of economic value comes from the labor that went into cultivating or fabricating the goods in question. And it is also undeniable that people make widely divergent contributions in this regard. So the only real way to undermine arguments for proportional justice is to undermine somehow the claim or assumption that people have a moral entitlement to the fruits of their effort and of their talents.

If the way we understand ourselves as democratic persons/citizens is to conform with and give support to the intuitions and imperatives of liberal distributive justice (i.e., egalitarian justice, in Aristotle's sense, or something akin to Rawls's difference principle), it therefore becomes necessary to define democratic persons in a way that denies them responsibility—and hence credit or blame—for the higher or lower amounts of labor or productive effort they contribute to the creation of wealth. It similarly becomes logically necessary to define democratic persons in a way that denies them a moral entitlement to the productive talents deployed in their labor and also in a way that would not make it seem a transgression of their personal "inviolability founded on justice" for society to appropriate these talents by regarding them as part of a pool of common assets:[29] that is, it must not seem a violation of the categorical imperative against treating some as means to others' ends for society to "view the greater abilities as a social asset to be used for the common advantage."[30]

These logical necessities thus dictate several of the most distinctive features of Rawls's conception of democratic persons—which also for the same reason represent logical corollaries of social justice liberalism's moral imaginary. The first of these is what was characterized in a previous chapter as the "shrinkage of the noumenal" within liberal anthropology. In order to remove the moral credit or blame from people's different levels of input into the production of social primary material goods, the moral agency of democratic persons/citizens in this context becomes reduced to the vanishing point. This represents, in effect, the obverse of Locke's maximizing his calculations of the percentage of economic value attributable to individual efforts for which people deserve credit. Whatever may be Rawls's or other social justice liberals' freestanding beliefs about the powers of personal agency, then, the confluence of deontology with social egalitarianism makes it necessary for them to delete deservingness from work efforts in the way Rawls does when he writes: "The assertion that a man deserves the superior character that enables him to make the effort to cultivate his abilities is equally problematic; for his character depends in large part upon fortunate family and social circumstances for which he can claim no credit. The notion of desert seems not to apply to their cases."[31]

If the moral agency of democratic persons must shrink in this way to deprive labor of its moral warrant when it comes to distributive shares, the dimensions of the person itself must also be stringently circumscribed in order to make it not only morally acceptable but also morally mandatory on grounds of justice to appropriate the economic fruit of personal talents for communal use. Now, no one can reasonably claim to deserve the talents bestowed upon him or her by God or the morally random and variable largesse of nature. No moral obstacle to the communal alienation of talents here. The more difficult barrier to such communal appropriation comes from the fact that it seems reasonable to construe one's economically fungible talents—such as strength, intelligence, energy, comeliness, diligence, and so on—as being themselves constitutive parts of the person in question. Were all these qualities to be taken from me, after all, could anything really be left of who I am? If everything distinctive, different, and particular to me disappears, I effectively disappear simultaneously—rather like Lewis Carroll's Cheshire Cat minus the smile. But if that be so, then the requirement that individual talents be considered subject to appropriation and redistribution by outside actors seems to contradict the core moral insistence upon the inviolability of persons. I am being used as a means to someone else's ends.

So here, Rawls, in order to contend that I am not so being violated, insists—must insist—that contrary to what I might suppose, my voice, intelligence, strength, and so on are not *parts of me* but things I relate to as *goods external to me*. My talents are "assets" I possess rather than aspects of my being. These assets may be appropriated on grounds of fairness without raising moral objections that my personal integrity has been violated—thus infringing the inviolability of persons that Rawls and Kant consider fundamental to rights—because the relevant "I" is the abstract rational being within/beyond the whole complex of traits that add up to my full identity.

The determination to undermine claims of proportional justice so as to depict social equality as the mandate of justice also requires one final feature of the conception of democratic persons.

CHAPTER FOUR

This is the attribution to us of the moral power to devise, choose, and affirm our own particular plan of life and the conception of the good informing it. Rawls specifically acknowledges the derivation of this tenet, once again, from the core moral intuitions at work. "The procedure is as before: we start with the basic idea of society as a fair system of cooperation. When this idea is developed into a conception of political justice, it implies that [persons/democratic citizens] can also take responsibility for their ends."[32] Thus, "free persons are responsible for their interests and their ends: they are able to control and revise their wants and desires, and . . . they accept responsibility for doing so."[33] Society has no responsibility for the wants and desires/conceptions of the good/plans of life chosen freely by its citizens. Nor does it place any constraints upon their content except for the requirement that they be compatible with the demands of political justice. Insisting upon this understanding of our unfettered capacity to choose and hence stand responsible for our wants and desires is necessary to justify the exclusion of claims that might be made on the basis of champagne tastes or on the basis of the moral weight of one's particular ends and purposes. Rawls makes that linkage explicit, following his account of our presumed moral agency regarding our wants, desires, and ends with these distributive implications: "Hence it is not by itself an objection to the use of primary goods that an index does not accommodate those with unusual or expensive tastes . . . [and] zealous aspirations for certain goals do not, as such, give people a claim to social resources."[34]

So the core logical sequence is this: in order to sustain a social democratic version of deontological liberalism's claims about both the role and the content of social justice—its status as first virtue of social institutions and its content as the difference principle or some simulacrum—it is necessary to suppose the moral propriety of a certain pattern of allocating responsibilities between the social collective, on the one hand, and particular individuals, on the other. This is what Rawls calls "a social division of responsibility." And its terms must be ones in which "society, citizens as a

THE DEONTOLOGY TRAP

collective body, accepts responsibility for [inter alia] . . . providing a fair share of primary goods for all . . . while citizens as individuals and associations accept responsibility for revising and adjusting their ends and aspirations in view of the all-purpose means they can expect." And the propriety of this scheme of allocation of social responsibilities in turn "relies on the capacity of persons to assume responsibility for their ends and to moderate the claims they make on their social institutions accordingly."[35] This division of responsibility also relies for the same reasons and to the same extent, though Rawls does not allude to it in this passage, on the presumed incapacity of persons to assume responsibility for their level of economically productive effort and not to have to accept proportional shares of primary goods accordingly.

The core dynamic of this part of the deontology trap is that the twin determinations to make social justice the moral foundation of a democratic society and to reject all claims of proportionality regarding the justice of distributive shares logically compels those so determined into untenable positions. Untenable positions here means the adherence to views or claims that cause deep and serious problems of basic empirical credibility, of logical coherence with other important claims we might need or want to make, and of moral attractiveness. What, then, are some of the particular components or examples of this pattern in the context of the conception of persons?

Probably the most salient credibility problem that presents itself arises out of the social division of responsibility required by egalitarian deontology and out of the understanding of the powers of human agency invoked to justify such a normative scheme. Perhaps people have different senses of the extent of their powers and their constraints when it comes to their wants, desires, and actions. But it would seem to stretch our credulity beyond the breaking point to suppose that real people are able to exercise the extent of unconstrained choice and control over their wants, desires, and ends essential to this conception. It additionally seems impossible to suppose that people of normal capacities are so utterly devoid

CHAPTER FOUR

of control over their "willingness to make an effort, to try, and so to be deserving in the ordinary sense" as this scheme also necessarily supposes.[36] And supposing simultaneously such a strong sense of agency in the first regard and such an utter absence of moral agency in the other regard beggars belief. If I pursue Hobbes's dictum that "this kind of doctrine admitteth no other demonstration" than to "read thyself,"[37] then I would have to say that, if anything, this conception of democratic persons and the powers of agency attributed to them gets things backward. Most of my wants and desires seem visited upon me by nature rather than being something I somehow chose. And even some of my larger ends, values, and conceptions of the good seem clearly to be heavily shaped and hence constrained by my social and family circumstances. It is hard to imagine, for example, that I could by some act of thought or will change my sexual orientation, my love of music and sport, or my taste for Cabernet and caramel. It is also hard to imagine, given the patterns of moral and emotional habituation visited upon me by the accidents of my personal biography, that I could ever really choose somehow to be a hip-hop artist or a Buddhist monk. Conversely, I believe that I do have a great deal of latitude over the extent to which I am willing to sacrifice my leisure or repose in order to engage in productive labors or contribute to the work of social organizations to which I belong. To the extent that my own sense of self is at all representative, then, we can say that the normative commitments of social justice liberalism encumber it with significant credibility problems. To undermine all claims of proportional justice so that social egalitarian aspirations can be mandated on grounds of justice forces its adherents into demanding that we accept—and conform our institutional practices and rules with—some fairly obvious misconstructions of the human condition. Both theoretically and politically, this is not a comfortable place to be.[38]

In addition to these credibility problems created by the dynamics of the deontology trap, social justice liberal theory runs into coherence and congruence problems for the same basic reasons.

THE DEONTOLOGY TRAP

The credibility problems surveyed above arose from the implausible assumptions about the human condition—specifically about the powers, the incapacities, and the resulting responsibilities of human beings/democratic citizens—we are required to affirm if we want to endorse the central moral intuitions of contemporary social justice liberalism. By coherence problems, I mean the similarly created contradictions internal to this theoretical persuasion. And by congruence problems, I mean the tension created between claims essential to this public philosophy and other important moral claims we arguably would not want to relinquish.

Two significant internal contradictions within Rawls's own theoretical argument that are generated in this way are the apparent logical incompatibility between his treatments of distributive and retributive justice and the seeming incompatibility between his domestic and international norms of distributive justice. The first of these problems has been remarked upon by other critics of Rawls.[39] The contradiction arises here because Rawls wishes to endorse both the distributive difference principle and the retributive doctrine of mens rea. To do the former requires denying that people are morally deserving of different economic rewards because of their different work efforts and economic contributions; to do the latter requires affirming that people are morally deserving of punishment for their criminal deeds. Rawls tries to dismiss this contradiction as an illusory one on the grounds that the purposes of distributive and retributive justice are entirely distinct. Retributive justice consists of moral sanctions, he says, whereas the functions of distributive principles are purely prudential. A propensity to commit crimes, he writes, "is a mark of bad character, and in a just society legal punishments will only fall upon those who display these faults. It is clear that the distribution of economic and social advantages is entirely different. . . . Variations in wages and income and the perquisites of position are simply to influence these choices so that the end result accords with efficiency and justice."[40] But this attempted defense of the logical disjunction between principles of distributive and

CHAPTER FOUR

retributive justice clearly fails on its face. It represents a petitio principii, presupposing precisely what it purports to justify—to wit, that it is logically and morally acceptable to construe the purposes and functions of the assignment of economic rewards and criminal sanctions as "entirely different." Rawls simply ignores the underlying contradiction between the premises he invokes in the two cases to sustain his stipulated categorical difference between the purposes of the two forms of justice: that is, the contradiction between justifying mens rea on the grounds that people can/must be held responsible for criminal acts stemming from their "bad character" while denying that considerations of moral desert and proportional justice have any relevance to allocating distributive shares on the grounds that people can/must not be held responsible for their economic acts that result from their character traits because their character should be considered as a product of "family and social circumstances" beyond their control.

The second internal contradiction emerged when Rawls addressed the question of international distributive justice in his *Law of Peoples*. He argues there that the difference principle is not applicable across the boundaries of nation-states. The reason he gives for declining to endorse at the international level the distributive norms he considers mandatory domestically is that "the crucial element in how a country fares is its political culture . . . and not the level of its resources," and therefore, "the arbitrariness of the distribution of natural resources causes no difficulty." He provides an illustrative case to make his point. Consider, he says, two liberal or decent countries of the same size and wealth:

> The first decides to industrialize and to increase its rate of real saving, while the second does not. Being content with things as they are, and preferring a more pastoral and leisurely society, the second reaffirms its social values. Some decades later the first country is twice as wealthy as the second. Assuming, as we do, that both societies are liberal or decent, and their

peoples free and responsible, and able to make their own decisions, should the industrializing country be taxed to give funds to the second? . . . This seems unacceptable.[41]

The question of theoretical coherence then becomes: why do the same considerations and the same logic not apply domestically? To the extent this argument makes sense, why then should we not say, pari passu, that it would "seem unacceptable" to tax someone whose secular and materialistic values drive her to work long hours to become wealthy in order to subsidize a fellow citizen who chooses to forego productive labor in order to pursue a conception of the good life centered on contemplation, prayer, and family activities?

The underlying difficulty this unaddressed contradiction brings to the surface is this. In order to sustain the moral irrelevance to distributive justice of both the content of people's particular plans of life/conceptions of the good and the different capacities or wills to work, claims necessary to sustain his domestic principles of justice, Rawls is forced to make a very radical distinction between people's responsibility for their ends and purposes, on the one hand, and their lack of moral responsibility for their labor contributions, on the other hand, construing the one as choice and the other as causally determined behavior. What the justification he offers for his demurral to carry the force of the difference principle across international boundaries reveals is that the work he makes this distinction do for him in his account of domestic social justice is not sufficient to its purpose. And that is because it is not only people's talents and willingness to work that determine their actual work contribution: as he acknowledges in his explanation of his refusal to apply the difference principle across national boundaries, the ends and purposes people choose also have a significant causal impact upon their work lives and therefore upon the share of primary goods they acquire by their efforts. If they are to be held morally responsible for their choice of ends, as Rawls's account of the moral powers of democratic persons demands, people are to that extent also morally responsible for the variance in their work contributions. The moral arbitrariness Rawls attributes to the latter evaporates (or is at least considerably compromised), and the moral geometry used to arrive at and sustain the difference principle thus falls apart.[42]

What I have referred to as the shrinkage of the noumenal realm in the conception of democratic persons that is necessary to permit the dismissal of any grounds for proportional distributive justice also creates difficulties when it comes to congruence with other moral intuitions important to liberalism and democracy. Rights discourse, liberal freedoms, and democratic self-rule all seem to depend upon convictions about the integrity, autonomy, and responsibility of democratic citizens, and these assumptions seem clearly to be threatened or compromised by diminishing moral agency and severing people's "selves" from their personal traits and talents in the way an egalitarian deontology seems to require.

Robert Nozick zeroed in upon these difficulties early on in his critical observations about Rawls. Regarding the rejection of moral agency and hence moral desert when it comes to "the effort a person is willing to make,"[43] Nozick writes: "So denigrating a person's autonomy and prime responsibility for his actions is a risky line to take for a theory that otherwise wishes to buttress the dignity and self-respect of autonomous beings. . . . One doubts that the unexalted picture of human beings Rawls's theory presupposes and rests upon can be made to fit together with the view of human dignity it is designed to lead to and embody."[44] And regarding the construction of people's traits and talents as external to and hence alienable from their morally inviolate selfhood, Nozick clucks acerbically that Rawls's claim that his principles of justice embody the mandate of Kant's categorical imperative against regarding some people as means to another's welfare can be defensible "only if one presses very hard on the distinction between men and their talents, assets, abilities, and special traits. Whether any coherent conception of a person remains when the distinction is so pressed is an open question. Why we, thick with particular traits, should be cheered that (only) the thus purified men within us are not regarded as means is also unclear."[45]

My intent here is not to endorse all of the constructive implications Nozick tries to derive from these critical comments.[46] It does not follow as a consequence of reinstating our talents as parts of our persons, for example, that taxation is, as he claims, tantamount to a form of slavery. Even according people a prima facie moral entitlement to the fruits of their labor does not necessarily lead to this radical conclusion because there are multiple relevant and morally defensible grounds for allowing this prima facie entitlement to be overridden by democratic consent in behalf of legitimate democratic purposes. The point instead is to acknowledge that Nozick makes very telling critical observations here and that the assumptions necessary to make social justice the sole and sufficient moral foundation of democratic aspirations plays into the hands of one's adversaries. For although there are, as I will say more about later, valid moral arguments for allowing democratic societies to impose taxes for redistributive purposes, the claim that the fruits of people's talents may be appropriated for collective goals because these talents are not part of their persons is not one of these arguments.

It is telling, I believe, that Rawls returns to these problematic claims about democratic persons in his final restatement of his theory of justice. He does so not to abandon his claims that moral desert should not factor into principles of distributive justice and that our talents can legitimately be treated as a pool of common assets but instead to reaffirm and bolster these claims by providing clarifications and alternative arguments on their behalf. Unfortunately, the clarifications prove incoherent and the alternative arguments unavailing. Rather than escaping the deontology trap into which he was driven by his central moral assumptions and political intentions, he simply flounders about within this trap, demonstrating its power yet again.

In his restatement of his position on the irrelevance of pre-institutional moral desert to principles of distributive justice, for example, Rawls tries to reconfigure his argument within the fundamental distinction he makes in *Political Liberalism* between political and comprehensive doctrines. By doing so, he tries to bypass his original arguments in *A Theory of Justice* that invoked propositions about the scope of personal agency and the causal power of external contingencies over human actions. If someone wishes to insist that they "do morally deserve certain things," he now writes, "justice as fairness does not deny this. Why should it?"[47] What he does insist, however, is that any and all such claims of preinstitutional moral desert that people make are made "from within their comprehensive doctrines." In a morally and religiously pluralistic society, these doctrines will differ and conflict with each other. And "since these conflicting doctrines say that we morally deserve different things in different ways for different reasons, they cannot all be correct; and in any case, none of them is politically feasible. To find a public basis of justification, we must look for a workable political conception of justice." And looking for such a workable political conception eventually "leads to the original position as a device of representation."[48] Recalling, then, that the original position disqualifies any considerations of moral desert from factoring into principles of distributive justice, the effect of this argument is to say this: claims of moral desert are always a function of comprehensive doctrines; these doctrines are incapable of demonstration and conflict with each other; the appropriate outcome, therefore, is to bracket all such claims; and doing so produces as the neutral, "political" default position principles based de facto upon the assumption that no claims of moral desert regarding primary goods are valid. In short, because all claims of moral desert allegedly depend upon comprehensive moral and philosophical doctrines about which we disagree, the right way to distribute social resources is to suppose that no one deserves any of them.

This recast argument fails for many reasons, however. Rawls here presents and defends the exclusion of moral desert from bearing upon principles of justice on the grounds that such dismissal is the proper way to deal with ideas situated within multiple and conflicting comprehensive moral doctrines. In alleged contrast with this situation of the idea of moral desert within these competing doctrines, Rawls says that justice as fairness—together with its enabling assumptions—is "political" in the sense of not depending upon controversial comprehensive moral views and therefore is in effect neutral among them. And for these reasons, he continues, putting into effect the principles of justice as fairness to determine the allocation of social resources represents a uniquely "workable" and "politically feasible" resolution of what otherwise would be perpetual and irresolvable moral contestation and political conflict. The problem is that Rawls's principles of justice and the assumptions embodied in the original position are none of the above: they are not neutral; they do not represent the only or most logical default position in the context of conflicting viewpoints; they are not merely "political" in the sense of being devoid of implications vis-à-vis comprehensive doctrines; and they are not any more workable or politically feasible than are other alternative ways of dealing with the issues and problems at hand.

The principles of justice set out in justice as fairness are neither politically nor philosophically neutral. They function politically to enforce certain patterns of distribution morally acceptable to some and not to others. And by excluding any considerations of moral desert, these principles of justice are compatible with some comprehensive philosophical doctrines—such as the naturalistic conception of human behavior Rawls deploys in *A Theory of Justice* to exclude considerations of desert—and incompatible with many other philosophical doctrines. This is not accurately describable as choosing a political (i.e., not comprehensive) conception in lieu of competing alternatives all of which would entail imposing comprehensive moralities. The proper way to characterize justice as fairness is as de facto partially comprehensive. So why is the proper default solution here, in the context of the liberal principle of legitimacy, to impose one partially comprehensive conception of distributive justice over others? If there must be a political default position that brackets contestable claims about justice, why would not modus vivendi liberalism be the logically favored outcome? If we cannot agree on principles of justice, why should we not simply fall back upon some form of bargaining to determine the allocation of social resources? Or why would not the favored "neutral" solution be the libertarian one of letting allocations be determined by the aggregation of freely entered contractual arrangements among individual members of the society? (Rawls's standard account of why instantiating his principles of justice would be politically preferable to a modus vivendi solution cannot provide a convincing answer here. His argument in support of that claim is that justice as fairness provides a stronger basis for political legitimacy and therefore for political stability because it has moral content and hence moral power—by contrast with the merely prudential status of modus vivendi agreements.[49] This argument may be valid in the abstract, but it depends for its relevance upon the quite dubious assumption that a well-ordered democratic society will produce citizens whose moral judgments will converge upon the principles of justice as fairness.)

It is also importantly misleading to imply, as Rawls does, that beliefs that economic rewards should be proportional to contribution are inextricably dependent upon the affirmation of the entire content of some particular comprehensive conception of the good. That supposition, which is used to screen notions of moral desert from acceptable principles of political justice, is logically unsustainable and empirically false. As evidence for the latter claim, I could invoke both my crowd of tennis friends and students in my classes. Both groups include people of widely variant religious persuasions and also widely variant conceptions of what a humanly good life looks like. Despite all this variance and disagreement about matters of comprehensive morality among them, they almost uniformly endorse the proposition that people who work longer, harder, and better deserve to receive greater economic reward than those who work less hard and less well. That moral proposition arguably functions as a reasonable moral belief people can and do endorse, "each from [their] own point of view."[50] So there seems no reason to believe that this convergence upon a politically regulative moral norm from a wide range of different comprehensive moral viewpoints could not serve as the basis of the very kind of overlapping consensus Rawls valorizes and describes in his "model case."[51] In fact, it would seem on empirical grounds to serve as a much more likely candidate than the difference principle for the "workable" and "politically feasible" kind of overlapping consensus Rawls says he wants to see achieved.

The account provided in *Justice as Fairness: A Restatement* for the problems associated with conceiving people as coherently severable from their talents and the latter as therefore properly available to be regarded as part of a pool of "common assets" fares no better. Rawls tries here to evade the difficulties presented by this claim in two ways. First, he says that it is a mistake to suppose that his principles of justice depend upon the proposition that people's personal talents are actually owned by the collective society. The "question of ownership," in fact, he writes, "does not arise" at all. And "should it arise, it is persons themselves who own these endowments." By agreeing to the difference principle, however, "it is as if they agree to regard the distribution of endowments as a common asset." So the confluence of these propositions adds up to the claim that it is morally proper that (and reasonable people would agree to be subject to the rule that) a democratic society should have the power to allocate the product of people's endowments as if it owned them, even though it is not in fact entitled to claim ownership of them. And the obvious question, one Rawls simply begs, is why that de facto alienation and appropriation of the rights and powers of ownership over things that others in fact own are reasonable or proper.[52]

The other clarification/explanation Rawls offers in *A Restatement* regarding the "common assets" claim is that "what is regarded as a common asset is the distribution of native endowments and not our native endowments *per se*."[53] This is, however, a distinction without any force. A "distribution" apart from the things distributed is merely an abstract pattern. It makes no sense whatever to speak of it being itself an asset amenable to allocation. So Rawls goes on to say that it is "the variety of talents" that is a common asset, and he provides an illustrative example to explain what that means: "This variety can be regarded as a common asset because it makes possible numerous complementarities between talents when organized in appropriate ways to take advantage of these differences. Consider how these talents are organized and coordinated in games and in performances of musical compositions." Such variations of talent "allow for mutually beneficial complementarities, as economists have long known and formulated in the principle of comparative advantage."[54] Now, this formulation is at least intelligible, and it references an important feature of and motivation for social cooperation. Members of teams and members of orchestras have different talents, and they do combine them in a way advantageous to all the participants. But this meaningful example does not serve in any way to bolster Rawls's claims about the propriety of treating the various talents as "common assets." Economists invoke the principle of comparative advantage not to challenge the market's allocation of the fruits of such cooperative endeavor but precisely to explain and justify market allocations and free trade. Moreover, the participants in these cooperative endeavors make no claims that their mutually beneficial cooperation entails some kind of common ownership of each other's talents. The last time I looked, the players on the Boston Celtics and the players in the Boston Symphony were neither each other's keepers nor part owners. And they received and accepted as their share of the benefits of their association sometimes quite different allocations determined by the value and scarcity of what they could contribute to the group endeavor.

Rawls's final restatement of his views regarding moral desert and treating people's talents as common assets is significant, then, but not because it successfully resolves the profound problems that cluster about these central claims. His revisiting them reveals instead that he was aware of these difficulties but that his best attempts to deal with them were at the end of the day quite unavailing. He tries diligently to circumvent morally dubious claims about desert and people's relation to their natural endowments to which he was driven in order to justify the idea that the aspirations of social democracy can be based entirely on claims of distributive justice. But in doing so, he winds up landing himself in logically untenable claims in their stead. The lesson here is that once liberalism casts aside its traditional teleological goals and succumbs to the sirens' call to seek justice alone, the iron grip of the deontology trap will not be cheated.

We have now looked at the difficulties created by the attempt to extend the reach of social justice and also at the difficulties created by holding fast to assumptions necessary to identify social justice with social equality. The last component of this pattern of social justice liberalism undermining its own aspirations concerns the problems created by reliance upon the sense of justice as the motivating force of democratic idealism. This question regarding the motivating power of the sense of justice is particularly pertinent, of course, when it comes to asking people to accept the sacrifices and obligations mandated by egalitarian allocations.

In justice as fairness, Rawls tells us, democratic citizens "undertake to avail themselves of the accidents of nature and social circumstances only when doing so is for the common benefit." So the relevant question here is why? What is it that motivates people so to devote themselves to the common benefit—to "agree to share one another's fate?"[55] Rawls argues that there is a profound symmetry between "the requirements of the difference principle" and those of the traditional "ideal of fraternity" in democratic theory: in his words, the difference principle "corresponds to . . . the principle of fraternity."[56] What he clearly has in mind here is to claim that complying with the mandate of the difference principle corresponds with two core features of civic friendship in Aristotle's classic treatment of that issue: mutual care and concern and the willingness to help each other in times and circumstances of need.

"Brothers and comrades go shares in everything," writes Aristotle.[57] So living in accord with the difference principle has the same effect, more or less, since there, we are likewise sharing our fate.

If the presumed effects of fraternity and the difference principle are similar, however, the similarity clearly cannot extend to the motives involved. Friendship, as Aristotle writes, "is an expression of community."[58] It is a product of mutual affection, understanding, and appreciation, which come in turn from the shared pursuit of common goods. But these cannot be the sources of allegiance to the difference principle in a large and pluralistic society, Rawls says. For a well-ordered society is not a community or association constituted by common devotion to the same conception of the good life, and the "ties of sentiment and feeling" in question would be "unrealistic to expect between members of the wider society."[59] So if these ties of affection and the common devotion to a conception of the good life cannot be available to produce a disposition to share one another's fate, what is it that motivates the disposition to act in that same fashion as justice as fairness requires?

Considering how important this question is to the practical political efficacy an account of social justice could have, it seems safe to say that it does not receive the serious attention it would seem to demand from social justice liberals. As Patrick Neal writes of Rawls and Charles Larmore,

> I cannot see that either actually gives an account of moral motivation, though each seems to assume himself to have done so. . . . They give an account of belief, but treat it as if it were an account of motivation. With regard to Rawls, for example, what is actually argued is a descriptive link or match between elements of individuals' conceptions of the good and elements of the public conception of justice. But what is not explained is why the existence of that analytical link provides the individual with a motivation (moral or otherwise) to adhere to the public conception. . . . Note as well

that Rawls's and Larmore's stability arguments assume not simply a link, but an extremely powerful one, between moral belief and motivation, one sufficient to override the force of whatever non-moral motivations move us.[60]

In this important respect, one can say once again that social justice liberals follow in Kant's footsteps by taking a perilous gamble sustained by great faith. For Kant struggled greatly with this question of an effectual motivating power sufficient to inspire fidelity to maxims of justice in defiance of strong impulsions of interest to the contrary. As he recognized, the obvious worry is that reason may "impotently raise its wings in the empty space of transcendent concepts . . . without being able to move."[61] But he expresses nonetheless his confidence in the power of "the pure concept of duty" to move "the human heart through reason alone." Indeed, he writes, "this influence is so much more powerful than all other impulses which may be derived from the field of experience, that in the consciousness of its dignity it despises such impulses and by degrees can become their master." He later adds that "to what extent [virtue] then eclipses everything else that charms the inclinations one may readily perceive with the least exertion of his reason, if it be not wholly spoiled for abstraction."[62]

The explanatory aporia regarding the motivational efficacy of beliefs about justice that Neal observes in contemporary liberals such as Rawls and Larmore seemingly must reflect a similar confidence. The basic hope must be a deontological adaptation of Aristotle's optimism about the relationship between the mind's apprehension of the human good and the will's disposition to seek it. Aristotle's view was that the will always seeks what the mind presents to it as good. Considering St. Paul's rueful lamentation about his own sinful will not doing what he knows to be good but doing what he knows to be bad, Aristotle may be overly sanguine in his expectations about the power of cognition of the good to motivate its pursuit. Given his eudaemonistic conception of the good, however, this tight linkage between knowing and doing is at least plausible: in pursuing the good, one may be forced to suppress lower desires and subordinate immediate gratification to longer-run flourishing. But it is ultimately one's own happiness that is being pursued, and the attractive force of that goal upon the will is easy to conceive and understand. The same considerations were what warranted Plato's attribution of erotic attraction to the Good. So, making the appropriate substitutions, the deontological version of this hopeful confidence in the moral rationality of the will is a belief that the will can be expected to comply with mandates presented to it by the sense of justice. Buying into this hopeful assumption about the motivational efficacy of beliefs about justice probably accounts for the lack of attention by Rawls and Larmore to questions about the linkage between belief and motivation that so puzzles Patrick Neal.

In a very real sense, it can be said that social justice liberals have no choice except to buy into this Kantian optimism about the moral will. Once the motivational moral sentiments that fueled classical civic friendship and traditional liberal fraternity—that is, mutual affection, attachment to community and common goods, and Hume's "nobler virtues" of caritas and friendship—are spurned as unavailable and/or inappropriate for large pluralistic societies, it becomes a necessity to depend upon the sense of justice having the twofold power not only to ascertain clearly what justice is but also to motivate compliance with its dictates. If this works, all is well: democratic society has a genuine "moral foundation" and motivational resources to bring it about. If it doesn't work, however, the deontology trap has struck once again: what liberalism is forced by its own logic and commitments to do leaves it in a problematic situation from which there is—on its own terms—no successful exit. (In the present context, the result of failure would seem to be an unavoidable fall back into a modus vivendi version of liberalism. If Aristotle's natural sociability is deemed unavailing and Kant's rational willpower doesn't work, it's back to reliance on Hobbes's rational bargain to provide the animating purposes of democratic liberalism. It is no accident, then, that Neal's skeptical animadversions about what he sees as the inadequacy of justice-centered liberalism's treatment of motivation appear within his own argument on behalf of what he calls "vulgar liberalism"—that is, an account of liberal purposes and sources of stability based in Hobbesian logic.)

However necessary it may be for deontological liberalism to buy into Kant's avowed confidence in the capacity of pure practical reason to perform the crucial motivating role left to it by the forced abdication of the nobler virtues and common goods from playing this role, that leap of faith leaves reform liberals' democratic hopes in a perilous position. For Kant's optimism about the will doing the right thing is not, for reasons mentioned earlier, as credible as is Aristotelian optimism about the will naturally seeking the good. It is one thing to be motivated to flourish as a human being, quite another to be motivated to sacrifice goods or advantages given by nature or social contingencies for the benefit of someone else. This is why Kant's worrisome image of deontological reason "impotently raising its wings" in the "empty space" of logical concepts is so prescient and directly on target. Eros, recall, was always depicted as winged. But it was powered by emotional longing, and it did not have to fly in an ontological vacuum. So Madison's admonition about not relying upon moral and religious motives to overcome factional interest is especially pertinent to the strategic imperatives a social justice–based liberalism places upon itself out of necessity.

The place where the motivational issues surrounding the sense of justice come to a head for social justice liberals is where they have to contemplate making their appeal to those who are going to be required by principles of justice to make sacrifices to benefit others. In *A Theory of Justice*, this crossroad is reached where Rawls ventures his response to the rhetorical query "Now what can be said to the more favored man?" Rawls responds more cryptically to this query than its seriousness demands, I think. But his answer is essentially a composite of two appeals. The first appeal is the only one Kant himself would countenance: that is, he simply invokes the authority of moral reason itself. Distributive principles are morally acceptable "only if the terms of the scheme are reasonable," Rawls writes. And "the difference principle seems to be a fair basis on which those better endowed, or more fortunate in their social circumstances, could expect others to collaborate with them." To give an added boost to this principled answer—so that his invocation of moral reasonableness might not "impotently raise its wings" and fail to fly, as it were—Rawls throws in a supplemental prudential appeal: without terms of social cooperation people will accept, "no one could have a satisfactory life."[63] Kant himself would have disapproved this auxiliary argument: responding to a question about why moral instruction often seems so ineffectual despite its being "convincing to reason," Kant complains that moral instructors create this problem by adulterating what should be an uncluttered and uncompromising appeal to precepts of reason, right, and duty. They are guilty of "suggesting all kinds of motives for moral goodness and in trying to make their medicine strong they spoil it."[64] Nonetheless, Rawls seems to realize that a pure and unadorned appeal to principle might lack weight in bending the will of the more favored to acquiesce in the sacrifices they are asked to make and that it might accordingly be wise to throw in a reminder of his audience's interest in civil peace and a commodious life.

It is instructive to note here how Rawls's rhetorical strategy mimics almost perfectly the rhetorical strategy of an earlier—if fictive—Kantian hero. I have in mind here the lead character, Frederick, in Gilbert and Sullivan's *Pirates of Penzance*. This pattern of inadvertent replication is likely no accident, for Gilbert clearly had been given somewhere during his education a competent exposure to Kantian ethics, and he equally clearly had not found what he heard very compelling. So he subtitles their operetta *The Slave of Duty* and lampoons Kant's moral doctrine by depicting its main protagonist as a fool for living his life by Kantian precepts. For example, Frederick agrees that he must remain in indentured servitude for four times the twenty-one years he expected because his birthday happened to fall on the twenty-ninth of February in a leap year.

Frederick's version of Rawls's rhetorical appeal to the more favored members of society comes when he, who has been at sea with pirates all his life, stumbles for the first time upon a bevy of young women and decides he would like to make one of them his own. Just as Rawls abjures appealing to the kinds of sentiments traditionally appealed to in such circumstances, Frederick first makes his case on strictly deontological grounds: "Oh, is there not one maiden breast which feels the moral beauty of making worldly interest subordinate to sense of duty?" When this high-minded opening sally falls flat, he—again like Rawls in his appeal to the more favored—reverts to a backup appeal to self-interest: "Oh, is there not one maiden here whose homely face and bad complexion have caused all hope to disappear of ever winning man's affection?" Once again, Frederick's appeal falls upon deaf ears: "No, no—not one!" the maidens reply. But then, unexpectedly, Frederick is bailed out by one of the maidens, who steps forward to accept his proposal. What is interesting, however, is that this positive response turns out to have been elicited by neither Frederick's invocation of duty nor his appeal to self-interest. Instead, his savior of the moment avows that she has been moved by natural pity: "Oh, sisters, deaf to pity's name, For shame!" He may have "gone astray," she sings, "but is that a reason good and true why you should all be deaf to pity's name?" So, Gilbert intimates, Frederick should have listened to Rousseau instead of Kant when it came to devising his rhetorical strategy. But even this is not his final word upon the relevant motivations in such circumstances, for he has the rest of the maidens voice to each other their suspicion that yet another sentiment might have been more important here: "The question is," they sing, "had he not been a thing of beauty, would she be swayed by quite as keen a sense of duty?"

Gilbert was no political theorist. But his fanciful vignette carries a moral quite pertinent to the problems of social justice liberalism. As rationalists and individualists, liberals are inclined to forget or to marginalize on principle the role of sentimental, affective, and libidinal forces in political bonding. At the deepest level of political theory, Paul Kahn has recently argued, this principled neglect of the animating role of eros and faith produces an anomalous situation in which "the internal morality of the liberal community is at war with the normative conditions of the community's existence." The result is that "liberalism offers a theory of political order, but liberalism cannot understand the conditions of the political upon which it depends."[65] Whether or not that be so, Gilbert's story carries a warning lesson that bears directly upon the motivational assumptions of social justice liberalism and hence upon its prospects in practice. That lesson is that when it comes to success in asking people to sacrifice their own welfare for "the common benefit," to recall Rawls's account of the practical effect of social justice, pity and eros are likely to trump not only conceptions of moral reasonableness (and especially heroic ones) but cool and calculating self-interest as well. This same point was made in other and different ways by a claim of Richard Rorty and a blunt query of Ralph Waldo Emerson. Rorty's claim is that "the novel, the movie, and the TV program have, gradually but steadily, replaced the sermon and the treatise as the principal vehicles of moral change and progress."[66] Emerson's query was a rhetorical response to those who would "tell me of my obligation to put all poor men in good situations: Are they my poor?"[67] The basis for Rorty's claim is his insistence that human solidarity "is to be achieved not by inquiry but by imagination, the imaginative ability to see strange people as fellow sufferers."[68] The basis of Emerson's query and its implicit challenge is his unapologetic insistence that he is obligated and willing to care and sacrifice only for people who "belong to me and to whom I belong."[69] Taken together, these two men of letters are admonishing both political theorists and liberal humanitarians that they should not be too beguiled by the powers of reason and justice when we set out to create a world where all can prosper. We had best attend carefully

THE DEONTOLOGY TRAP

instead to practices and conditions that can create sympathetic understanding and some form of civic friendship—or, to use Emerson's phrase, "spiritual affinity."

In the context of the central concerns of this book, then, the point is this: if you want a democratic society in which its members are willing to "share each other's fate" and to make the necessary accommodations and sacrifices for that to happen, it is a singularly bad idea, tactically speaking, to disdain communal attachments of affection and identity. For absent these motivating sentiments, based to some extent in what Todd Gitlin calls "common dreams,"[70] invocations of reasonableness, fairness, and justice are likely to be an exercise in futility—especially in light of the reasonable disagreement over the content of these ideals. But it is precisely this tactical blunder that the theoretical hegemony of social justice within contemporary high liberalism invites.

THE POLITICAL COSTS

If the foregoing discussion of the public philosophy of contemporary social justice–based liberalism seems somewhat abstract and academic, its central claims and conclusions can be stated in more straightforward terms. The dominant public philosophy within contemporary American liberalism tries to make the concept of justice do too much, placing upon it burdens it cannot carry. It claims a determinate specificity for justice it cannot in fact attain. It claims for justice a moral hegemony it cannot legitimately exercise. It assumes for justice a motivating power it does not have in the absence of communal purposes and social sentiments. In seeking to disqualify any consideration of proportional desert and to equate justice with maximum prudentially feasible equality, moreover, this contemporary version of liberal public philosophy finds itself logically driven into defending claims about human agency, personal responsibility, and individual integrity that conflict with widely shared moral beliefs informing other important democratic principles and practices. I now want to argue that the consequences and costs of these problematic claims are not confined to the theoretical realm. The philosophical arguments of rights-based liberal theorists both reflect and have informed a moral imaginary that has in turn shaped the political stance and social policy of American liberalism over the last several decades. The various moral conundrums and normative tensions visible at the theoretical level have therefore spilled over into the political arena and have exacted their toll there.

The epigram for this section is William Galston's claim that "Rawls offers us a dangerously one-sided reconstruction of the liberal tradition, the inadequacies of which are mirrored in the national electoral disasters of contemporary liberalism." And these political misadventures occur because "Rawls's conception of free and equal moral personality"—one that, as I have argued above, emerges from the determination to place democratic ideals on a deontological foundation—"diverges radically from [the dominant] American understanding of freedom and equality and leads to principles of justice significantly different from those most Americans embrace." Particularly important in this context, given the striking electoral fact that the putative liberal party in this country has not carried the white working class in a presidential election since the year 1964, is that this public philosophy "in effect if not in intention rejected the beliefs and undercut the interests of the working class."[71]

The cumulative defections from what political scientists used to deem the electorally "normal" Democratic majority have resulted, of course, from a host of changes in the demographics of the American public and changes in the relative saliency of different political issues. Among these changes, those associated with race, religion, and to some extent perceived positions on national security loom the largest. The post–civil rights defection of the South from its previous—and somewhat anomalous—place in the New Deal Democratic coalition, the politicization of culturally conservative evangelicals, and the lingering perceptions that

Democrats are weak on security issues are surely central factors in the demise of the Democratic majority.[72] I believe, however, that Galston is right to see intertwined with these political causal forces a general decline in the appeal of liberal rhetoric and policy—and also to see this decline as associated with what I have termed the transformation and what he calls a reconstruction of liberal public philosophy. The best way to explain this phenomenon is to ask: what do the core claims and the moral imaginary of today's justice-centered liberalism look like when taken off the pages of academic theory and translated into concrete political values and policies? The answer, I fear, bears a nonfortuitous resemblance to some of the unflattering stereotypes traded upon by liberalism's adversaries and does not bode well for this kind of liberalism's hopes for political resurgence.

The moral and conceptual centerpiece of the transformation of liberalism's public philosophy, recall, was the abandonment of self-rule and self-realization as the ultimate goals of liberal policy and the establishment in their stead of distributive justice as the axial goal. This fundamental displacement carries with it a number of important and costly political and rhetorical consequences.

One consequence is that liberalism has forfeited some of its traditionally "idealistic" cast and taken on the guise of a more "materialistic" public philosophy. The result has been something of an ironic reversal in recent American political discourse and popular perception regarding which party is about "values" and which is about "greed" in the sense of focused-upon material concerns. This claim may seem scandalous and perverse to liberal partisans. What, after all, is more moral than their dedication to social justice and to the welfare of the disadvantaged? Conversely, it has always been the conservative party, from Alexander Hamilton right down to today's Republicans, that has been the party apparently dedicated to material abundance and concupiscence to the neglect of higher goods. "The business of America is business" and "what's good for General Motors is good for America" were mantras of Republican conservatives, and it is liberal Democrats who have been the ones inclined toward starry-eyed idealism. It seems a curious misunderstanding to perceive liberal goals and policies as materialistic, and it equally seems to take a lot of gall to depict the historical champions of bourgeois acquisitiveness as the party of "moral values."

The underlying problem, however, is this. If the animating purpose of liberalism is to achieve social justice, if social justice is conceived as distributive justice, and if distributive justice means the reallocation by state action of "primary goods," then it appears that liberalism is in a broad sense "all about the benjamins." This inference and the attendant characterization of liberalism's purposes is not simply one purveyed by the spin doctors of the new conservatism. It is on display also in representations of contemporary liberal politics and philosophy provided by political theorists and commentators who are themselves sympathetic to programs and policies aimed at greater civic and social equality. Contemplating the dominant mantras of American liberalism in places such as Democratic Party platforms and *The Nation*, for example, Mickey Kaus winds up using the phrase "money liberalism" to characterize what he finds there. And Iris Marion Young, contemplating the dominant rhetoric of contemporary liberal theory, worries about the inadequacies of what she calls its devotion to "the distributive paradigm."[73]

It is no doubt true that the degree of material inequality in contemporary American society is excessive by almost any relevant measure. Even conceding the contestability of notions of distributive fairness, it seems hard to conjure any plausible definition of either fairness or public good that could comport with currently existing extremes. Moreover, these extremes seem inconsistent with the requisites of democratic self-governance and a healthy civil society. So it is both dismaying and galling to liberals like myself to drive to meetings of Democratic precinct workers in upscale homes past trailer parks with Bush-Cheney or McCain-Palin signs on display. Don't these people get it? Are Roger Ailes and Republican advertising gurus really that effective in their campaign to distract the working class from its real interests? Thomas Frank captures this dismay and incredulity quite well when he writes of recent political patterns in his home state of Kansas:

> For decades Americans have experienced a populist uprising that only benefits the people it is supposed to be targeting. In Kansas we merely see an extreme version of this mysterious situation. The angry workers, mighty in their numbers, are marching irresistibly against the arrogant. They are shaking their fists at the sons of privilege. . . . They are massing at the gates of Mission Hills, hoisting the black flag, and while the millionaires tremble in their mansions, they are bellowing out their terrifying demands. "We are here," they scream, "to cut your taxes."[74]

Frank's counsel to Democrats and liberals, in line with that of many other commentators, is to disenthrall these misguided conservative populists from their self-defeating behavior by driving home to them the way they are hurting their own economic self-interest. Without necessarily gainsaying this counsel, it is an important corollary of my argument that this strategy is not sufficient. False consciousness, actively and skillfully encouraged by the propagandists of today's reactionary right, may indeed be part of the picture. But that is not the whole story, and to leave it at that misses an important part of the equation for which liberals and their problematic public philosophy are themselves partly responsible. For the fact is that a sizable segment of these seemingly perversely self-damaging voters are broadly aware that they are to some extent acting against their own specifically economic interests, but they do so to prioritize other nonmaterial values and goods more important to them. When it comes to the task of winning over these voters, it will not be enough to chant "it's the economy, stupid." It will instead require reflection upon how it is that the dominant public philosophy of liberalism fails to link its concern with economic distribution, aka social justice, with any larger and more compelling vision of a good democratic society.

Today's liberals, who combine a fixation upon greater equality in possession of primary goods with a principled neutrality, agnosticism, or reticence about good character or the good life, need to attend carefully to the historical observations and theoretical complaints of sympathetic critics such as Michael Sandel and Ronald Beiner. Sandel argues that progressive social reformers in the American liberal tradition up to and to some extent through the New Deal embraced what he calls a "political economy of citizenship." American liberals from Thomas Jefferson to Hubert Humphrey took an active interest in social justice, advocating policies that would distribute economic resources more widely and evenly across the society and fighting against laws and policies whose effect would be to deepen inequalities and concentrate economic power. But their focal concern was not with economic equality per se, nor were their concerns with distributive issues driven principally, much less entirely, by some putatively valid standard of distributive justice. Instead, their concerns with distributive issues and with the institutional arrangements of economic production were driven by their larger preoccupation with personal development and with the social requisites of effective democratic self-governance. A good political economy for them was not simply one that scattered wealth as widely as possible in the name of fairness but one that helped to foster among the citizenry the capacities and civic virtues upon which a democratic society depends: independence, competency, civic awareness, and social responsibility. This was what Sandel calls a "formative project" devoted to the cultivation of the character and capacities required of democratic citizens. Louis Brandeis expressed this position clearly in his argument on behalf of what he termed an "industrial democracy" that would have, as one of its consequences, accorded a larger share of wealth and power to working people. "We must bear in mind all the time," he wrote, "that however much we may desire material improvement and must desire it for the comfort of the individual, that the United States is a democracy, and that we must have, above all things, men. It is the development of manhood to which any industrial and social system should be directed. . . . We Americans are committed not only to social justice . . . ; but we are committed primarily to democracy." And that priority requires "striving for the development of men" because we could achieve distributive justice but still "have a nation of slaves."[75] The political economy of traditional American liberalism, in short, contextualized social justice within and subordinated it to a preoccupation with the character and personal development of the self-governing civic equals who constituted its citizenry. This way of tying distributive criteria to larger concerns about good character and a good society thus converged logically with and therefore reinforced the social goals traditional liberalism made paramount: self-rule and self-realization.

What the deontological character of contemporary American liberalism has done is to decontextualize social justice from these deeper republican and Whitmanesque concerns and to set it up as a freestanding paramount social goal on its own. But this disentangling of the right from the good and the dismissal of concerns with character and personal development (as an allegedly tendentious and inappropriate imposition of a comprehensive conception of the good) winds up leaving contemporary liberalism apparently fixated upon material distribution per se. That makes it seem morally pusillanimous: "more goods for some, less for others" is not a morally elevated paramount social ideal, even when the some are the putatively "disadvantaged" and the redistribution is styled as demanded by fairness. Beyond that, it also makes it seem morally perverse in a way that Ronald Beiner captures well when he complains that on this conception, the criteria of justice and therewith the distributive policies of the liberal state apparently

> ought to be uncompromisingly neutral between on the one hand a conception of the good life centered on the principle of doing as little as one can get away with and endeavoring to

get others to subsidize one's indolence, and on the other hand a conception of the good life centered on notions of effort, conscientious work, and pride in what one does. It should be neutral between a conception of the good life geared toward the attainment of chemical euphoria at every opportunity and a conception of the good life focused on ideas of social responsibility.[76]

And it is not only the moral concerns about character and the good life associated with the civic republican political economy of citizenship that get jettisoned by contemporary liberalism's principled agnosticism about the good: the important pragmatic and prudential concerns addressed by that formative project are left unaddressed as well. For the fostering of good character in the citizenry was not just a good end in itself: it was an instrumental good to the end of successful democratic self-governance. How, then, shall we expect the latter good to come about? As Beiner observes in this context, "The central puzzle in [this brand] of liberalism is the notion (verging on blind assumption) that it will be possible to sustain within the private domain character formation, constitutive attachments, socialization into substantial ways of life, *Sittlichkeit* . . . within the horizon of a public philosophy" centered upon social justice that insists as a corollary upon "neutrality or agnosticism concerning the relative superiority of different conceptions of the good life."[77] This combination of certitude about what is just and relentless skepticism about what is good—a pattern dictated by the moral and philosophical premises of today's high liberalism—has the practical result, then, of making liberals seem not only unconcerned about the core features of a good life but also so unconcerned about the cultural requisites of democratic self-governance as to be dangerously foolish. Liberal rhetoric thus loses appeal and liberal policies lose credibility with an electorate that at a deep intuitive level shares the conviction of classical philosophers and Judeo-Christian clerics that there are such things as noble and base lives—and that also is intuitively skeptical of Kant's optimism that even a race of devils can be well governed.

The transformation of the normative political economy of contemporary liberalism—consequent upon the substitution of justice-as-distributive-equality for self-rule and self-realization as its axial goal—also cuts it off from the implicit classical/Christian teleology and the civic republican resources that informed traditional American liberalism and enhanced its political appeal. Traditional liberalism contextualized its normative political economy and the formative project so central to it within the republican commitment to public spirit and democratic community. These commitments have been important to American political aspirations from John Winthrop to John Dewey. They also have a profound if often tacit affiliation and resonance with powerful religiously based norms of caritas, stewardship, and (before gender-neutralized discourse) brotherhood.[78] Divorced from these larger moral and communal aspirations, the presentation of liberal reform policies as imperatives based solely upon principles of justice and the claim rights of the putatively disadvantaged leaves them politically weakened and morally diminished. Especially once the blatant injustices of Jim Crow and other discriminatory practices are prohibited by law, expressing broader aspirations for greater social equality in the form of individual claim rights—rather than as a function of principled aspirations to deepen the bonds of a democratic community within which all people are, in Whitman's phrase, "complete subjects for freedom"—can leave these aspirations sounding like little more than somewhat truculent and imperious demands for social handouts. Whereas traditional liberals presented themselves as the champions of a noble and heretofore unattained form of society in which "all could be free," contemporary liberalism winds up looking—at least to those unpersuaded of their obligation to redress every inequitable and arbitrary misfortune visited upon humankind by fate or circumstance—more like a front for aggressive panhandling. That perception is surely neither fair nor accurate, but it is what happens when the

CHAPTER FOUR

expansive and ambitious social hopes of liberalism get reduced to demands for equalization based exclusively upon a problematic construction of distributive justice.

The reconstitution and reconstruction of American liberalism as an alternative form of individual rights discourse represent not only an unfortunate deflation and narrowing in the substance of American liberal aspirations. They also represent a serious tactical mistake. To put it in military terms, this strategy not only abandons the high ground to the enemy but also leads to fighting the battle on the enemy's home territory and most favorable terrain. Reform liberalism's strong suit is communitarian, republican, and democratic rather than liberal in the technical sense of privileging what Constant termed the liberty of the moderns: that is, individual freedom from the demands, concerns, or controls of the larger society and the state. Reform liberalism's rhetorical strength comes from invocations of community, solidarity, and the general welfare—and therefore of the mutual support and succor democratic citizens need to offer each other in their common and cooperative pursuit of essential public needs and important human purposes. Turning reform liberalism into nothing more than an alternative rights discourse places it in a vulnerable position because rights talk induces most people—and certainly an American audience—to focus upon individuals and their rights to be free of the domination or depredation of others. Trying to build the case for democratic civic equality, civic friendship, and legitimate public purposes upon axioms of individual entitlement is a very bad strategy induced by an overextension of—and insufficient reflection upon—the notion of civil rights. Certainly, anyone of reform liberal sympathies who attended to the way that Robert Nozick was able to skewer Rawls so easily by spotlighting the dubious claims needed to derive egalitarian terms of distributive justice from individual rights claims should have been filled with deep foreboding. If the aim of political rhetoric is to frame the issues at stake in a manner that induces your audience to favor your side of the debate, this was a strategy on the terrain of political discourse reminiscent of ill-conceived military charges like those of George Pickett's cavalry and the Light Brigade. Ask Americans to concentrate their attention upon distributive justice, and most of them immediately think of individual desert. To demand a focus on distributive justice and then to dismiss the relevance of desert is a very bad idea indeed. It simply invites the kind of withering fire Nozick directed against justifications of the difference principle, and it simultaneously deflects attention from the important and pertinent fact that libertarian distributive norms are themselves not reflective of what people can reasonably claim to deserve.

A moral imaginary that presents reform liberal ideals as the answer to the question "what's a fair distribution of social goods when no one can be said to deserve anything?" also has the damaging effect of divorcing these ideals from the "work ethic." Indeed, it seems to turn contemporary liberalism into a force that actively seeks to derogate and undermine that ethic. By the work ethic, I do not here mean the full and specific version of that ethic famously provided by Max Weber in his attempt to characterize the moral psychology purportedly fueling capitalist entrepreneurialism. Work ethic here has a simpler, more straightforward, and less theological meaning. It refers to the interrelated moral intuitions that people have an obligation to contribute to their society by "answering the bell" (to recall John DiIulio's phrase) and being economically productive, that fulfilling this obligation provides the basis for valid claims of moral desert, and that being a productive worker and a contributing member of society in this way entitles people to a certain degree of social status and self-respect. Indeed, this is what makes Melancthon Smith's "respectable yeomanry" respectable and gives them their social identity.[79]

From the Olympian and insular perspective of well-meaning academic and suburban liberal elites, "the poor" or "less advantaged" whose welfare they take as their proper concern may appear as a largely undifferentiated mass identified most importantly by the subaverage economic status they have in common. If there be any relevant distinction among them, it is simply the quantitative one of degree of poverty; it is, then, the poorest or least advantaged among them who have the strongest claim upon society's concern. From the perspective of the working class, in contrast, in the minds of those who see themselves as "working hard every day" to "keep this country turning around,"[80] a bright line of moral and social status distinguishes them from those who make no similar sacrificial (of time and effort) contribution to the public weal. The latter group—the relevant "others" in this moral perception—does not include the disabled but encompasses the able-bodied who live off the labor of someone else: including those "disadvantaged" who could work but don't, wealthy "coupon-clippers," and college kids who drive BMWs supplied by their parents. Nothing could be better calculated to offend and alienate this large sector of the American public, the same respectable yeomanry whose welfare and dignity were, until recently, absolutely central to the mission and self-definition of liberal progressivism, therefore, than to do what the moral imaginary of contemporary liberalism has done: to dismiss as a gigantic irrelevancy what working people see as their most important contribution to the public weal and their proudest claim to civic virtue. When Michael Tomasky speaks of "the left's decreasing empathy with the conditions faced by working-class Americans" and the rise of "a liberal elite that was failing to represent the interest of many working people," surely this subversion of traditional liberal rhetoric and values—this moral devaluation of work itself—is an important part of the story.[81] It not only alienates the natural constituency of liberal progressivism—the "common people," the working class, the "simpleman" (John Adams), the "respectable yeomanry." It also cuts contemporary liberalism off from what has always been one of liberalism's most important normative and rhetorical reference points: the entitlement of those who labor to the fruits thereof. Jefferson invoked this moral touchstone when he spoke in his first inaugural of government not "taking from the mouth of labor the bread it has earned." Lincoln invoked it in his rhetorical construction of the core injustice of slavery. "In her natural right to eat the bread she earns with her own hands without asking leave of any one else," he said in a speech on the *Dred Scott* decision, a black woman "is my equal and the equal of all others." This right, he said, has been "made so plain by our good Father in Heaven, that all feel and understand it, even down to brutes and creeping insects." "From the beginning of time," he added in his final debate with Stephen Douglas, "this common right of humanity" has struggled with the "tyrannical principle . . . that says, 'You work and toil and earn bread, and I'll eat it.'"[82] The Populist Party platform began with the charge in its opening paragraph that "the fruits of the toil of millions are boldly stolen to build up colossal fortunes for a few." And so on.

The problem with abandoning this traditional liberal moral imaginary regarding the obligations and entitlements of labor is not only that it is widely perceived—and especially by the working class—as a dismaying doctrine of exculpatory fatalism. It also serves to incapacitate liberals in important political battles by depriving them of precisely the moral language and logic they need to make their political arguments. Consider in this context the recent contest over the repeal of taxes on inherited wealth. In their recent study of the successful campaign for repeal of the estate tax, Michael Graetz and Ian Shapiro found that there was a "stunning . . . lack of opposition" to this measure. Given the issues at stake, what was especially remarkable was that "there was no moral argument on the opposing side."[83] This is a tax that has been on the books since 1916, is levied only on the wealthiest 2 percent of Americans, and was extolled early on by Andrew Carnegie, an industrial magnate of the Gilded Age who was an apologist for the inequalities of corporate capitalism and who violently suppressed striking workers. In Carnegie's words,

> Of all forms of taxation [the estate tax] seems the wisest. . . . The growing disposition to tax more and more heavily large estates left at death is a cheering indication of the growth of a salutary change in public opinion. . . . It is desirable that

nations should go much further in this direction. Indeed, it is difficult to set bounds to the share of a rich man's estate which should go at his death to the public through the agency of the state.... By taxing estates heavily at death the state marks its condemnation of the selfish millionaire's unworthy life.... [And] under the sway ... [of this tax,] we shall have an ideal state, in which the surplus wealth of the few will become, in the best sense, the property of the many.[84]

So the real mystery becomes: how could a tax on inherited wealth extolled in forthright moral terms by someone such as Carnegie wind up today being repealed with "no moral argument on the other side"? Graetz and Shapiro try to answer this conundrum by citing political dynamics and tactical problems faced by groups that might have been inclined to oppose repeal. They mention, for example, the current weakness of organized labor. And they note that charities and nonprofits, which might stand to lose from repeal, "were behind the eight ball in many ways because they didn't want to annoy their donors." These are, no doubt, relevant considerations. But equally important in accounting for the rhetorical dog that didn't bark in this mystery, I would argue, is the self-incapacitation caused by contemporary liberalism's principled disdain for the moral privileging of work; for without invoking this staple tenet of traditional liberalism, the most obvious and pertinent moral argument against repeal of the estate tax cannot be made. That argument can best be put in the form of the question: Why should little Johnny Rich-kid be utterly exempt from taxation on wealth he did nothing to earn while I must pay taxes—and at an even higher rate precisely because of his exemption—on every dime I earn by the sweat of my brow? Why, indeed, does this make any sense at all by reference to the moral and practical imperatives of a democratic society?[85] But contemporary liberals find such obvious objections doubly difficult to make: on the one hand, they seem inhibited by their own worries that enshrining work might open the door to proportional conceptions of social justice; on the other, these same inhibitions have already made them unconvincing spokespeople for the moral entitlements of labor. In the case of the largely one-sided battle over estate tax repeal, as a consequence, the defenders of the entitlement of little Johnny Rich-kid were themselves actually permitted to style themselves as the champions of the work ethic. As Michael Graetz (who aptly says that opponents of repeal should have called it "the Paris Hilton Benefit Act") reported with suitable incredulity, "What won the day for the forces of repeal was a moral argument based in the great U.S. tradition of hard work and thrift."[86] What the fight over estate tax repeal thus brought into sharp relief is one important element in the ironic political self-immolation of contemporary liberalism. By trying to promote a more ambitious conception of social and economic equality on the basis of a rights-based theory of distributive justice devoid of any conception of moral desert, today's liberals have undercut their own efforts to defend the legitimate moral claims of working people and the important goal of civic equality against the political machinations of the American plutocracy.

The same dynamic has also served to undermine, in the mind of the American electorate, the legitimacy of and need for a strong and active government to provide the financial and institutional support necessary (in Lincoln's words) "to give all a chance" and "to do for the people what needs to be done, but which they can not, by individual effort, do at all, or do so well, for themselves," including countervailing the oppressive potential of concentrated wealth. In the well-chosen words of Mickey Kaus, contemporary liberalism's "disparagement of the work ethic has cost tens of millions of votes for almost all government programs."[87] This happens because the paradigmatic and self-defining public policy of contemporary liberalism became Aid to Families with Dependent Children (AFDC), aka "welfare," aka the dole. To the extent that the right has used this identification to characterize and attack "New Deal liberalism," this is misleading and inaccurate. Cash relief was a temporary emergency expedient for New Deal

Democrats in the depth of the Depression. It never was justified as a good policy in principle or one that a democratic society should seek to regularize in the long term. But to the extent that AFDC came to be taken as the paradigmatic expression of the policies and goals of contemporary liberalism, this was neither surprising nor inappropriate, for two important reasons. First, endorsing income redistribution in the name of social justice without regard to the work contribution of recipients—either as a reference point for determining economic desert or as an emblematic expression of good democratic citizenship—arises directly from the principles of justice in its public philosophy. Second, as Steven Teles's excellent study of the politics of welfare policy makes clear, liberal elites made it a point of pride and principle to obstruct a clear public consensus about welfare policy. As Teles notes, by consistent and overwhelming margins the American public "supports quite generous levels of public provision," but people want such provision to center on the provision of jobs and job training. They "oppose welfare but support assistance to the poor: They believe that work is of supreme importance, both for its own sake and because of its connection to upward mobility."[88] When welfare reform proposals were introduced around 1970 that embodied what Teles calls this "culturally integrative mode of political reasoning" that supported "the traditional values of work, family, and self-reliance through an expansion of the government's role in income support and employment," liberal elites joined conservative elites in an "incredible political alignment" to defeat them. This was a double disaster for contemporary liberalism's political goals and political credibility. Not only were proposals defeated that "would have meant, for millions of the nation's poor, greater income and integration into the American social mainstream,"[89] but contemporary liberalism indelibly marked itself as a political force whose leadership would go to the mat to protect welfare recipients from having to shoulder the burdens and social obligations carried by the working class. It is this devastating combination of what was widely perceived as moral obtuseness, imprudence, and contempt for public opinion that the right could thenceforth conjure merely by mouthing the phrase "tax-and-spend liberals." Never mind the right's own fiscally irresponsible counterpolicy of running up huge deficits through taxing less and spending more. Contemporary liberalism left itself a rhetorical easy mark—and to some extent deservedly so.

Many contemporary liberal apologists want to insist that their recent political travails represent the price paid for their valiant defense of civil rights against a retrogressive and racist public. Although some defections from the traditional New Deal coalition can in fact be accounted for in that way, this insistence is for the most part a self-protective delusion that seeks to represent the price of folly as the stigmata of virtue. Almost uniformly, the American public now recognizes the destruction of Jim Crow laws and attitudes as a signal accomplishment that saved American society from its deepest sin and ugliest anomaly. What has damaged contemporary liberalism's credibility and electoral appeal has not been its role in achieving the long-overdue civil and political rights so scandalously denied to African Americans—something for which even partisans on the right such as Newt Gingrich feel compelled to give it credit. Instead, that moral capital was lost and converted into a political deficit when the defense of civil rights metamorphosed into the defense of welfare rights—when the face of "civil rights" became not Rosa Parks, who wanted to ride equal on the Montgomery city bus, but the welfare moms on the National Welfare Rights Organization (NWRO) bus, who demanded to ride free on someone else's labor.

When welfare reform came in 1996, it came on terms significantly less favorable to recipients than those offered in legislative proposals that liberal legislators had torpedoed some twenty-five years before. Understandably upset at the complicity of a Democratic president in some of the harsher provisions of the legislation, Peter Edelman wrote a famous article entitled "The Worst Thing Bill Clinton Has Done." One passage in that article is worthy of note here. "For some people," Edelman wrote, staying on welfare was dictated by economics, because it involved a choice between . . . welfare . . . and the even worse situation of a low-wage job, with its take-home pay reduced by the out-of-pocket costs of commuting and day care, and the potentially incalculable effects of losing health coverage. With time limits these people will no longer have that choice, unappetizing as it was, and will be forced to take a job that leaves them even deeper in poverty.[90]

What is so remarkable about this passage is that it seems to treat the "even worse situation of a low-wage job" into which the welfare reform bill might force former welfare recipients as though it were heretofore a null category: that is, only a potential situation currently devoid of inhabitants. It is instead, of course, the real situation of millions of working poor in this country. The "worst thing Clinton has done," therefore, was to have approved policy changes that would eventually force those currently on welfare into the "even worse situation" of people who work for low wages. There seems to have been in Edelman's mind no sense at all that the greater moral scandal might have been that the net result of the existing American social service and income policies had been to make many people who went to work and tried to be productive and self-supporting citizens worse off than others who made a "choice . . . dictated by economics" to "stay on welfare." I certainly have no wish to lay the blame for this melancholy state of affairs entirely at the door of contemporary liberals such as Edelman. It is not liberals who stand in the way of a universal health care system whose absence is a key feature in this picture, for example: the major culprit is a conservative right that prates endlessly about the work ethic and does little to reward the working poor who live up to that ethic. But one is nonetheless driven to wonder who is left to play the traditional liberal role of champion of the working class when the moral imagination of contemporary liberalism leaves it so fixated upon the welfare of the "least advantaged" that it seemingly becomes oblivious to the interests and the just deserts of those whom FDR's secretary of labor, Frances Perkins, said that she "came to Washington to work for": namely, "the millions of forgotten, plain, common, working men."[91] As Michael Tomasky has written in his own attempt to account for the political decline of the American left, "Voters get no hint that we [i.e., the left] acknowledge the existence . . . of a group called 'workers.' . . . I suppose most lefties greet the word worker with some residual toleration, although once in a while, if you express concern for workers, you are challenged: what about people on welfare? . . . Besides, the argument goes, most of the working class, i.e., the white working class, votes conservative."[92] Perhaps, then, the electoral defection of many working-class voters, however perverse it may seem to liberal partisans like me, is not so inexplicable after all.

5 New Democratic Vistas

So what are the future prospects for American liberalism? That becomes the crucial issue, and about that we can only speculate. I learned early on in my academic career from one of my mentors that it is hazardous for any political scientist to commit himself or herself in print to prognoses about what is to come. This teaching came by example and inadvertently: he concluded a study of a particular country by predicting it was on the road to political stability, only to see civil war erupt there just as the study was published. But I would nonetheless be willing to hazard the guess here that if American liberalism remains confined within the limitations of justice as fairness or some close simulacrum (academically) and of "money liberalism" (in the popular mind), and if it remains tethered to the moral intuitions, the normative sociology, and the conception of democratic persons that have informed and sustained this conception of liberal purposes, its future will not be a bright one. The historical trajectory of American liberalism could wind up mimicking the biological trajectory of those Alaskan salmon that expend extraordinary energy to swim upstream to their home waters, where they fulfill their biological mission and then simply disintegrate. In that case, the historical mission of twentieth-century American liberalism will have been to lessen the collateral damage of a capitalist economy and to break down an inherited racial caste system. Bereft of a new animating mission and saddled with an unpopular public philosophy, it would conclude its life cycle by breaking apart into a minority coalition of the dispossessed, various grievance groups, public employees, left-leaning sectors of the intelligentsia, and some of the more tender-hearted members of the middle and upper classes. And if the Democratic Party occasionally achieved national electoral success, that good fortune would be fueled more by reaction against the extremism and incompetence of a socially conservative plutocracy or by the serendipitous appearance of an unusually charismatic candidate than by the intrinsic appeal of its own social ideals.

A happier scenario for the future of American liberalism will, in my view, require the realization among those of liberal sympathies that what I have called the transformation of American liberalism should be seen as a diversionary detour rather than an evolutionary step forward—more of a historical aberration that, like bell-bottoms and tie-dyed shirts, perhaps made some sense at a particular place in time but makes much less sense as a public philosophy for the long term. Such a recognition of the narrowness and time-boundedness of a liberalism fixated upon a more egalitarian distribution of primary goods will not occur as a result of academic treatises such as this one. It will occur because of changing political demographics, because of the continued consolidation of the civil rights revolution, because of the appearance of new exigent social and economic problems, and perhaps most importantly because of the different lived experience of a new political generation. Thomas Kuhn observed in his analysis of scientific revolutions that fundamental changes in prevailing scientific paradigms are definitively accomplished only when an older generation of scientists committed to older theoretical models dies off.[1] Death is more decisive than debate can ever be. That pattern is even more apparent when it comes to changes in the dominant paradigms of public philosophy; for history is more mutable than nature, and the social problems that function as the paradigm-generating "anomalies" are lodged in the psyche by the formative events of people's lives. In the case at hand, deontology is to some extent locked into the perceptual prisms and emotional responses of those American liberals whose moral and political sensibilities

CHAPTER FIVE

were crystallized in the sixties and seventies. In contrast, those for whom the Selma march is something in a history book and who grew up in a multicultural world where most college graduates are women see the American political landscape differently than my own generation does. They will be preoccupied by different social issues, they will perceive other forms of social disorder and injustice, and their political ideals and agendas will be likely to change accordingly. They will, among other things, be much less intuitively and prereflectively deontological than the previous generation of liberals.

If Kuhn and I are right about the existential dynamics of changes of dominant paradigms in both science and politics, then, it is likely that American liberals now in their fifties and sixties will spend the remaining years of public life largely reinscribing the patterns of the rights-based liberalism gestated through their experience and interpretation of the civil rights revolution. Given the historical specificity and the internal weaknesses of this conception of liberal ideals, however, it is a public philosophy that will be subject to reform by the emerging generation. Some of the differences between the older and younger generations within the Democratic Party, for example, were clearly put on display during the recent presidential primary contest between Senators Hillary Clinton and Barack Obama. The age cohort of voters was a significant predictor in this contest. Older female voters who grew up while women were fighting to redefine their social roles in the seventies and eighties were emotionally more disposed to identify with Clinton and to insist upon the importance of breaking what could be seen as the final glass ceiling, but younger women who have experienced less inertial resistance to their own social aspirations and who take it as natural and normal that they have full access to and representation within schools of law, business, and medicine found gender much less of a concern and voted for Obama in considerably greater numbers. Similarly, older voters seemed psychologically less comfortable at the prospect of an African American president, whereas younger voters, who grew up seeing Derek Jeter as the face of baseball and Tiger Woods as the face of golf, found that prospect not only unthreatening but largely unremarkable.

It is this emerging new generation of American liberals to whom I am most concerned to speak here. Substitute the word *liberal* for the word *naturalist,* and I feel much like Charles Darwin did at the end of his *Origin of Species,* where he wrote: "I by no means expect to convince experienced naturalists whose minds are stocked with a multitude of facts all viewed, during a long course of years, from a point of view . . . opposite to mine. . . . But I look with confidence to the future—to young and rising naturalists—who will be able to view . . . the question with impartiality."[2] To this "young and rising" generation of American liberals, I would say: the prospects for your future success will depend—at least in part—upon the success of what might best be styled as a liberal reformation.

A reformation has three main components. The first step is disenchantment and divestment: the process begins with the recognition of problematic features of prevailing belief systems that need to be revised or rejected. The second step is one of remembrance and recovery, as the reformers attend carefully to some of the verities of their tradition that have been compromised or neglected. And the final step is one of creative adaptation, as these reappropriated ideals are reinterpreted and put to work in new and changed circumstances. In the Protestant Reformation, for example, the process of reform originated with the growing conviction that certain clerical practices such as the selling of indulgences were corrupt and the soteriological and ecclesiological doctrines behind them unacceptable. The reformers then sought to reinvoke core features of their faith tradition and use them as reference points for developing the conceptions of justification by faith and the priesthood of all believers, which in their turn informed important changes in religious practices and institutions.

My stylized narrative of American liberalism's historical trajectory and critical analysis of its recent public philosophy in the

CHAPTER FIVE

preceding chapters lead to the suggestion that the cause of American liberalism would be well served by its undergoing a similar process. It is not that recent American liberalism has been engaged in corrupt practices such as the selling of indulgences. In fact, its problems and failures have been for the most part the product of good and generous intentions. But these are problems and failures nonetheless. Driven by a laudable passion to overcome the exclusions and oppressions of the American version of racial apartheid and also to dismantle other exclusions and inequalities of gender and sexual orientation, American liberals were lured into the misconception that the historical social aspirations of the democratic project were essentially encompassed by principles of distributive justice. And that fundamental narrowing and misunderstanding led in turn to entrapment in dubious corollary moral claims and at times to the endorsement of imprudent social policies.

It would be both presumptuous and futile to try to specify in any great detail the changes needed to transcend these misdirections and to set American liberalism on a better path to achieving its best and noblest goals. That will be the work of the rising generation to whom I speak. But it would also seem a failure of nerve to say nothing at all, even in general terms, relevant to this reconstructive challenge. So let me conclude by giving a brief sketch of what the reshaping of the moral imaginary of a reformed American liberalism might look like, what the main features of a social agenda guided by this revised moral geography might be, and how those changes might provide the basis for a new liberal majority.

RESHAPING LIBERALISM'S MORAL GEOGRAPHY

The moral geography of recent American liberalism, as we have seen, has been centered on a capacious and ambitious ideal of social justice. It is social justice that is seen as providing the moral foundation of democratic society. It is social justice that is seen as providing the proper justification for liberalism's historical aspirations for a society marked by civic equality instead of political hierarchy and social oligarchy. And it is a hoped-for agreement about and common devotion to egalitarian principles of justice that is counted upon to provide the moral consensus needed for liberal progress and democratic social stability. But justice cannot bear these burdens that have been placed upon it. The attempt to redeem the promise of American liberalism as a function of justice and right not only has led to an inflation of justice beyond its moral purchase but also has entailed the endorsement of moral claims in tension with other democratic values and purposes. In contrast, recent liberalism has been extraordinarily reticent about democratic teleology. It relies upon a conception of the good life that is as constrained as it can be while still explaining the point of justice—what Rawls calls, approvingly, a "thin theory of the good." Its conception of democratic civic virtue and good democratic citizenship is similarly somewhat atrophied by historical standards. Normatively speaking, its democratic citizens possess only those virtues and capabilities—tolerance, civility, and reasonableness—necessary for them to be "subjects of justice." And although these are indeed important virtues for democratic citizens to possess, it seems perfectly acceptable to contemporary liberalism to attribute—as we have seen—very limited powers of agency and very limited sentiments of "that harmony and affection without which liberty and even life itself are dreary things" (per Jefferson) to these same good citizens. For American liberalism to regain its moral equilibrium and appeal, therefore, it needs to demand less of justice, to bolster its hopes for democratic community, and to expect more of its people.

I have increasingly come to see contemporary liberalism's fixation upon social justice in Wittgensteinian terms. The concept of justice functions as an invisible conceptual fly-bottle, constraining liberalism's social vision and frustrating its best efforts to conceive—much less achieve—the larger purposes of democratic progressivism. In academic liberalism, that constraining and distorting power of the deontological fly-bottle displays itself when the highest and deepest moral aspirations of liberal theorists are blunted and misshapen by their entrapment within the limitations of the concept of justice. Rawls's deepest moral aspiration for democratic society is that it be a form of human association whose members "share one another's fate." But he winds up fostering the delusive hope that people who are in effect political strangers rather than political friends would nonetheless share each other's fate and share their resources with these others simply by virtue of having a sense of justice—failing to see that the specific content he ascribes to this sense of justice as fairness could only come about as a product of antecedent moral bonds. No merely formal sense of justice could on its own produce the sense of common fate upon which the moral motivation to endorse any redistributive principle of justice must depend. Or consider the way that Iris Marion Young's deepest aspirations for democratic society become distorted because of her compliance with the contemporary presumption that such progressive aspirations must be conceived within the ambit of justice. For Young, social justice should be understood along the lines of critical social theory as the overcoming of or liberation from concrete forms of social oppression. But what constitutes triumph over "oppression" for her turns out, definitionally and conceptually, to be something that looks much more like achieving human flourishing—the full deployment and enjoyment of our human faculties—than achieving adherence to a distributive principle. Indeed, she explicitly expresses her disdain for what she calls "the distributive paradigm" even as she presents her social ideals as matters of justice.[3] Young's democratic aspirations are in many ways quite similar to those of Whitman's democratic vistas. She, like Whitman, wants to see an inclusive democratic community where a wide variety of human types can all lead free and flourishing lives. But by clinging to the operative assumption that these goals are all circumscribed within the orbit of justice, she leaches out some of their content, distorts their true moral basis, and encourages the false implication that people have a claim right to a flourishing life that can properly be made legally actionable upon other people or upon society at large. As a result, what holds promise at the outset as an inspiring vision of a democratic community of autonomous and flourishing civic equals turns into a template for a hyperpoliticized society intent upon deploying an extensive array of legal directives and mandates to achieve and enforce political and economic equality among all social identity groups.

Just as Wittgenstein sought, in his *Philosophical Investigations,* to disenchant himself from his bewitchment by the mirage of a perfect language that had previously captured his imagination by posing all manner of questions about the functions of language unanswerable within the confines of that delusive ideal conception, so an American liberalism seeking renewal of its power and appeal needs to disenchant itself from its imprisoning bewitchment by the delusion that we have at our disposal a conception of social justice that can function as the perfect political language of a democratic society. People, including the morally serious, will always disagree about what is most fair—or, given the world's scarcities and tragedies—what is least unfair. If we, as human beings, treat people in an arbitrarily inequitable fashion, we can certainly be said to have acted unjustly. But either random nature or a God whose ways are not our ways, together with a myriad of historical accidents, produces such arbitrary inequalities all the time. What, then, is the morally proper way for us to deal with this palpable unfairness? How can the costs of gratuitous suffering be "fairly" allocated? What about gratuitous distributions that are themselves morally worthy and practically important, such as gifts of love or friendship? What redress is proper here? Our very selves/existences are gratuitous (products of grace or accident) and unequal in hugely important ways. What redress is due or effectual here? Members of decent societies will certainly seek to provide whatever assistance is possible and necessary for those who are disadvantaged by these natural and social tragedies to lead good lives. But do these situations really constitute moral language games in which the concept of justice is the most appropriate tool? Or is it not more appropriate to conclude that, by trying to do work it was not designed to do, the concept of justice has gone on holiday here?

Putting justice in its place—back into its suitable language game—certainly does not mean setting it aside or ignoring it altogether. Within its proper domain, indeed, it is correct to insist that demands of justice morally trump utilitarian calculations. So what is this "proper domain"? I would suggest that it is composed of three categories of "rightness." The first of these subdomains of justice comprehends the basic human rights that Kant would have seen as essential to the respect for persons as rational beings—the rights to basic liberty, to the integrity of one's own person, and to property acquired and held in accord with duly enacted law. The second subdomain is that of democratic rights—modes of fair dealing with people as constituted by the democratic postulate of moral equality and by the requisite conditions of democratic procedural legitimacy. These are the democratic civil rights and the right of equal treatment before the law. (These two central components of democratic justice are actually well stated in Section One of the Fourteenth Amendment of the Constitution of the United States, especially had the "privileges and immunities" clause been given the content and taken with the seriousness it deserved.) The third subdomain of justice is fuzzier, perhaps, but still a legitimate part of the moral grammar of justice. This is the moral requirement for some credible degree of proportionality between social contribution and social reward. The reward in question need not be monetary: it may consist in honor, deference, or public office. When it comes to economic reward, market allocations may serve as prima facie grounds for calling a distribution just, but these grounds are not properly dispositive. It is, for example, entirely appropriate to insist that it is "only fair" that soldiers who return wounded from combat receive the best care the society can give them, as well as the best transition to civilian employment the society can devise. It is not acceptable to say, "Well, you volunteered and knew what you were getting into—or were drafted by random lottery. Thanks, and so sorry."

There is, then, a significant place for justice in the moral geography of democracy and of American liberalism. Within this domain, it is perfectly appropriate to speak with Rawls about "the primacy of justice" and to insist that "each person possesses an inviolability founded on justice that even the welfare of society as a whole cannot override."[4] What is not appropriate is for this primacy or inviolability to be construed as extending to some specific and determinate standard for allocating all the resources a society can control or to some specific moral algorithm for redressing the inequities and gratuitous suffering that are a deplorable but inescapable and to a considerable extent incompensable part of the human condition. As a democratic citizen, I am entitled to demand that my government and my fellow citizens respect the integrity of my person, my liberty, my duly held property. I am entitled to demand that the laws of the land be neither arbitrary nor discriminatory against me. I am even entitled to ask, I will argue momentarily, that my fellow citizens set into place policies and institutions that allow me to develop my talents and capacities to the fullest extent possible. But I have no right to insist that they are somehow obligated to compensate me for my being less talented or less favored by fate than they are. I can, of course, argue that both collective prudence and social solidarity call for social insurance arrangements to protect each other against unmanageable adversities. But that is not at all the same as claiming that any adversity, failure, or disappointment that befalls me creates a debit in the ledger of all those who did not suffer the same or worse fate. Placing such a demand on my fellow citizens is a piece of moral effrontery, and imposing that demand upon a democratic society is a certain recipe for making it seem illegitimate.

Justice is thus not banished from the moral geography of a reformed liberalism. It remains a central concern. But it needs to be constrained to its proper place within the moral economy of a good society and not expected to provide the content of all the

CHAPTER FIVE

ambitious moral aspirations of democratic liberalism. Justice has to be complemented by and contextualized within a reclaiming and reaffirmation of the classic democratic teleological goals of self-rule by all and the self-realization of all. The ultimate moral purpose of democracy—and therefore the central animating concern of a renascent American liberalism—should not be simply getting the allocation of the society's goods right by some conception of distributive justice. And it cannot be a delusional and quixotic quest to somehow make the whole world fair. Instead, the ultimate goal of American liberalism has to be to make of our society a democratic moral community: a cooperative association of moral equals able to govern themselves and lead flourishing lives. The relationship between democratic teleology and democratic justice within liberal public philosophy should be similar to Thomas Aquinas's conception of the relationship between grace and nature: democratic teleology does not abolish justice but transcends and perfects it. The ends of self-rule and self-realization neither justify nor require infringements upon the sphere of basic human rights and democratic justice. But they do represent a reassertion of Hume's "nobler virtues," higher ends that transcend the conditions of justice and provide the context within which the achievements of justice are "perfected" by their role in enabling the creation of a humanly fulfilling way of life. This account also provides the proper way to understand the relationship between civil rights and "the beloved community" in Martin Luther King Jr.'s moral geography of the good society. Civil rights are essential, but even beyond their status as imperatives of right is their function as a necessary condition for the kind of moral community where, as King put it, children of different races can join hands and live well together.

It is also pertinent to note that these core teleological democratic aspirations have a legitimate role to play in the distributive policies of a regrounded American liberalism. Democratic justice has a relatively clear and definitive nucleus composed of basic human rights, but it also has an important but more ambiguous and contested peripheral circle where several morally legitimate distributive criteria reside in some tension with each other. In this latter circle, the formal norms of distributive justice serve to disqualify allocative policies that are arbitrary, partisan, or "rent-seeking." But claims based on desert, need, and entitlement remain in a kind of legitimate contestation. These latter claims inevitably and properly have to be balanced and adjudicated through legitimate democratic procedures. A liberal public philosophy should here acknowledge the prima facie legitimacy of entitlement to holdings obtained without rights violations—in part because it is both morally proper and collectively prudent to recognize and honor the willingness of people to work and sacrifice to provide for family and friends. A liberal political philosophy should also warmly and fully endorse the moral claim of desert to resources people create by the labor of their hands and minds. But a liberal public philosophy will also invoke the democratic goods of self-rule and self-realization to justify some overriding of these claims of entitlement and desert on grounds of teleological need/necessity. It will further use these same ultimate purposes as the basis for defining need as what is necessary to achieve, so far as humanly possible, the civic competence of all members of the society. Like the social justice liberalism of recent decades, this reformed liberalism will deny the moral sacrosanctness of Nozickean/libertarian entitlement. Instead of brushing aside invocations of entitlement or desert on grounds of fairness, however, it will argue for balancing and compromising these valid concerns on the basis of a commitment to democratic purposes that themselves have overriding moral import.

This change in the moral geography of liberal public philosophy implies, in terms of moral philosophy, an unapologetic reassertion of the moral significance of classical phronesis and eudaemonia—prudence and happiness. I use the modifier "classical" because prudence here does not signify mere calculations of personal advantage and because happiness here does not stand for mere hedonistic gratification. This conception of liberal purposes assumes that Bentham was wrong to make all pleasures morally equivalent, that Kant was wrong to consign all human desires to moral insignificance, and that liberalism's devotion to freedom and equality does not require it to be neutral about the good. This is a liberalism that sides with the insistence of Mill and Aristotle in attesting that there are profound qualitative differences among the vast variety of human desires and that the aspiration to live in a democratic community of moral equals capable of competent self-rule and the pursuit of personal fulfillment has a moral weight commanding our allegiance in a way that lesser appetites do not.

This, then, is in a real sense a perfectionist liberalism. But "perfectionism" is a crude label that invites serious misunderstanding. No liberalism and no good democratic theory can demand or be predicated upon the acceptance of a particular "fully comprehensive" conception of the good in Rawls's sense. No liberalism can claim to have solved the mysteries of human existence and thereby to have discovered one single right or best way for people to construe or pursue their own plans of life and personal narratives. All liberal public philosophies—and all good democratic societies—must acknowledge the limitations and fallibility of our moral knowledge, must account for what Rawls terms "the fact of reasonable pluralism," and must respect the human right of self-determination. So the democratic good championed by a renascent "partially perfectionist" form of liberalism has—just like democratic justice—its own principled constraints. There is, nonetheless, nothing anemic about the democratic good that should occupy a privileged place in the political aspirations of American liberalism. This conception of democratic good is dictated by the democratic moral postulate of the moral equality of all citizens, by the definitive democratic aspiration that "all shall be free," and by the requisites of institutionalizing felicitous democratic self-governance.

In effect, the understanding of the democratic good in the moral geography of a reformed liberalism would represent a beefing up of the ideal of democratic personhood. The conception of democratic persons played a logically crucial role as a "freestanding normative" ideal in Rawls's account of his deontological liberalism, as well. But his democratic persons were construed in a narrow and specific way: democratic persons in his account were "subjects of justice," people with the competencies and dispositions proper to participants in a contractual relationship embodying fair terms of social cooperation. By contrast, the democratic persons of a populist and perfectionist liberalism possess the more extensive competencies and dispositions required to function as members of a sovereign democratic public who can govern themselves collectively in a system of deliberative self-rule and individually as free people seeking their own personal development and happiness. Rawls's democratic persons could be quite passive citizens who simply accepted and abided by what they understood to be fair principles for the distribution of their society's resources. The more robust democratic citizens envisioned by a populist perfectionist liberalism have to be more active, deliberative, and self-actualizing people who assume responsibility for their personal welfare and for the public good as well. They are the "full grown men and women" of whom Whitman spoke—the kind of people who are both the essential basis and the final fruit of the new kind of society he foretold in "Democratic Vistas."

This more robust conception of the democratic good, together with its implicitly more ambitious and demanding understanding of democratic persons, is of course not beyond challenge—both from within and beyond the liberal camp. There are other perfectly respectable conceptions of liberal purposes and other morally decent nonliberal conceptions of a good society. What, then, can we say to those who challenge this moral geography and its endorsement of an ambitious democratic teleology? We need not be quite so peremptory and dogmatic in our reply as Richard Rorty suggests we should be when liberal ideals are challenged—that is, to treat these critics as if they were "mad."[5] But

CHAPTER FIVE

the truth behind Rorty's somewhat tongue-in-cheek suggestion here is that all societies and all ways of life are ultimately based upon the acceptance of certain moral assumptions that are neither demonstrable nor universal. So with that in mind, we can simply respond to liberals more skeptical about conceptions of the good in general and to those who champion undemocratic or illiberal conceptions of a good society by saying: somewhere else in other times and places or in other kinds of human society, your skepticism or your alternative account of the political good might be entirely appropriate. But here, we are all moral equals. Here, the people rule. Here, we strive that all may live free and fulfilled lives. That is who we are as a people, and here, these are the moral beliefs and aspirations that will guide and animate the particular way of life to which we are committed. These are, in effect, our self-evident truths.

REVISING AMERICAN LIBERALISM'S SOCIAL AGENDA

The reformed liberal moral geography mapped in the preceding section is not intended to be something entirely new. Instead, it can more properly be seen as an attempt to articulate the moral assumptions implicit in the traditional democratic liberalism of people such as Whitman and Dewey in terms that compare to those found within deontological liberalism's account of the moral foundations of democratic society—so that the contrast between these two moral imaginaries is brought into focus. The most fundamental contrast between these two conceptions of democratic ideals is that the updated "populist perfectionist" liberalism I have sketched has a less determinate and dogmatic understanding of what democratic distributive justice entails and a more capacious and ambitious vision of the possibilities and imperatives of the democratic good. The other major and related contrast is that between the Rawlsian conception of good democratic citizens as "subjects of justice" and Whitman's conception of these democratic citizens as "separate and complete subjects for freedom, . . . happiness, . . . and growth" who "rule themselves." The question then becomes, what might be the implications of moving from one account to the other for the social agenda of American liberalism? If the most important and distinctive feature of late twentieth-century high liberalism has been its promotion of social and economic equality, what might be the changes in this social agenda logically consequent to the shift in liberal moral geography I am endorsing? Are the differences between these public philosophies mostly abstract and rhetorical, or does the choice between them have concrete practical bearing upon the social goals American liberals should pursue and the policy strategies it should adopt?

I believe that the reclaiming by American liberalism of the populist and perfectionist aspirations found in its lineage would carry implications for changes in liberal social policy. There is a lot of distance, of course, between the very general precepts of a public philosophy and the content of concrete social policies. Trying to negotiate that space is a perilous undertaking: there are reasons that the term *casuistry* has unflattering connotations. But a public philosophy that carried no practical implications would be empty and barren indeed. So let me in this section try to fill at least some of this space by indicating what my colleagues on the more empirical side of political science have found it useful to call "middle range principles." Principles of the middle range are more concrete than global principles such as—in this context—self-rule and self-realization but not so specific as, say, the details of a tax code. Judgments about these latter very specific policies are inevitably dependent upon epistemically hazardous calculations better left to economists or psychologists and ultimately to the collective judgment of the democratic electorate. But logic and a fairly basic understanding of politics and economics can permit us to put some flesh upon the more abstract bones of political philosophy. With a cheerful openness to additional or contrary suggestions, then, I want to argue that the social agenda of a reformed

American liberalism should incorporate among its principal features the continued protection and extension of democratic civil rights and liberties, a dedication to developing to the fullest extent possible the democratic human capital and civic competence of the entire citizenry, the building of a neorepublican political economy, and the promotion of a robust democratic public sphere.

First, the moral postulates and enduring democratic purposes of a populist and perfectionist liberalism make it not simply appropriate but imperative for American liberalism to make it a special concern to protect and further the democratic civil rights and liberties of all members of the society. This imperative is a matter of basic justice among the moral equals who constitute a democratic society; beyond that, it is a requisite for the legitimate functioning of the institutions of democratic self-rule. These rights and liberties, moreover, also provide part of the institutional framework within which members of a democratic society are able to pursue their own personal projects of self-realization.

The moral equality of democratic citizens, the procedures of democratic self-rule, and the possibilities of personal self-realization all depend upon the instantiation and protection of civil rights and civil liberties. For that reason, the civil rights revolution of the sixties has just as fundamental a place in the self-defining narratives and the moral priorities of the reshaped American liberalism I am endorsing as it did within the deontological liberalism of recent decades. Within this specific policy arena, the difference between the two liberalisms is in a sense mostly academic: that is, the difference is more one of theoretical rationale than of concrete policy imperatives. In any case, it should certainly remain a constant concern of American liberalism to consolidate the achievements of the civil rights revolution, to extend them where necessary, and to strengthen the legal and institutional infrastructure required to sustain them. Now that de jure racial discrimination is prohibited by law, it is probably safe to say that all of the respectable political persuasions in this country endorse democratic civil rights and liberties in the abstract. But further work and continued vigilance are needed to make the enjoyment of these rights and liberties both real and universally enjoyed rather than merely formal. Just as the Supreme Court recognized in the landmark case of *Gideon v. Wainwright* that the formal rights guaranteed to citizens in criminal proceedings require the provision of competent legal representation in order to be meaningful,[6] so it should be an essential liberal concern to identify and deal with real-world circumstances and spillover effects of otherwise seemingly unobjectionable practices that compromise or negate the actual enjoyment and exercise of these rights and liberties.

As part of its eternal vigilance on behalf of the universal enjoyment of democratic civil rights and liberties, it also falls to any American liberalism worthy of the name to exercise special concern for those who fall into the category of what the Supreme Court famously recognized as "insular minorities."[7] These may be ethnic, racial, religious, or cultural groups that are clearly distinguishable from the dominant majority in ways that may motivate adherents of the majority culture or holders of majority attributes to confine, limit, or closet them. As part of this special concern for those whose full civic equality and civil liberties may be threatened by majority prejudice, for example, liberalism's commitment to the ideals and goals of the civil rights revolution requires its adherents to defend the right of gay and lesbian citizens to form legally recognized households with all the attendant privileges and protections. It also imposes a moral obligation to follow through on the rectification of the social and economic disadvantages imposed upon African American people by the historical legacy of slavery and Jim Crow apartheid.

The next feature and the logical centerpiece of the social agenda of the reformed liberalism I am recommending would be a passionate commitment to the greatest possible development of democratic human capital. This focus follows directly from taking the democratic teleological goods of self-rule by all and self-realization by all as the axial purposes of liberal social action. The key shift here is from a focus upon a more equal distribution of goods and social resources in the name of justice to a focus upon the development of the core human and civic capabilities of all members of our democratic society. In the context of canonical democratic theory, this represents a reaffirmation of the proposition of Wilhelm von Humboldt famously endorsed by John Stuart Mill that "the grand, leading principle towards which every argument unfolded in these pages directly converges, is the absolute and essential importance of human development in its richest diversity"[8]—and a reinvocation of Walt Whitman's insistence that democracy's ultimate moral significance is that it constitutes a "grand experiment of development, whose end . . . may be the forming of a full-grown man or woman" and that its deepest purpose is to develop and perfect the "measureless wealth of latent power and capacity . . . of the people."[9] In the context of more contemporary theories of democratic purposes and morality, this core feature of a reformed liberal social agenda represents an endorsement of the arguments of A. K. Sen and Martha Nussbaum that it is more fitting for us to focus upon the maximizing of personal capacities and capabilities than upon the distribution of wealth and income per se.[10]

What are these capabilities whose fullest possible development should be a primary concern of a revitalized and recentered American liberalism? They fall under two basic headings—headings that parallel in their defining adjectives the deontological categories of human rights and democratic rights. First are those basic human competencies necessary to be a fully functioning adult. Second are the competencies necessary to perform those tasks and to fulfill those roles incumbent upon citizens of a democratic society. It is possible for people to disagree about exactly what specific competencies warrant inclusion under each of these two headings, and I will not try to explore or adjudicate those possible disagreements here. But whatever ambiguities may remain at the margins, surely there are core features under each category that seem fairly obvious. To be a fully functional human adult, for example, surely requires having the capacity to form and pursue a plan of life of some sort, the capacities needed to manage one's own affairs, and the capacities necessary to associate with other people. These capabilities in turn depend upon the acquisition of basic social skills, upon having some level of ability to engage in practical reasoning, and upon some degree of communicative ability. Similarly, in order to be a competent member of a democratic public engaged in self-rule, certain civic capacities seem essential. Competent democratic citizenship requires having the ability to engage in or at least understand public discourse and to arrive at reasonable public judgments, the intellectual and characterological capacity to understand and acquiesce in the rule of law, and the ability to be a contributor to the tasks required by the terms of social cooperation governing the communal life of the society. These competencies, moreover, depend in turn upon the attainment of certain basic reasoning, communicative, and productive skills.

The argument here, then, is that—pursuant to its axial principled commitment to the democratic purposes of universal self-rule and self-realization—the fundamental imperative of the social agenda of a reformed American liberalism should be to develop the human and civic capabilities of its members rather than to deliver them a certain measure of primary goods. But if this imperative tells us what is to be developed, it leaves unanswered the question of the relevant distributive criteria. Even if the central goals are teleological rather than deontological—derived from democratic purposes instead of from principles of distributive justice—the allocative issues still remain. Developing the human capabilities necessary for people to become self-ruling democratic citizens with a real chance to pursue their plans of self-realization requires resources, after all. Indeed, successful pursuit of some plans of life—or even unsuccessful pursuit, for that matter—can be extraordinarily expensive. Does that mean that the principled imperative of a liberal social agenda to develop human and civic capabilities is infinite in its scope? Does it logically demand an open-ended public budget? Not at all. The relevant conception of "self-realization" in this context is, to borrow a phrase from Rawls, political and not comprehensive. The public responsibility incumbent upon a democratic society to finance the human and civic competency of its citizenry will always be a quite substantial one. But it does not by any means require some kind of blank check on the public treasury.

The proper distributive standard for a capabilities agenda grounded in the central aspirations of democracy is therefore a threshold criterion. This allocative principle would require that all members of the society have access, one way or another, to those resources they need to develop their personal abilities to a level sufficient for them to become full participating and contributing democratic citizens. Beyond that, there is no principled imperative and no algorithm of justice that mandates additional redistributions of wealth and income—or offices or honors or social status—from some individuals to others. In a free society, there will always be inequalities in these respects as a result of individual choices, different individual efforts, different personal talents, and sheer luck. But so long as everyone enjoys the opportunity and resources to develop their human and civic capabilities, there is no moral scandal and nothing that needs redress here.[11]

In saying that a liberal social agenda should give pride of place to the development of human capital, it needs to be emphasized in case it is not clear from context and examples, that I do not mean to construe that term in a narrowly economic sense. We are not speaking simply of economic investment in factors of production here. Certainly, a developed capacity for engaging in productive economic activity is important for the welfare of both the society and the individual. So that is part of the story—but only part. We are talking here about developing people into democratic citizens and not merely into producers and consumers. The goal of developing human capital in a democratic society therefore has to include equipping its members to be not merely contributors to that society's gross domestic product (GDP) but also capable participants in the larger tasks of political self-governance and community life.

In practical terms, this principled focus upon human development logically begins with a commitment to universal access to high-quality education and health care. Recent national rankings of both educational achievement and public health make it clear that we in this country have serious work to do in both of these areas. In both, we do extremely well at the top levels of the pyramid: we have world-class universities and extraordinary advanced medical technology. It is the middle and lower ranges of the pyramids that need enormous improvement.

Any serious social agenda for American liberalism would have to include an insistence upon some form of universal health care, therefore. With a spouse who works as a health care delivery system business consultant, I am keenly aware of the enormous complexities and potential pitfalls in getting this done effectively and efficiently. But the simple fact is that all other countries of similar economic status are able to do this, whereas we have more than 50 million uninsured citizens even though we spend a greater percentage of our GDP on health care than any other nation. We have, then, strong principled reasons to solve this problem and equally strong prima facie grounds for knowing it is possible.

In the area of education, a serious human capital agenda would require making every effort to eliminate—or at least minimize—what Jonathan Kozol has termed the "savage inequalities" that characterize our system of elementary and secondary education.[12] Every capable student should have access to a "world-quality" education with skilled teachers. As part of that effort, moreover, vast improvements are necessary in our national program of civic education. As Thomas Jefferson insisted long ago, in the context of democratic self-rule it becomes a matter of the first priority to equip citizens with the knowledge and understanding sufficient to "render the people the safe, as they are the ultimate, guardians of their own liberty."[13] For Jefferson, this suggested that the

CHAPTER FIVE

earlier stages of education should be primarily historical—the idea being that this would provide students the vicarious experience and evidentiary base to judge "the actions and designs of men," in order to "enable them to know ambition under every disguise it may assume; and knowing it, to defeat its views."[14] A more contemporary version of a minimal civic education for competent democratic citizens, I would argue, would require all students to acquire a basic knowledge not only of world history and American history but also of American constitutionalism and political institutions, together with some understanding of basic economics. This is by no means an unreasonable expectation or something all that hard to do, but we currently fall far short of meeting this standard. Moreover, in this day and age, everyone needs to have some minimal understanding of science and technology: to give but one example, it would seem a matter of basic competency for someone summoned to serve on a criminal jury to know what DNA is.

Especially in the context of a globalized market system, where jobs are subject to rapid appearance and disappearance with the easy mobility of capital and information, a commitment to development of human capital would also seem to require providing wide access to job-training programs for adult workers as well as for advanced secondary or community college students.

Finally, I would offer a more general point under the heading of human capital development. Even a conservative and libertarian political economist such as Milton Friedman is willing to recognize that for a variety of reasons, most economies, including our own, suffer from imperfections in the capital market that result in underinvestment in human capital.[15] Even someone who, like Friedman, denies the existence of sufficient positive externalities or neighborhood effects to justify public subsidy of advanced education and occupational training therefore should be, as he is, willing to support something resembling student loan programs to rectify these capital market failures. And were we, more realistically I believe, to recognize the positive externalities of making such funds available (not only in terms of additional future tax revenue but also in terms of diminishing inequalities of wealth and income), then it becomes reasonable to think of making some of these funds available in the form of grants rather than loans. Proposals along these lines have been put forward recently, as, for example, by Bruce Ackerman and Anne Alstott, who argue for providing a basic capital grant of some $80,000 to every young adult at the age of maturity.[16] It is also worth noting that a similar proposal was advanced some two hundred years ago by the Enlightenment mathematician and social theorist Condorcet in the same paragraph in which he sketched out the model of modern Social Security programs. One way to mitigate the "inequality, dependence, and even misery, which ceaselessly threatens the most numerous and most active class in our society," he wrote, would be to "provide all children with the capital necessary for the full use of their labor, available at the age when they start work and found a family, a capital which increases at the expense of those whom premature death prevents from reaching this age."[17] For a host of practical reasons, proposals such as these are not likely to come to fruition anytime soon. And to some extent, current programs such as Pell Grants and Federal Housing Administration (FHA) loans function to serve some of the same purposes. The theoretical case on behalf of doing more to remedy the inadequacy of available funds for investment in human capital is nonetheless a strong one—both on narrowly economic grounds and on the broader grounds of the central human developmental aspirations of a democratic society. So proposals of this sort deserve a place on the long-run human capabilities agenda of a twenty-first-century version of American liberalism. If even a former economic adviser to Barry Goldwater is willing to testify to our current underinvestment in human capital—and that without going beyond the economic case alone—that situation should be seen as an important public policy challenge and not as a mere theoretical curiosity.

One great virtue of a liberal public philosophy that focuses upon developing the basic human capacities and civic competencies of its citizens is that it benefits from a happy convergence between its democratic principles and collective prudence. A program of capabilities maximization works to strengthen the social foundations of a democratic society's ability to function effectively at the same time as it serves the accomplishment of democracy's deepest moral aspirations. This is the happy causal circularity at the heart of Mill's account of the prerequisites and the justification of democratic governance. The ultimate virtue of representative government, Mill argued, is (in addition to its responsiveness to the interests of the voting public) that it is the form of government best suited to foster the improvement of the intellect and character of its citizens. But it is these very virtues of mind and spirit that provide the cultural requisites for the survival and efficacy of a democratic polity.[18] These prudential virtues of a capabilities agenda give it political appeal, therefore, even among those who may be less persuaded by the moral argument on its behalf.

The logic of an American liberalism in the spirit of Mill and Whitman also lends itself to the promotion of what Richard Dagger has called a "civic economy" and what Michael Sandel has characterized as a "political economy of citizenship."[19] What these conceptions have in common is the claim that some of the central ideals of the civic republican tradition should be used as touchstones for a contemporary democratic political economy. Civic republicanism accorded special importance among its political goals to achieving civic equality, the avoidance of dependency or subjection to social domination, and the development of those civic virtues necessary for democratic governance. A neorepublican political economy is thus one constructed with careful regard to the question: "What economic arrangements are most hospitable to self-government"?[20] The critical claim shared by Dagger and Sandel is that the dominant normative political economics in American public philosophies—liberal or conservative—are essentially devoted to aggregative and/or distributive goals and that the traditional republican concern with the impact of economic arrangements and institutions upon the character and capacities of the citizenry has largely been ignored. They also agree in regarding this neglect as a mistake that begs remedy.

Although the provenance of the notion of a neorepublican political economy is not identical with what I have characterized as the populist perfectionism of traditional American liberalism and although I am not entirely in agreement with Sandel's account of who the culprits have been in causing the neglect of republican concerns or with some of his prescriptive recommendations, I would argue that the central conception here of a civic economy or a political economy of citizenship coheres very nicely with the capabilities/human capital agenda I have set out.[21] That complementarity is hardly surprising, since creating the conditions for successful self-rule is one of the central concerns of both republicanism and the democratic perfectionism of people such as Mill and Whitman.

There is no definitive catechism—either historical or contemporary—that specifies some agreed-upon template of the particular tenets or components of a civic or neorepublican political economy. Fleshing out this notion instead constitutes an exercise in hermeneutics and casuistry—an attempt to draw out what might be the most logical and appropriate implications of civic republican political ideals for a normative political economy. A model of a neorepublican political economy thus embodies an attempt to answer the question: what seem to be the most likely features of a political economy oriented toward institutionalizing the conditions of republican/democratic/representative self-governance and creating both as a means to that end and as a worthy end in its own right a citizenry composed of nondependent, politically competent, and public-spirited civic equals? All readers are welcome to offer their own answers to this question, but for the sake of argument, my own answer would incorporate the following principal features: broad ownership of property, an emergency economic safety net, universal (not means-tested) social insurance, institutionalized human capital development, a commitment to making work pay, a moderately progressive tax code, and enforceable expectations of personal social responsibility.²²

The first of these elements of a neorepublican civic economy, the desire to create a broad ownership of property, goes back a very long way. Aristotle insisted long ago upon the prudential benefits of having a large middle class, for example. And both liberal and conservative republicans during the early days of our own country advocated policies to spread property ownership accordingly. Jefferson's comments and proposals along these lines are widely known. But his more conservative republican political adversary, John Adams, likewise saw it as a highly desirable goal "to make the acquisition of land easy to every member of society; to make a division of the land into small quantities so that the multitude may be possessed of landed estates." Such a policy, he said, was necessary in order to preserve equal liberty and to ensure consideration of the "liberties, virtues, and interests" of the people in all acts of government.²³ More recently, John Rawls has also invoked the notion of a "property-owning democracy" as one of the two models of political economy that might "be designed to satisfy the two principles of justice." And although his endorsement of this model is, not surprisingly, couched in terms of social justice, he strikes a republican—and populist perfectionist—note by citing the value of "putting all citizens in a position to manage their own affairs."²⁴

Because the principal wealth-creating assets in a contemporary economy are no longer found in land but in capital and since we no longer are a frontier society, the old "forty acres and a mule" strategy that appealed to Jefferson and Adams no longer gets us very far. So unless we want to advocate some version of the "expropriate the expropriators" strategy—as I do not, for all sorts of reasons both practical and moral—this devotion to widely dispersed property ownership should be understood as a regulative ideal that should guide economic policy and property law when multiple otherwise acceptable laws and policies are on the table. Relevant examples under this heading include laws and policies relating to corporate acquisition and concentration (especially but not exclusively in areas where such concentration confers political power and influence, such as ownership of media outlets, thus violating one of the main principled "blocks" upon the use of wealth in a legitimate democratic society),[25] laws and policies relating to homeownership, laws and policies governing the acquisition and running of small businesses and family farms, and laws governing the inheritance of property. Regarding the latter, we should recall Tocqueville's valid if somewhat hyperbolic pronouncement that laws of inheritance

> ought to be placed at the head of all political institutions, for they exercise an incredible influence upon the social state of a people. . . . Through their means, man acquires a kind of preternatural power over the future lot of his fellow creatures. When the legislator has once regulated the law of inheritance, he may rest from his labor. . . . When framed in a particular manner, this law unites, draws together, and vests property and power in a few hands; it causes an aristocracy, so to speak, to spring out of the ground. If formed on opposite principles, its action is still more rapid; it divides, distributes, and disperses both property . . . and power [and] signals the coming of democracy.[26]

With this admonition in mind, it should be a standard part of a liberal social agenda to tax inheritance in a manner that permits people to convey their earned assets to family and friends in ways that secure their economic security and comfort but that offer strong incentives to philanthropy and the dispersal of very large estates. As far as tax policy more generally is concerned, a neorepublican political economy will also include a moderately progressive schedule of income taxation.[27] There is here neither punitive animus nor confiscatory intent—of the sort embodied in the determination once expressed by a British Labourite to tax the wealthy "until their pips squeak." Superior productivity should be honored and the legitimate claims of proportionate justice respected. But a populist perfectionist liberalism incorporates the civic republican assumption that popular government is a common enterprise, and it is a standard feature of common enterprises that those with a greater stake and ability to pay should contribute more.

The social insurance sector of a neorepublican economy includes two components. The first is a safety net to prevent outright destitution, based on need alone and justified on grounds of human decency, civic friendship, and collective prudence. There is no set template for the form or amount of this safety net, although adequacy, efficiency, and the avoidance of perverse incentives are the pertinent criteria in making such decisions. Any further social insurance programs should be universally applicable to all citizens on the model of our current Old-Age, Survivors, and Disability Insurance (OASDI, or Social Security) program.[28] As Theda Skocpol has been reminding us for some while now, programs of social provision in this country that have both functioned well and received broad and continuing support exhibit two important characteristics. First, successful programs "have never been understood either as poor relief or as mere personal 'entitlements.' Socially provided benefits have been morally justified as a return for service to the community, or else as preparation for individuals who would subsequently contribute to the larger community." Second, these successful programs "have built bridges between more and less privileged Americans, bringing people together—as worthy beneficiaries and contributing citizens—across lines of class, race, and region."[29] Social Security has been a successful program enjoying broad support because it satisfies these criteria. People earn their benefits by years of productive labor and making contributions. Benefits bear some proportionality to contribution levels, but those at lower income levels enjoy a higher ratio of benefits to contribution. The program thus combines earned rewards, social solidarity, and protection against impoverished old age for people who contributed to the nation's economic productivity during their working years. In moral terms, it therefore reflects and helps to reinforce proportional justice, civic friendship, and civic equality—while serving collective prudential purposes as well.

A neorepublican political economy, unlike the political economy of the social justice liberalism of recent decades, is thus not need-based (except where the safety net comes into play). Nor is it simply rights-based. Instead, it is devoted to creating the social and economic conditions conducive to the achievement of a populist and perfectionist liberalism's goals of competent self-rule and self-realization. It aims to foster and reward competent and responsible democratic citizenship and to promote the general welfare by enabling ordinary Americans to pursue their plans of life with reasonable hopes of success. The ethos of this kind of political economy is therefore unapologetic about imposing a work expectation upon all its members who are able of mind and body. It assumes that all citizens should be willing to "do their bit," to borrow the Britishism Stuart White invokes in his conception of "fair dues social reciprocity," in contributing their time and effort to the productive labors of the community.[30] The important complementary correlate of this expectation/demand is a commitment to "making work pay," to invoke another current maxim. There are, of course, significant practical limitations to the extent of regulatory intrusion into labor markets that are feasible and benign. But any liberal social agenda would include a reversal of the recent decline in the (real) minimum wage and strong support for and possible enhancements in the Earned Income Tax Credit—which is not only one of the most effective antipoverty programs but one that sustains the work ethic while not interfering unduly with the economic rationality of the labor market. Health care reform should make a real contribution to this effort, as well, because any serious and rational reform will involve elimination of the moral anomaly and perverse incentives of providing care to the impoverished via Medicaid and subsidizing care for upper-income people via tax shelters for employer contributions to

CHAPTER FIVE

health insurance while leaving lower-income workers exposed to ruinous financial burdens (made even heavier and more inequitable because private payers are billed about double the cost to insurance companies) in the event of accident or serious illness. Finally, creative ways should be sought to incentivize and reward employers who treat their salaried employees more favorably and who avoid exploitative and demeaning policies toward them. In my own city, for example, there are companies such as Costco that clearly make efforts to do well by their employees in terms of benefits and conditions of work and other companies who take advantage of the powerlessness and social disadvantage of their workforce to treat them abusively in order to squeeze every last drop of output from them. The marketplace offers its monetary inducements to the latter type of employer, so counterbalancing favorable treatment available to the government—whether in tax arrangements, regulatory regimen, or whatever—should be deployed to lessen any market disadvantage the better kind of employers might have to shoulder as a consequence of their salutary labor practices.

The fundamental intent and presumably the effect of the movement toward this kind of civic/neorepublican political economy in general terms would be to restore to the twenty-first-century "respectable yeomanry" the pride of place they enjoyed within the normative sociology of an earlier American liberalism prior to their moral demotion within the social justice liberalism of the past several decades. The same policies bolster our society's chances of success in attaining the central populist and perfectionist goals—what Whitman called the "ulterior object of political and all other government"[31]—of giving this body of average citizens the conditions and capacities necessary for democratic self-governance and pursuit of their personal plans for a humanly good life. In Theda Skocpol's blunt words, a failure to create such a political economy of citizenship that provides the necessary national systems of social support for our average working families "is ethically obtuse and politically dumb." Such a failure would represent not only a forgetting of what she calls "the best traditions of U.S. social policy making, stretching all the way back into the nineteenth century," but also, and not adventitiously, a loss of connection with the best traditions of American liberal public philosophy.[32]

The final component in my sketch of a reformed social agenda for American liberalism is a renewed determination to protect and promote a healthy public sphere within the nation's civic life. The term *public sphere* is here intended to denote two things: first, it refers to public spaces and venues for common life and civic events open to all citizens qua citizens; and second, it refers to institutional mechanisms and forums for public political conversation in the service of what Habermas calls "rational will formation."

A well-ordered democratic society embodies, among other defining characteristics, balance and complementarity between its public and private domains. Both are essential. We are social animals and, in a democracy, civic equals engaged in common endeavors on behalf of the general welfare. As such, we need to establish some elements of common identity, some sense of common purposes, and some degree of common values. Without a vital public sphere, these functional necessities for making democracy work are difficult if not impossible to develop. We are also separate, different, and distinctive individuals with different talents and different, in some respects divergent, conceptions of the good life. We need, therefore, protected space and places for these activities of personal happiness and self-realization to occur and flourish. If the public domain of society becomes too extensive and encompassing, it turns intrusive and oppressive. At the extreme limit, it becomes in effect totalitarian; in those circumstances, Sartre's famous and otherwise implausible claim that "hell is other people" turns into reality. However, if a democracy's public sphere shrivels and atrophies, the consequences are a different kind of social pathology. If the lives of democratic citizens are wholly submerged within an all-encompassing sphere of entirely private pursuits, these lives become narrow and impoverished in a different way. The limit condition under this heading would be lives of solitary confinement, where people go slowly insane, or a world of hermits, whose denizens lead lives of slightly daft self-absorption. The more plausible and less extreme social pathology produced by an atrophied public domain, however, is the condition that Tocqueville attempted to describe under the term *individualism*. That did not mean a condition of negative liberty and personal self-reliance, in his lexicon. It meant instead a social world that "disposes each member of the community to sever himself from the mass of his fellows, and to draw apart with his family and friends; so that, after he has formed a little circle of his own, he willingly leaves society at large to itself." Individualism "at first," Tocqueville continues, "only saps the virtues of public life, but in the long run, it attacks and destroys all others, and is at length absorbed in downright selfishness."[33] The danger to which a democratic society devoid of a vital public sphere is subjected is that it becomes a world of strangers who pass one another by, unknowing and indifferent. And then, because they have competing interests but no compensatory bonds of mutual association, affection, or common identity, these strangers turn increasingly into competitors simpliciter, if not into enemies.

America's individualistic and libertarian version of conservatism has characteristically been largely oblivious to the latter dangers and has actively denigrated the public sphere as useless and coercive. In recent years, for example, the libertarian humorist P. J. O'Rourke has quipped that if you want to know what public means, you should think about public toilets. And Milton Friedman has counseled us to auction off Yellowstone National Park and the Grand Canyon to private owners: "If the public wants this kind of an activity enough to pay for it, private enterprises will have every incentive to provide such parks. . . . I cannot conjure up any neighborhood effects . . . that would justify governmental activity in this area."[34] In contrast, American liberals have traditionally promoted and defended the value of public spaces and institutions such as public schools, public libraries, public parks, and public hospitals.

One of the significant but underremarked consequences of American liberalism's deontological turn—its centering itself on distributive justice—has been a corollary neglect of this traditional liberal concern with a vibrant democratic public domain. The problem here is that if the axial goal of liberalism is to get the allocation of goods to separate people right, to get the right funds into the right pockets as it were, then regardless of how egalitarian the mandated distribution might be, it can be accomplished in a purely private and individual way. There is no need for any kind of common life. You need only to have an authoritative bureaucratic mechanism to shift resources from one private pocket to another. Rawls may talk about democratic citizens as "sharing one another's fate." But all this might amount to in hard, concrete fact could be in effect to do what Nozick says the difference principle entails: namely, according some separate and private individuals a kind of de facto partial ownership of other individuals' equally private productive activities.[35]

In the real world, this tunnel-vision fixation upon a rights-based maximization of the private interests or desires of less well-off individuals has resulted in the erosion of the integrity of the public sphere and therefore of its ability to function effectively in pursuit of the purposes that justified it in the first place. If, in the name of equal rights, it is insisted by liberal groups such as the ACLU that winos be allowed to appropriate space in public libraries to use as their drying-out tanks or that public parks have to be available to the homeless population and to drug addicts for use as shantytowns, the inevitable result is that these spaces deteriorate and become abandoned by those who would otherwise have enjoyed them for their intended purposes. And then, with O'Rourke's disparaging allusion to public toilets having been unnecessarily validated as a seemingly accurate description of public spaces in general, the public support for these venues evaporates, funds needed to sustain them are withheld, and they disappear from the scene.

My claim here is that, when vibrant and healthy, the functioning of these public spaces and institutions makes an extremely

CHAPTER FIVE

important contribution to an ethos of civic equality, to the cultivation of civic friendship, and to the presence of a sense of common life and purpose in a democratic society. Their successful functioning can also add immensely to the quality of life of particular communities—and especially to the quality of life of those of lesser means who lack access to private libraries and cannot afford to join private clubs for their recreational needs. Since these are all important democratic goods in and of themselves and since these goods also are conducive to successful democratic self-rule and personal development, a reformed liberal social agenda needs to include a renewed concern for creating and sustaining such public spaces and venues for common life. Contrary to O'Rourke's sneer about public spaces and in support of my claim here, I offer the illustrative case of the small town near my family's longtime summer home. This town has only some 1,500 inhabitants, and it is in one of the poorest counties of its state. But it offers its residents a very commodious place to live, in large part because of the vibrant community life afforded by the town's public spaces. These include two public parks, an attractive public library, a community meeting house, an older citizens' community center, and a small amphitheater. In one of the parks, all manner of people play on the two tennis courts, teenagers play into the night on the well-lit basketball court, and families with small children make good use of the playground. The other park, on the shore of a small Lake Michigan inlet, boasts grassy spaces with a large picnic shelter and yet another playground—a place constantly bustling with activities such as fund-raising fish fries sponsored by civic groups, farmers' markets, and evening concerts. More music and occasional theatrical productions take place in the amphitheater and in the community hall. (A community chorus that grew up partly in response to the availability of these venues now makes concert tours to other areas of the country and even abroad.) People regularly bring their children to the library for book readings. Moreover, the relationships developed in these venues and events seem to spill over into the conduct of the town's business and help it run

NEW DEMOCRATIC VISTAS

effectively—much along the lines of the impact of the civic culture Robert Putnam cites as a crucial feature of what makes democracy work much better in some Italian locales than in others.[36] No doubt, this little town encompasses its own petty animosities and tensions, as do all societies composed of us cupiditous and vainglorious human beings. So though I do not want to embrace Whitman's characteristically excessive effusiveness in its entirety, this is a place that comes to my mind when I read his envisioning of

> a community, today and here, in which, on a sufficient scale, the perfect personalities, without noise meet; say in some pleasant western settlement or town, where a couple of hundred best men and women, of ordinary worldly status, have by luck been drawn together, with nothing extra of genius or wealth, but . . . industrious, cheerful, resolute, friendly, and devout. I can conceive such a community organized in running order, powers judiciously delegated—farming, building, trade, courts, mails, schools, elections, all attended to; and then the rest of life, the main thing, freely branching and blossoming in each individual . . . , a true personality, developed, exercised proportionately in body, mind, and spirit.[37]

What it is about this pleasant little town that brings Whitman's bucolic reverie to mind could and would in no way, shape, or form be able to exist and sustain itself apart from the kind of public spaces and communal activities I have described. It is true, of course, that some of the social dynamics I have cited are more pertinent to smaller communities than to larger metropolitan areas. But even if the specific patterns and possibilities for public spaces and events are somewhat different within larger cities, other parts of the process work in a similar fashion to promote social capital and improve the quality of life for large sectors of the population. Try, for example, to imagine New York without Central Park, Washington Square, the Bronx Zoo, the New York Public Library, or the major museums that host public functions.

CHAPTER FIVE

Or imagine Chicago without Grant Park and all the concerts, festivals, and other public events that happen there. Or imagine Boston without its Commons, or Washington without the Mall and Rock Creek Park.

The other important subset of the public domain deserving specific mention in this context is the public sphere in the sense that Jürgen Habermas uses the term: that is, the public forum or deliberative sphere—all those places and mechanisms and occasions for public dialogue and discourse to take place. If democratic self-rule is actually to occur, these places and mechanisms need to be plentiful and need to perform in nonsystematically distortive ways. It is through the functioning of these venues that two things crucial to democratic governance occur: first, what Habermas characterizes as the social practices of rational will formation, and second, the creation of what Condorcet spoke about as the "tribunal" of public opinion.[38] By rational will formation, Habermas means to signify those processes of idea formation and contestation through which democratic citizens are enabled to conceive, test, and decide what their public purposes and regulative norms should be. And by a tribunal of public opinion, Condorcet is optimistically anticipating the systematic creation of a level of public knowledge and awareness sufficient to police the self-aggrandizing actions of the powerful by subjecting them to continuous and effective public scrutiny.

Recent developments in information technology have essentially consummated the empirical grounds for Condorcet's optimism. His comments about the emergence of a new and powerful tribunal of public opinion were actually nested within his reflections upon the political consequences of the invention of the printing press. ("Has not printing freed the education of the people from all political and religious shackles? . . . It is enough for there to exist one corner of free earth from which the press can scatter its leaves," he wrote.) Today, it is even less possible "to seal every crevice through which truth aspires to enter," as he put it.[39] As people like Bill Clinton, Karl Rove, and John McCain discovered to their chagrin during the 2008 election campaign, if you contradict yourself or deny saying something you in fact said, your prevarications will be available to public view on the Internet the very next day. At the same time, however, these very technological devices serve as powerful vehicles for the massive dissemination of outright falsehoods and fabrications to the vulnerable and credulous. The standard assumptions of optimistic liberals such as Condorcet about the unproblematically benign consequences of technological advances, here and elsewhere, are misleadingly sanguine. Maintaining the health and efficacy of a democratic public forum therefore requires constant battle against the studied and systematic efforts of the politically powerful and ambitious, the socially ascendant, the wealthy, and the ideologically driven to dominate and/or degrade the functioning of the public forum for their own purposes.

In the abstract terms of political theory, what this means is that one of the ongoing tasks on a liberal social agenda is to minimize "systematically distorted communications" in the public sphere. That fight can be carried on in both affirmative and defensive ways. Affirmatively, the goal is to create and strengthen the channels and institutional sites within which well-informed public deliberation and opinion formation can take place. Defensively, the goal is to work actively against those forces seeking to exert dominance over or to degrade the public forum through monopolization, exclusion, and pollution in the form of deliberate misinformation. The specific ways and initiatives through which these tasks might be best accomplished I am happy to leave to the creative imagination of my readers. There are already on the table, however, a number of suggestions along these lines that have been made by thoughtful advocates of strong institutions of democratic deliberation such as Benjamin Barber, Bruce Ackerman, and James Fishkin. Among these proposals are lower postal rates for journals of political information and discussion, various manner of deliberative assemblies, the creation of an institutionalized national "Deliberation Day" prior to national elections, increased access to and use of television for civic information and discussion, and the creation of authoritative Internet sites that make important political and economic data easily available to the voting public.[40] On the defensive side of the agenda, it would seem important to combat concentrations of ownership and control over newspapers and television outlets. And it would also be useful to promote a renewed journalistic ethos of service to the public through independent and aggressive fact-checking and investigative reporting.

Theoretically, one would think that the protection and promotion of the democratic public forum should not be a partisan or ideological matter. All those who care about the health and legitimacy of democratic governance should be united in this enterprise. And certainly, liberals can find strong and principled allies across the political aisle here. But it is nonetheless hard to deny that the efforts of social and economic elites to fend off democratic reform by campaigns of divide-and-rule, cover-ups, and misinformation did not disappear in the eighteenth or nineteenth century. What Enlightenment liberals thematized as the epic confrontation between Reason and Authority is a perennial one that gets fought on new fronts all the time. As a consequence, the active promotion of institutionalized ways to inform the public and enable them to make competent judgments on their own behalf in the common interest needs to be a continuous part of the social agenda of a political persuasion whose central concern is to sustain the proud boast of American democracy that here the people rule and here all shall be free.

CONCLUSION: TOWARD A NEW LIBERAL MAJORITY

Two related questions have animated the discussion in this chapter. First, what would the moral imaginary of a reformed American liberalism recentered on the traditional liberal goals of universal self-rule and self-development look like? And second, what might be the shape of a social agenda devoted to these goals?

My answer to the first question is that the moral geography of a reformed liberal public philosophy would demand less of justice and expect more of its people. It would display considerably less certitude about what constitutes a fair distribution of social resources within a morally complex—and, in some respects, a morally tragic—world where some have more talent than others, where some have greater misfortune than others, and where people make different choices about how to distribute resources they are morally entitled to control. It would exhibit greater realism about the extent to which it is possible for even the most well-intentioned political society to redress the deep and inexhaustible arbitrary inequalities of the world—and more humility about what it is proper to demand in this regard of people who bear no causal responsibility for these inequalities. In addition, this moral imaginary would embrace a conception of the democratic good—a community of civic equals who not only treat each other with mutual respect but who "share one another's fate" through their mutual devotion to practices of deliberative self-rule and to institutionalized conditions enabling everyone to pursue their own conceptions of personal fulfillment whatever these may be—subject only to the demand that they be consistent with the requisites of good democratic citizenship. This revised moral imaginary would also incorporate a normative conception of democratic persons who are strong and capable moral agents and not simply people who may have a sense of fair play and the ability to decide what they want but who otherwise are depicted as the passive sport of chance.

My answer to the second question regarding the kind of social policies most appropriate to this conception of liberal public philosophy was to suggest a social agenda composed of four principal parts. The first of these was to continue the work of the civil rights revolution in universalizing the attainment of full democratic

CHAPTER FIVE

rights, with special attention to the rights and full civic inclusion of all those subgroups of the American public vulnerable to being subordinated or marginalized by self-serving majorities. The second major feature of this agenda was the development of policies and institutions devoted to the fullest possible development of human and social capital, maximizing the human capabilities and democratic civic competencies of the people as a whole. The third component was the creation of a civic or neorepublican political economy—a set of economic institutions and allocative arrangements conducive to popular self-governance and the development of the democratic civic virtues as well as to material productivity. And the last element of this freehanded sketch of a populist perfectionist social agenda was the promotion and sustenance of a robust democratic public sphere to complement a strong private realm of families and associations.

One way to understand this social agenda—and the moral intuitions that drive it—is to see it as the embodiment of an alternative conception of what Rawls called the social division of responsibility. In his account of a well-ordered democracy, society as a collective body assumes responsibility for protecting civil liberties and "fair" equality of opportunity while also providing all individual citizens with the amount of primary goods dictated by the society's putative moral obligation to redress arbitrary inequalities. The correlative responsibilities of individual citizens are to choose their own goals in life and to accommodate their pursuit of these goals to the level of resources the society allocates to them. In the conception offered here, by contrast, society as a whole takes responsibility for protecting democratic civil rights and liberties and providing all its citizens with an economic safety net and with the resources and institutions necessary to enable all of them to develop their talents and capabilities in ways that allow them to be full participants in the political and economic life of the society. Individual citizens in turn are expected to respect each other's equal democratic rights, to contribute to the economic efforts of the society to the extent of their abilities, to take full advantage of the opportunities and resources made available to them to develop their political and economic competencies, and to assume responsibility for the pursuit of their personal projects of self-realization as dictated by their own conceptions of a good human life.

In both of these accounts, the democratic society as a whole assumes important responsibilities in order to enable all of its members to become competent self-governing agents of their own self-actualization. On neither account is the state construed as no more than a night watchman who tells everyone, no matter their specific endowments and circumstances, that they are on their own. The major difference on the side of collective responsibility is that in the conception I am endorsing the society makes no pretense to know in any complete or determinate sense what distributive justice consists in (beyond its mandate to adhere to formal principles of democratic right), much less to be able or obligated to produce it. It instead conceives its own responsibility to be creating the conditions that allow all its members to become capable and competent people and democratic citizens. On the side of individual responsibility, the major difference is that in my conception, individual citizens are expected to do more than simply exercise the freedom to choose their own ends in life and then to adjust these in light of the level of resources allocated to them: they bear the additional obligations to "do their bit" economically, to develop their ability to manage their own lives, and to participate conscientiously in the collective self-governance of their society.[41]

I believe that this understanding of the democratic social contract—its terms of social cooperation and its allocation of social responsibilities—coheres much more closely with the median moral sensibilities of the American public than does the contrasting understanding promoted by the rights-based liberalism of the past several decades. If there is such a thing as an "overlapping moral consensus" in this country, it does not consist in a broad allegiance to an egalitarian interpretation of distributive justice.

It instead incorporates a strong belief in the reality and moral importance of personal freedom and powers of agency, an insistence upon the moral and practical importance of work, belief in moral desert and therefore in standards of proportional justice, insistence upon civic equality and a correlative disdain for social snobbery and condescension (aka elitism), and a widespread acceptance of obligations of mutual assistance among "fellow Americans." Evidence for this reading of the modal moral imaginary among the American public can be found not only by attending to the ubiquitous tropes of standard moral rhetoric in this country but also by consulting empirical surveys of public opinion and the results of relevant experiments by social psychologists.[42]

American conservatives have traded heavily upon the public's devotion to the work ethic and to norms of desert and proportional justice in order to justify their championing of free enterprise, market distributions, and repeal of inheritance taxes. They have also cynically exploited the American disdain for snobbery to turn populist sentiment away from economic to cultural resentments. And they mostly give lip service to norms of mutual assistance ("compassionate conservatism") while cheaping out on concrete policies that might seem to follow from them. Liberals, because of their egalitarian sentiments and awareness of the power of historical and social circumstances, often seem relatively oblivious to or dismissive of norms of strong agency and moral desert. They often are uncomprehending about how they can appear to be socially condescending and imperious. And they tend to denigrate and underestimate the power of fraternal sentiment in favor of relying upon claims of rights and justice when it comes to their exhortations on behalf of programs of mutual assistance and communal provision. As a result, they transgress important values and sensitivities of their intended audience while simultaneously forswearing or heavily subordinating appeals to norms and sentiments of common identity and civic friendship that could generate support for important liberal social aspirations and policies.[43]

The practical political benefit that the reconfigured public philosophy I am commending can bring to American liberalism in this context is that it is an excellent fit within and a potentially valuable resource for the most plausible strategy for rebuilding a liberal electoral majority in this country. For decades prior to the pivotal year of 1968, what political scientists refer to as the "normal majority" in American national elections was Democratic. That is to say, the distribution of political opinion and the pattern of political affiliation in this country were such that—absent short-run perturbations—national elections would produce a Democratic majority. Since the election of 1968, however, the normal outcome has produced a Republican majority. To borrow a metaphor from Samuel Lubell, liberalism has, over the four decades since that date, functioned as the moon rather than the sun in the American political cosmos.[44] For eight years, it was the mission of George W. Bush's chief political aide, Karl Rove, to consolidate and extend this Republican majority for the next generation. Although that mission, seemingly within reach a few short years ago, may have run aground as a consequence of the series of calamities, blunders, and failures of that very administration, we will not know for some time whether the Democratic success in 2008 marks the entry into a new liberal era or whether it will turn out to have been merely what political scientists call a "deviating election" within a longer era of continued conservative electoral dominance.

Karl Rove's vision was, in effect, to build a long-term Republican majority on the model of the William McKinley coalition at the turn of the last century. For Democrats, the relevant historical reference points lead understandably toward aspirations to reconstitute some version of the New Deal or Progressive coalitions. Serious obstacles confront any efforts to reconstitute either of these coalitions in their original form, however. The obvious central problem vis-à-vis the New Deal coalition, of course, is that the seismic events of the sixties pried the so-called solid South out of that coalition for reasons that make this loss irretrievable for at least the midterm future. Attempts to reconstitute the original

Progressive coalition, moreover, confront difficulties generated by important social changes that distinguish our time from theirs. Important among these changes, as Jeffrey Isaac has pertinently observed, are the decline of the liberal form of Protestantism that played such an important role within the Progressive movement and the corresponding burgeoning of politically and culturally conservative Protestant evangelicalism, the decline of a praxis-oriented social science in favor of a more putatively scientific and value-neutral kind of academic social science, and the decline of both class politics and the power of organized labor.[45]

If it is unlikely that either the Progressive or the New Deal coalition can be resurrected in toto, there are promising strategies nonetheless available to American liberalism in the years ahead. The repeated declarations of conservative pundits that we are a Center-Right country are not truly convincing. By most standard measures, this country is more liberal today than it was fifty years ago—more tolerant, more socially inclusive, and less dominated by a traditional social oligarchy.[46] Liberalism's recent electoral struggles have not been a result of the country somehow becoming more politically, economically, or socially conservative. They are, instead, mostly a result of liberalism, through a combination of historical circumstance and their own missteps, allowing itself to be framed coming out of the Vietnam era as being soft in foreign policy, as being on the wrong side of the culture wars, and as being out of touch with the values and interests of Middle American working people. But now, the Madisonian electoral coalition that the Republicans were able to cobble together between a minority economic persuasion and a minority social persuasion may be beginning to unravel. Moreover, younger voters are now entering the electorate leaning predominantly toward the liberal side of the political spectrum. The challenge for American liberals is to rise to the occasion and take advantage of the opportunity thus presented to them.

Against this backdrop of challenge and opportunity, the most promising approach to building a new liberal electoral majority is what could be called the Garrison Keillor–Studs Terkel strategy. This strategy encompasses a dual reclamation project. The first part of this strategy is directed at reclaiming a central component of the Progressive coalition, and the second part is directed at reclaiming a central component of the New Deal coalition. The first of these—the Garrison Keillor component—is geographic, the second—the Studs Terkel component—demographic.

The geographic target for liberal reclamation is the progressive upper-midwestern section of the country. The original Progressive coalition was essentially a tricentric one, with New York, California, and Wisconsin as its principal axes. As American liberalism became increasingly individualistic, rights-based, secularist, and antipopulist, this Progressive coalition suffered something of a rupture. The tension between the eastern and urban liberalism of a Richard Hofstadter and the midwestern progressivism of Madison (Wisconsin) historians such as Merle Curti, canvassed in a previous chapter, reflected this breakdown. So we have in recent years become accustomed to thinking about the electoral map of the country being one of coastal blue states with a sea of red states in between. The demographic part of this electoral reclamation project is the white working-class voter. It was not simply the loss of the so-called solid South that broke apart the New Deal coalition. Equally if not more important was the defection of white working-class voters from the Democratic Party. Sometimes, these voters are characterized as Reagan Democrats. But their defection from liberalism began over a decade before the Hollywood actor/California governor appeared on the national political scene. The watershed year, once again, was 1968—that fateful year in so many respects in American politics. In that year, after decades of being a reliable component of the liberal majority, the white working class voted predominantly for Richard Nixon, and it has since then never returned to its New Deal Democratic electoral affiliation.

The causes of the white working class's shift from its previous electoral support of the liberal party and its social agenda are multiple and controversial. In both its timing and its battle lines, it can be said that the paradigmatic expression of the political and class fault lines at issue here was the conflict between the Chicago police and the mostly young, mostly middle- and upper-class antiwar demonstrators in Grant Park at the 1968 Democratic Convention. But which aspects of the animosities here revealed were most important is not entirely clear. George Wallace's attraction of some northern voters in that year indicates that racial tensions played some part in this. But it is also sometimes forgotten that much of Wallace's political rhetoric embodied a class-based revolt of the "little guys" against student radicals, suburban liberals, and "pointy-headed intellectuals who can't park their bicycles straight." When Wallace said that he had a four-letter word for student protestors, that word was not R-A-C-E but W-O-R-K. What those students, the coupon-clipping limousine liberals, pointy-headed intellectuals, and welfare recipients were presumed to have in common was their abdication or escape from the burdens of ordinary hardworking and patriotic folk who answered the bell each workday and answered their country's call on the battlefield as well. From the vantage point of the white working class, it seemed more and more that the powers-that-be within American liberalism might talk a lot about social justice, but on the ground, this seemed to consist mostly of shielding their own privileged children from burdens and dangers placed on working-class kids and favoring those seeking handouts above people of modest talent and limited resources who tried to pull their own weight. And although liberals understandably saw their war on poverty as a moral cause exemplary of their good social conscience, those who earned modest livings equally understandably saw it as largely irrelevant and oblivious to their own economic struggles. As one bumper sticker I saw on a battered car about that time read: "I fight poverty. I work." Whichever element in this multidimensional pattern of disaffection and resentment one might choose to emphasize, the basic problem can be stated in general terms: since the sixties, members of the white working class have not perceived American liberalism as taking their own values and interests to heart.

The dual reclamation strategy mentioned earlier, then, is targeted at these two constituencies who were once reliable members of the liberal electoral majorities fashioned by Progressivism and the New Deal: the communitarian social progressives of the upper Midwest and the more geographically dispersed, class-based populists among the white working class. Both of these constituencies remain groups that arguably should logically be members of a liberal coalition, the one because of its progressive social ethos and the other because of its economic interests. And if American liberalism wishes to regain its former status as sun rather than moon within the political universe, it needs to devote its principal energies toward bringing these spiritual kin of Garrison Keillor, on the one hand, and Studs Terkel, on the other, back into their fold.

The relevance and value of the project of liberal reformation outlined in this chapter to this very concrete and practical electoral enterprise, then, is this: the reconfiguration of liberal public philosophy I have defended in these pages provides a much more favorable basis for reclaiming the allegiance of these two crucial constituencies than does the moral and political imaginary more characteristic of postsixties liberalism. One can reasonably argue, in fact, that these constituencies did not abandon their liberal affiliations so much as liberalism abandoned or marginalized them, their moral ethos, and their legitimate concerns. The dominant ethos of the Minnesota Farmer-Labor Party and the Wisconsin Progressive Party—an ethos reflected in the academic political theory of Minnesota's Harry Boyte and Wisconsin's Charles Anderson, for example—is one of pragmatic communal self-rule.[47] But social justice–centered liberalism at best subordinated and at times actively disdained this populist progressive ideal. And the normative sociology of social justice liberalism placed the least well-off at its moral center, depriving the average working man and woman of the focal role they played in traditional liberal

CHAPTER FIVE

normative sociology and leaving them only the tenuous hopes of speculative calculations about "trickle-up" economics exemplified by Rawls's musings about "chain-connection." Both of these constituencies, moreover, hold firm convictions about the moral importance of personal agency and responsibility, the importance of community, and the fairness of reward for effort—convictions that seem to them in some respects positively violated by the criteria of social allocation championed by recent liberalism in the name of justice. The reconfigured moral geography and refashioned social agenda depicted and endorsed in the body of this chapter, in contrast, conform much more naturally and congenially to the values and interests of these two constituencies. By rediscovering and rededicating itself to the populist and perfectionist aspirations of an earlier liberal imaginary and bolstered by the entry into the electorate of a new generation more attuned by their own formative experiences and socialization to these aspirations than were the generation they are replacing, American liberalism therefore has before it the opportunity to lay claim to a bright future.

Afterword

Queries and Responses

It was a standard convention among Scholastic authors to conclude their disputations by responding to what they saw as the most logical objections that could be levied against their argumentative claims. I want to follow that practice here. Given the relevant philosophical and political landscape, there are three major questions or complaints likely to be raised in opposition to my central thesis that American liberals should dislodge social justice from its place as primary virtue within their public philosophy and replace it with the historic liberal dedication to achieving democratic self-rule and self-realization—as those goals might best be understood and realized within the setting of a large postindustrial society. First, what happens to the quest for social justice? Second, how can liberalism embrace the perfectionist goal of self-realization without violating the principled liberal prohibition against forcing a particular comprehensive conception of human flourishing upon those members of a pluralist society who hold to a different understanding of the human good? And third, don't the recognized shortcomings of the American public when it comes to political competency and commitment to central liberal and democratic values turn the populist ideal of self-rule into a potentially dangerous fantasy? These are reasonable and important concerns I need to address here. I also will say a few words in response to some who have asked how my argument compares with those of Richard Rorty, who

AFTERWORD

called for returning to the liberalism of Whitman and Dewey in *Achieving Our Country*, and Michael Sandel, who has also criticized rights-based liberalism and endorsed a neorepublican political economy of citizenship in *Democracy's Discontent*.[1] Finally, I will conclude with a brief comment about the 2008 election.

THREE ISSUES

The most common worry voiced by those with whom I have shared my conviction that American liberalism should, in effect, move away from Rawls and build upon the legacy of democrats such as Walt Whitman is quite simply "But what about social justice?" For them, the idea of a liberalism without social justice as its moral and rhetorical centerpiece seems unimaginable and improper. My response to their dismay depends upon what exactly they are worried about losing here. If what they want to hold on to is a moral insistence that distributive justice is the constitutive goal of American liberalism and that distributive justice is defined by social and economic equality, my response is an unapologetic "Good riddance." For reasons explained earlier, identifying social justice with the most equal practicable distribution of primary goods presupposes the rejection of any claims of moral desert based upon different choices and levels of effort. These rejections are logically sustainable, in turn, only on the basis of assumptions about human agency and responsibility that are morally problematic, incompatible with other liberal and democratic moral axioms, and unacceptable to most of the American public. If, then, the plaint "What about social justice?" means you would hold fast to these problematic moral claims and have them drive the core social purposes of liberalism, my response is "Let it go." Liberalism properly understood is an aspiration to empower rather than to level, and it seeks to expand the scope and power of human agency rather than to deny it a legitimate place among the criteria for allocating social goods in a democratic society.

The query "What about social justice?" often expresses a different kind of concern, however, one to which I would give a more sympathetic and reassuring response. Perhaps the worry here is simply this: if social justice is not the central purpose of liberal politics, what happens to the welfare of the disadvantaged? The demand for social justice of an egalitarian sort as the first virtue of a well-ordered democracy, whatever its collateral baggage, had the effect of prioritizing the welfare of those toward the bottom of the socioeconomic hierarchy. With my recommended return of liberalism to its more venerable preoccupation with the virtues of self-rule and democratic development, are these folks going to be thrown under the bus? Would they be left unmourned and unattended to suffer from costs imposed upon them by moral luck, market forces, historical inequalities, and arbitrary social contingencies? My response to these concerns would not be dismissive. Instead, I would say that these more vulnerable and disadvantageously situated members of society are the people who would benefit the most from the goals and the policy agenda of a new populist perfectionism—even if the distributive benefits they receive would come more de facto than de jure. That is to say, they would certainly come out well ahead in distributional terms, but that consequence would be a collateral benefit pursuant to other teleological democratic goals rather than being itself the focal goal in the guise of a deontological imperative.

The central causal dynamic at work in this distributional context is captured by the familiar maxim that a rising tide lifts all boats. Programs of universal communal provision and social insurance function in exactly that way. Moreover, there is a corollary effect at work here directly pertinent to any concern with the welfare of the least advantaged. For although a rising tide lifts all boats, it does not benefit all boats equally: the boats benefited the most are those that were stuck on sandbars. So crafting social policy to raise everyone at least to a certain level of adequacy—as defined by the needs and social goals of the society—will benefit those on the bottom the most.

AFTERWORD

It is, practically speaking, extremely important, moreover, that social welfare policies geared to universal provision are much more appealing to the American electorate, hence much more likely to be enacted. And the reason that these policies are more popular is not simply that their benefits are more broadly distributed. The superior attractiveness of these policies by contrast to means-tested ones is a function not merely of the electorate's self-interest but also of their values and moral intuitions. The underlying principles and rationale are much more important here than many seem to appreciate. The fairness-as-equality arguments invoked on behalf of means-tested welfare programs stand at odds with widely held beliefs about moral agency and personal responsibility. The rationale for public subsidy of certain basic resources essential for people to function as democratic citizens, in contrast, relies upon a more complex set of values that are more widely accepted.

There are at least five major strands of the rationale for redistributive programs such as Social Security, publicly funded education, and universally accessible health care. The first is simple compassion toward the needy: a humane people helps those who are down on their luck and in bad circumstances. Second, a broad sense of fairness is indeed a factor, but this is based more upon a sensed obligation to provide what Whitman called "a fair chance for growth" to every member of society than it is upon some sense that all should, at the end of the day, have relatively equal shares of primary goods.[2] This sense of social obligation is especially pertinent, moreover, to remedying the undeserved inequality of life chances among children, who clearly bear no responsibility for their family circumstances. This is where Rawls's notion of redress seems quite appropriate and thus garners wide support. Third is something that Michael Walzer claims can be found in almost all societies: namely, a concern for making accessible to all members of the society those goods necessary for them actually to participate in the life of the society—for them to be real members and not de facto aliens excluded for financial reasons.[3] A fourth justification for universal provision of some social resources is essentially prudential: it is a practical imperative for any society that wants to be successful (stable, strong, productive, reasonably harmonious, etc.) to create a competent citizenry—in both a political and an economic sense. And finally, there is the fundamental principled dedication of a democratic people to creating a social setting in which everyone can flourish, have a good life, and so become one of Whitman's "separate and complete subjects for freedom." So although self-interest is surely a factor in the superior appeal of a universal communal provision strategy, the availability on its behalf of a complex and robust set of justificatory moral principles and social values is also a large part of the story.

Moreover, this robust set of principles and goals has the capacity to sustain support for an agenda of quite substantial social investment in human capital that simultaneously will produce greater upward social mobility among historically disadvantaged sectors of the population. Certainly the historical evidentiary base for comparing the relative efficacy vis-à-vis social equality of universal and means-tested strategies favors the former. Correlation is not causation, of course, and the relevant causal forces are many and complex. But it is nonetheless worth noting that what has been called the "Great Compression" in American income distribution occurred under the aegis of the public philosophies of Progressivism and the New Deal: between 1919 and 1947, real manufacturing wages went up 70 percent while the real income of the top 1 percent remained constant. The "Great Advance" in which all classes roughly doubled their real incomes came between 1947 and 1973. And the era of the "Gilded Age Revisited" from 1980 up to the present, in which real manufacturing wages were flat while the real incomes of the top 1 percent rose by some 235 percent, has been the period in which the focus upon distributive justice has been dominant within the house of liberalism. The point here is not that the ascendance of social justice–centered liberalism was causally responsible for the recent resurgence of income inequality. Instead, the point is that universal provision programs and arguments were at the very least compatible with—and presumably played some causal role within—achieving greater social equality, whereas constant pleadings for social justice have seemingly had little capacity to attenuate significant backsliding on this front.

A second major objection to my proposals is that they are ipso facto "oppressive" in practice. This complaint centers on my reaffirmation of the traditional teleological democratic goal of self-realization—my endorsement of what Whitman called "the grand experiment of development, whose end may be the forming of a full-grown man or woman."[4] The burden of the complaint runs like this. The goal of self-realization, it may be said, depends upon the acceptance of a specific comprehensive conception of a humanly good life. We live, however, in a society in which people subscribe to many different conceptions of the human good. A democratic society could therefore dedicate itself to an experiment in development, runs this complaint, only by privileging some people's idea of the good life over others'. And these others will consequently not be treated equally and will in practice be improperly constrained in their efforts to live out their own plans of life. In short, a democratic society cannot seek the "self-realization" of its citizens without violating its own obligation to accord all its citizens equal liberty. Hence, the argument and attendant objection go, a perfectionist liberalism must be oppressive toward some members of the society, whereas a liberalism devoted to social justice will not suffer from the same disabling flaw.

There are several strands to my response to this objection. The first is that social justice liberalism, contrary to its protestations and self-presentation, enacts its own oppressions. Second, the form of perfectionism I endorse and the accounts of self-realization espoused by Whitman and Dewey are not oppressive in the way and to the extent alleged. Third, the privileging of some ways of life over others is morally defensible on liberal grounds.

First, tu quoque: social justice liberalism enacts its own oppressions and exclusions. Rawls does assert his determination to do what he terms applying the principle of toleration to arguments about the good life. And he counsels, as a consequence, what he calls a "method of avoidance" when it comes to entering into such debates. But whenever the validity or the priority of what he terms his "political virtues" is challenged, he acknowledges that his underlying presuppositions about these elements of the good life must—however reluctantly—be acknowledged and insisted upon. As Rawls puts it: "In affirming a political conception of justice we may eventually have to assert at least certain aspects of our own comprehensive religious or philosophical doctrine . . . and hence to maintain the kind of thing we had hoped to avoid."[5] Moreover, "even though political liberalism seeks common ground and is neutral in aim, it is important to emphasize that it may still affirm the superiority of certain forms of moral character and encourage certain moral virtues."[6] My point here is not that these reluctant affirmations are necessarily inappropriate; my point, instead, is that they reveal the stance of studied and principled impartiality vis-à-vis criteria of the good life and moral character to be a bit of a sham. This is a show of alleged neutrality vis-à-vis the good put on for (perhaps admirable) political reasons: to express tolerance and seek consensus. Whenever push comes to shove, however, the gun is there beneath the table, as it were, ready to be pulled out and used—accompanied perhaps by expressions of regret that "there is no social world without loss."[7] In short, despite its ostensive stance of principled neutrality vis-à-vis conceptions of the good, social justice liberalism has and requires its own commitments in this regard—along with all the bias, privileging, and "oppression" that might come with these commitments.

The second and more important response to the objection that a liberal and democratic perfectionism of the sort found in people such as Mill, Whitman, and Dewey requires the oppressive establishment (the First Amendment term is here quite apt in characterizing the alleged impropriety) of a contestable comprehensive conception of the good life is that no one who reads "Democratic Vistas" or the famous third chapter of *On Liberty* could possibly levy that charge unless they were in the grip of some highly misleading form of academic scholasticism. These classic perfectionist texts, these paeans to the centrality of personal development and self-determination to democratic purposes, are also and at the same time classic invocations and celebrations of the plurality and great variety of fulfilling and morally legitimate modes of life. Their authors were among the first to "celebrate diversity" as a valuable by-product and intrinsic good—an outcome to be welcomed and prized as one of the benefits consequent to the self-realization of all the people. In Mill's account, the "blend" of the "ideal of self-development" and the "ideal of self-government" allows and encourages people to "cultivate . . . all that is individual in themselves." And the happy result is certainly not the production, much less the imposition, of some "uniform" comprehensive way of life but rather the opposite: "By the same process human life also becomes rich, diversified, and animating. . . . There is a greater fullness of life . . . [and] human beings become a noble and beautiful object of contemplation."[8] In like manner, Whitman's vision of "perfect personalities" is certainly not the endorsement of what he derogates as some "stereotyped éclat of history or poems." It instead eagerly anticipates the emergence of a "rich, luxuriant, varied personalism," a social platform providing "full play for human nature to expand itself in numberless and even conflicting directions" and producing "a large variety of character . . . freely branching and blossoming in each individual."[9] There is nothing here and nothing in the kind of democratic perfectionism I endorse remotely resembling some single, determinate, all-encompassing conception of the good human life—some all-prescribing moral or religious catechism that embodies the defining features of the term *comprehensive*. It is true that the openness, multiplicity, and permissiveness of democratic perfectionism's conception of good human lives are not infinite. Resident within the notion of self-realization is a conception of democratic character or democratic civic virtue that is not entirely up for grabs. But this conception of democratic character is simply a different version of what Rawls acknowledges as a crucial touchstone of his own democratic theory: a "normative [and] . . . political conception of the person . . . suitable for the basis of democratic citizenship."[10]

In short, the version of perfectionism found in Mill and Whitman that I am endorsing here is itself "political not comprehensive." Just like Rawls's "freestanding" ideal conception of the kind of personhood commensurate with the demands of democratic citizenship, so the content and limits of a democratic perfectionism are established by reference to its own understanding of what Rawls calls "political virtues." In logical form and social function, these two conceptions of normative democratic personhood are identical. Both embody their respective understandings of the capacities and dispositions necessary for people to function as competent citizens who abide by the behavioral norms essential to the successful functioning of democratic governance. The differences between the character ideals of social justice liberalism and those of a populist perfectionist liberalism are substantive, then, and not a matter of their formal status. The one conception of democratic persons encompasses those capacities and dispositions requisite for citizens of a political regime organized about liberal principles of distributive justice. The other conception encompasses those capacities and dispositions required of citizens of a political regime devoted to self-governance by moral equals seeking self-realization consonant with their various plans of life. These two normative conceptions of democratic character and its constituent political virtues, in fact, actually overlap considerably. The political virtues specified by Rawls include civility, tolerance, reasonableness, and a sense of fairness.[11] The political virtues of democratic populist perfectionism include each of those virtues, with one major distinction: the populist perfectionist reading of the virtues of reasonableness and sense of fairness does not include the supposition that possessing these attributes compels their possessors to endorse the specific range of distributive principles and policies insisted upon by Rawls.[12]

AFTERWORD

In addition to the amended particulars of Rawls's political virtues, the populist perfectionist ideal of democratic character would include those capacities requisite for participation in self-rule. It is not enough, on this account, to satisfy the norms of ideal democratic citizenship simply by being tolerant, civil, and willing to cooperate with others on fair terms. Instead, as people who rule and are ruled in turn, democratic citizens on this conception must develop the moral and intellectual capacities necessary for the performance of these roles. Ben Barber's conception of democracy in its perfection being an "aristocracy of everyone" is more than a nice rhetorical phrase: good democratic citizens must embody to some significant extent the virtues of Aristotelian phronimoi. They must be people capable of good practical judgment, able to deliberate about the common good and the best means thereto. These same capacities for contributing to what Habermas calls "rational will formation," it may be added, are also necessary for democratic citizens to conceive and pursue their own personal plans of life, their self-realization as guided by what John Tomasi has referred to as their "compass concepts"—that is, "those thicker, more identity-dependent concepts" by which individual liberal citizens steer "their lives as whole persons and not merely as members of the body politic."[13] Being self-governing in this larger transpolitical sense is one of the great privileges accorded to their citizens by liberal democratic societies, and it is therefore entirely appropriate for those societies to seek to equip their citizens to enjoy that privilege and to meet its attendant responsibilities. If this be oppression, we should all be happy to make the most of it.

The third major objection to my argument targets its populist component. Don't you ignore the great problems and dangers of popular self-rule? Doesn't the best evidence suggest that "the people" aren't really up to the job? And, particularly against the backdrop of those doubts, why should we worry so much about self-rule, anyway: don't substantive norms of democratic justice trump procedural norms of democratic legitimacy, since the latter are ultimately merely instrumental to achieving the former?

These objections are grounded, first, in reasonable worries about the competency of the demos to govern competently and, second, in a conviction that presumptively valid standards of social justice are ascertainable independent of the expressed will and judgment of the people. The proper responses to them are in part practical, in part principled, and in part empirical.

The practical rejoinder is: that horse is already out of the barn. We have now definitively and irrevocably institutionalized one-person, one-vote popular sovereignty, and liberals need to learn to live with it respectfully even if not to genuflect supinely before it. It is both self-defeating and self-delegitimizing for liberals to suppose on the basis of their devotion to certain substantive principles that they can ignore and circumvent the wishes of the democratic electorate whenever they consider those wishes benighted.

The principled rejoinders are based on a rejection of the premise that procedural norms are merely instrumental means to independently predetermined substantive outcomes. Procedural norms of democratic legitimacy are not purely instrumental to their outcomes but are instead grounded in their own moral imperatives: specifically, the moral imperatives of civic equality and self-determination. Universal suffrage and the principle of one person, one vote are not simply arrangements devised to achieve the right outcome by some independent objective standard, whether that be natural law, common good, or distributive justice. Universal suffrage and the one-person, one-vote rule are mandated by the postulate that the lives of all citizens are of equal worth and that, correlatively, all have the right to be treated as equal. They are practices also derived directly from the other democratic moral postulate that all citizens are entitled to determine their own destinies and are correlatively entitled to what William Godwin called the right of private judgment—the right to make up their own minds and to choose accordingly what principles and policies to support. Norms of democratic procedural legitimacy, in short, are not "means only" but embody and give effect to the core democratic categorical imperatives of liberty and equality.

AFTERWORD

Moreover, to the extent that democratic procedures are instrumentally valuable, the goods to which they are instrumental are not limited to the substantive content of the decisions they produce. We can always hope that the results of democratic procedures of self-rule will be substantively good ones. But it is important to emphasize what might be called the collateral substantive democratic goods generated by adherence to canons of democratic procedure. The first of these collateral goods is liberty itself. Justice Felix Frankfurter reminded us of the causal relationship here in his famous observation that "the history of liberty is the history of procedure." That is to say, liberty is not only an abstract theoretical principle from which appropriate democratic procedures are derived; in the sense of real and concrete embodied freedom, liberty is in practice created and experienced by the institution of these procedural norms in the actual conduct of law and politics. A second important by-product of fidelity to democratic procedural norms is political legitimacy. Once people have accepted and assimilated the core liberal values of equality and autonomy, the abrogation or circumvention of procedural norms of democratic self-rule compromises the acceptance as morally proper of any outcomes so generated. And when this abrogation or circumvention becomes systemic and continues over time, the unhappy consequence is what Jürgen Habermas has explored under the rubric of "legitimacy crisis." Finally, as Mill famously argued in his classic defense of representative government, participation in the tasks of self-governance requires people to expand their cognitive universe and to stretch their moral imagination. Abiding by the procedural norms of democratic legitimacy therefore pushes people to become competent democratic citizens and in the process to develop some of their most important human capacities.

The empirical objection to the insistence upon recovering popular self-rule as an important liberal purpose is that the democratic populace is simply not up to the job. Say what you will about government by consent and popular sovereignty, this objection goes, the warrants for political rule have always been wisdom and virtue, and today's democratic populace possesses neither of these in sufficient measure. Those who govern must first possess certain intellectual or cognitive capacities: they must be knowledgeable about politically relevant facts, must have good judgment, and must also be committed to the animating values and norms of a democratic society. Our studies of voting behavior, public opinion, and political attitudes, however, say liberals skeptical of populist norms of self-rule, reveal disabling failures and inadequacies in all these respects among the democratic public. The public's political knowledge seems woefully thin and their understanding of and dedication to democratic values alarmingly weak.

These are certainly reasonable worries. Even Walt Whitman, in the midst of his celebration of popular democratic governance, conceded what he called "the appalling dangers of universal suffrage." Anyone familiar with the dismal level of politically relevant knowledge among the American populace cannot escape concerns about the public's core civic competency and capacity to render the political judgments they have to make. The question is whether these concerns justify abandoning ideals of self-rule to fall back upon more tutelary or elitist conceptions of good governance. And here, I would insist that the undeniable limitations and occasional derangements of what Condorcet called the tribunal of public opinion are not so great as to justify liberal apostasy from Lincoln's ringing endorsement of government of, by, and for the people.

In the first place, it is a mistake to imagine that the ideal of democratic self-rule is contingent upon the sovereign public's possession of the kinds of knowledge requisite for elected officials and administrators who actually run the government. It is not the role of the sovereign public to make specific decisions about policy matters requiring expertise beyond its ken. We cannot expect and need not demand, for example, that the voting public have the kind of grasp of the history and political sociology of the Middle East required of our diplomatic corps or the understanding of capital flows and exchange rates required of those who manage federal monetary policy. The public's role in democratic self-rule is essentially twofold. First, the people must possess the capacities needed to run the constitutive social enterprises of a democratic society: the professions, the commercial enterprises, the educational institutions, the organizations of civil society, and so on. And second, they must be able to function in the role of, in effect, the board of trustees of the government, holding an ultimate fiduciary power over it and exercising a broad and general oversight over the political leaders they select and hold to judgment.

Almost all of us have our moments of serious doubt about the competence and rationality of the American public in these respects. And reasonable people may differ on exactly how high the bar should be set. Nonetheless, despite their fallibility and at times seeming perversity, the preponderance of evidence suggests that present-day Americans have at least the minimal competency needed not only to organize and administer the core institutions of civil society but also to perform the political oversight functions to which they are entitled by the fundamental norms of democratic consent. The public may exhibit rather low levels of factual knowledge about government and world affairs, and it needs to be one of our educational priorities to make significant improvements in this respect, but the best recent inquiries into citizens' political decisionmaking suggest that they use a variety of sources, cues, and informational shortcuts to render judgments that broadly conform to plausible perceptions of officeholders' performance and broadly cohere with their own values and policy preferences.[14] Moreover, political scientists who take the trouble to conduct in-depth interviews with selected members of the public on important political issues such as social justice, environmental policy, and the role of religion in public life have found that the people they interview generally exhibit passable levels of deliberative competency.[15]

In regard to worry about the fragility of the average American's devotion to civil liberties and core democratic values, its principal evidentiary basis is the literature canvassed in chapter 3 that led to John DiIulio's remark about learning as a graduate student that "many intellectuals had it in for us." "Us" here referred to "America's white working class," which was in this literature, DiIulio complained, depicted as composed of "racists and crypto-fascists."[16] Specifically and less tendentiously, this is the social science literature that investigates the public's views and attitudes about toleration, race, and authority. This literature does not speak with unanimity, by any means. But much of it offers an unflattering portrait of the American public as discouragingly intolerant, racially biased, and authoritarian in disposition rather than as genuinely dedicated to respecting everyone's civil liberties and democratic rights.

I did not, like John DiIulio, grow up in a working-class neighborhood in Philadelphia. With him, however, I share a considerable skepticism about the public opinion literature that has been used to justify the depiction of working-class and middle-class Americans as intolerant, racist, and authoritarian. This literature and the unflattering construction of the American public based upon it suffer from both external and internal problems. The external problem is that its claims are in tension with much prima facie evidence to the contrary. The internal problems are technical weaknesses within the literature itself.

How, for example, do depictions of the American public as inclined toward bigotry and intolerance square with Alan Wolfe's conclusion at the end of extensive interviews of people living in middle-income communities all across the country that his respondents "prefer to sit in the seat of nonjudgment. Reluctant to impose their values on others, they are committed to tolerance to such an extent that they have either given up finding timeless morality or would be unwilling to bring its principles down to earth if, by chance, they came across it." Moreover, reports Wolfe, "when we asked people how they felt about taking special steps to recognize and celebrate specific cultures, most of those with whom we spoke put aside their opposition to bilingualism and

AFTERWORD

indicated strong sympathy with multiculturalism."[17] How convincingly can the construction of the American working class and lower middle class as authoritarian cohere with the deeply individualist, libertarian, and even antinomian strains evident in the culture, personal style, and social practices of so many who fall into those demographic categories? And exactly what kinds and extent of racism are consistent with the massive rollback within a few decades of a deeply entrenched system of racial apartheid and with the widespread veneration not only of African American athletes and entertainers but also of public figures such as Colin Powell and Barack Obama?

The literature that purports to find widespread intolerance, racist attitudes, and authoritarian dispositions among the American public, moreover, is internally uneven and problematic. These problems are multiple and cumulative, incorporating difficulties that are epistemic, evidentiary, hermeneutic, conceptual, and normative. It would take a whole other volume to lay out all the relevant particulars here, but perhaps a few comments and examples can provide some sense of the problems I have in mind.

In the first place, the relevant data are systematically elusive, ascertainable only indirectly and through inherently speculative attributions. "Attitudes" are not directly observable events or behaviors. Their existence and content can only be inferred from purportedly relevant indicators. Those who try to ascertain and characterize other people's attitudes, therefore, face the same epistemic hurdles confronting researchers who seek to ascertain other internal phenomena, such as intensities of preference. And as Robert Dahl properly acknowledges, when we try to compare intensities of preference, "We do so by postulating certain types of overt behavior as crude measures of intensities. But we can do no more than postulate. We can never directly observe sensate intensities of want or preference; hence we can never know what the overt behavior we use as a measure really measures, unless it measures other kinds of overt behavior."[18] In the relevant public opinion studies of allegedly intolerant, racist, and authoritarian attitudes, the overt behaviors that are in Dahl's terms "postulated" as "crude measures" of the alleged psychic dispositions are verbal responses to survey questions. The "overt behaviors" are thus statements rather than actions. And that is not adventitious, for the researchers are seeking to ascertain mental states that may not be reflected in actual behavior. (Even in the 1960s-era study where many Tallahassee respondents said that an African American should not be allowed to run for mayor, for example, no one actually tried to interfere with the campaigns of a couple of such candidates who in fact stepped forward.) What concerns and worries these researchers is what their respondents might want to do or think should be done rather than what they actually have done.

Serious hermeneutic problems surround the questions and responses to the survey questions devised to try to smoke out the relevant attitudinal data, however. Before we could claim to know with any reliability what so-called attitudes stand revealed by respondents' answers, we must know very clearly exactly what these verbal responses mean. But the questions posed are almost invariably open to multiple plausible interpretations, and hence any inferences drawn from responses to them are hazardous at best.[19]

The conceptual and normative problems within this literature overlap. Racism, intolerance, and authoritarianism are presumptively bad and undemocratic, but it is not always clear what the definitions of these sins are and hence what opinions, actions, or attitudes are to count as instances. For example, must one believe all ways of life to be morally equivalent in order to be tolerant? Or is it being tolerant to respect the civil rights and liberties of people one considers mistaken in belief and/or immoral in behavior? If intolerance consists of a willingness to abridge people's civil liberties or democratic rights, what exactly is the scope of these liberties and rights assumed to be? Is the content of what shall count as such a liberty or right not itself to some extent a matter of legitimate disagreement and contestation in democratic politics?[20] Clearly, whether or not a particular person or group gets designated as intolerant depends greatly upon the answers given to these questions. Researchers who equate tolerance with acceptance and who begin with an expansive set of rights and liberties they see as uncontestably definitive of democratic norms, then, predictably depict their respondents as much more intolerant than researchers who define toleration by forbearance rather than acceptance and who define democratic rights and liberties more circumspectly. The danger with using the more expansive standards for what counts as tolerance is that, in the words of Paul Sniderman et al., the result is "to equate the liberal position on an array of issues with support for democratic rights, . . . to collapse the distinction between conceptions of justice and of rights, and to represent commitment to democratic liberties as a distinctive virtue of the left. But ideology and support for democracy are not the same thing, and it does no good, analytically or normatively, to confuse the one with the other."[21] The associated and additional consequence is that the American public becomes depicted as considerably less committed to core democratic norms, including the respect for standard civil rights and liberties, than it in fact is.

Similar contestable judgments regarding important conceptual issues have likewise contributed to constructions of the American populace as incorrigibly racist.[22] Moral passion on behalf of overcoming social inequalities produced by America's long legacy of racial oppression is admirable. And ascertaining the motives and attitudes that shape people's policy preferences is intrinsically difficult and somewhat speculative. Between them, however, these traits have helped produce a literature that often falls prey to the temptation to ascribe unworthy motives to those who seemingly stand in the way of what appear to the researchers as morally impeccable goals. Opposition to busing and affirmative action policies becomes construed as ipso facto evidence of racial animus, and some underspecified form of "conjunction" between "traditional values" (such as individualism and the work ethic) and agreement with propositions such as "It is wrong to set up quotas to admit black students to college who don't meet the usual standards" is taken as grounds for labeling survey respondents as racists.[23]

Finally, it is clear that much of the literature on the "authoritarian personality"—and certainly, this is true of the seminal book that created this psychological construct—tends to operate upon the normative assumption that any predisposition to accept the pronouncements or to comply with the orders of authority figures is problematic and possibly even protofascist. The implicit assumption seems to be that Henry David Thoreau provided the definitive conception of the proper attitude toward authority in a democratic society in his essay *On Civil Disobedience*, whereas, in contrast, Abraham Lincoln's plea in his Lyceum Address that "every lover of liberty . . . swear by the blood of the Revolution never to violate in the least particular the laws of the country" would earn him points on the F-scale—never mind that his dual concern was to insist upon the integrity of democratic rule of law and to protect people such as Thoreau from getting lynched. It is worth insisting, then, that the most rational and morally appropriate predisposition toward authority figures in a democratic society is not necessarily captured by "Question Authority" bumper stickers. In a reasonably well-ordered democratic society—one whose laws arise from genuinely democratic procedures and one whose constitutive social enterprises are well governed—both the prudent and the morally appropriate stance toward admonitions and pronouncements of duly constituted authorities arguably is not one of blind obedience but nonetheless one of holding a (rebuttable) presumption on behalf of acquiescence. It is a sign of neither rationality nor democratic civic virtue to treat a police officer's signal to stop or the collective judgment of professional biologists about evolution as entitled to no more respect than advice or opinion from some random person on the street. With that in mind, it makes little sense, pari passu, to treat any expressed presumption of respect for authority among respondents to sample survey instruments as an indicator that those respondents would

AFTERWORD

be easy prey for some Führer wannabe who might appear on the political horizon.

In the context of this book's concerns, the reason for subjecting the literature on public opinion and political psychology to skeptical interrogation is that this body of work was produced and became influential during the time frame within which the transformation of liberal public philosophy took place. This chronological coincidence was not entirely adventitious. Instead, the generally denigrative picture of the political knowledge, values, and motivations of the American public it generated wound up serving as evidentiary grounds for the shift in core goals and political strategies characteristic of the new version of liberal public philosophy. Specifically, the unflattering depiction of the public's low level of political competency and awareness and its tenuous commitment to liberal values played a significant role, sometimes tacitly and sometimes quite explicitly, in liberalism's antipopulist turn—its backing away from its traditional identification with and dedication to the goal of democratic self-rule. And it offered at the same time both moral and prudential warrant for liberalism's juridical-bureaucratic turn—its embrace of strategies to circumvent public judgment rather than to inform and persuade it in the service of forming successful electoral coalitions. It is, therefore, entirely appropriate and even mandatory to hold this literature to very high standards of proof. As Sniderman and Philip Tetlock rightly observe: "Labeling an individual or viewpoint as racist is a serious matter."[24] It is likewise a serious matter to label people as intolerant or as having a psyche that suits them better to be fascist subjects than to be democratic citizens. And it is likewise a very serious matter to make empirical claims whose "value slope," to borrow Charles Taylor's relevant phrase, serves to undermine important democratic norms such as that of popular sovereignty.

So the burden of my skeptical remarks upon the literature on the American public's attitudes toward race, toleration, and authority is that the unflattering and worrisome generalizations it has created are in considerable measure distorted and misleading.

It is no doubt true that the modal positions of the American public on questions of race, tolerance, and authority are not identical to those commonly held by most academics and liberal elites. For example, the general public is more likely to construe toleration as respect for the rights of people whose opinions you reject and whose behavior you may deplore—and not as the affirmation and recognition of all ways of life other than one's own. The public is more likely to think that racial propriety consists of nondiscrimination—and not in the institution of laws and policies designed to produce greater socioeconomic parity among different racial and ethnic populations. And the general public is more inclined than academics and liberal elites to believe that they are obligated to comply with the mandates of duly constituted public authority. But it is by no means clear that these disparities place the public's values and attitudes beyond the pale of democratic norms.

It should nonetheless certainly be not only acknowledged but also emphasized that the creation of a competent democratic public represents a perennial and difficult challenge facing every democratic society in the world. Every live birth amounts, in effect, to the admission of a political barbarian into the citizen body: no infants arrive in the world predisposed toward democratic values, and they all arrive incompetent, unreasonable, and intolerant of anything and anybody disruptive of their personal comfort. This challenge has been very imperfectly met by our own society. But even if perusal of the morning newspaper or electoral decisions that seem obtuse may occasion democratic despair, not to mention outright misanthropy, no sober assessment of the competency and values of today's democratic publics both here and abroad provides compelling grounds for abandonment of the fundamental principled democratic goal of popular self-rule. Indeed, we might profitably worry somewhat less about the alleged incompetency and perversity of the general public and worry a good deal more about the failure of today's democratic elites to perform their own roles in democratic governance honorably and competently. As Anna Greenberg recently wrote: "It is

AFTERWORD

ironic that many of the pathologies of the mass public lamented by policymakers and opinion leaders are, in part, a result of the incentives elites have to obscure their positions, their efforts to shape opinion to their own ends, and the standard measurement techniques they employ. We worry that our democracy rests on a shaky foundation of collective ignorance, apathy, and cynicism, while ignoring the ways our representatives and political operatives are complicit in creating such a state of affairs."[25]

For members of the sovereign public to perform their responsibilities in democratic governance adequately, they need the help of their political leaders. Among other things, democratic political elites need to treat the public and its problems with respect by conducting their public discourse at a level appropriate to the gravity of public decisionmaking. It is particularly depressing in that context, then, to read the report that

> during the 2000 debates George W. Bush and Al Gore spoke, respectively, at a sixth and a high-seventh grade level. (The Lincoln-Douglas debates were carried out at about a twelfth-grade level.) . . . As disheartening as this sounds (it's safe to say that most Americans would prefer leaders with post-pubescent rhetorical skills), the voters themselves inspire more confidence. At the third debate in 2000, in a "town meeting" setting where Bush and Gore responded to questions from the audience, the candidates logged their lowest scores of the campaign (low sixth grade for Bush, high seventh grade for Gore). The audience's questions, in contrast, were at the ninth-grade level on average.[26]

As political sovereigns, a democracy's people have the right to expect their leaders to inform them of the facts relevant to public decisions, to anticipate and alert them to public challenges and problems on the horizon, to develop and explain the range of viable policies calculated to meet these challenges, to focus upon general interests and long-term solutions rather than upon particular interests and temporizing expedients, and to appeal to the public's better motives and higher aspirations rather than seeking to promote their purposes by engaging in what Henry Adams called "the mobilization of hatreds." If these indeed count among the responsibilities of democratic leadership, I leave it to the judgment of the reader whether current derangements in American politics should be laid mostly at the public's door.

To summarize, the three most substantial worries about my counsel that American liberalism rediscover its historical dedication to "populist" self-rule and "perfectionist" universal self-realization and my responses to them are these. Query: What about social justice? Answer: The important and valid social ideals and aspirations that drive liberalism's concern with social justice will be safeguarded and more successfully pursued as corollaries and requisites of self-rule and self-realization—without the attendant problems created by the twin suppositions that liberalism is all about distributive fairness and that fairness and social equality are coterminous. Query: Doesn't endorsing self-realization as a central liberal purpose require the illegitimate imposition of a particular comprehensive conception of the human good? Answer: No. Liberal perfectionism is receptive to a riotous plentitude of ways of life its citizens find fulfilling, subject only to the insistence that these ways of life be compatible with the requirements of democratic citizenship. Question: Don't the public's incapacities and shortcomings make a principled dedication to democratic self-rule dangerous? Answer: Yes. The dangers are real, even "appalling," to recall Whitman's own characterization. We have, however, no real alternative to living with these dangers. Moreover, the principles behind democratic self-rule—that government derives its legitimate powers from consent and that all are created equal—are unassailable, and the collateral benefits are very important. The only proper liberal strategy, therefore, is not to imagine that the will and judgment of the people—such as it may be—can be circumvented by judicial fiat or by bureaucratic legerdemain when we don't like it. Instead, that strategy

AFTERWORD

has to be to minimize the dangers by improving the competency of the democratic public and by cultivating leaders who don't try to trade upon public ignorance.

TWO COMPARISONS

Finally, because recent arguments of Michael Sandel and Richard Rorty exhibit certain similarities to arguments I have made in this book and because some readers have wondered where I differ with them, let me state as succinctly as possible what I see as the major agreements and disagreements between their views and mine. The relevant texts here are Sandel's *Liberalism and the Limits of Justice* and *Democracy's Discontent* and Rorty's *Achieving Our Country*.[27] In both cases, I concur in part but also dissent in part.

Take Sandel first. I have always considered *Liberalism and Limits of Justice* to be an insightful and ingenious excavation of the underlying presuppositions about human selfhood that seem necessary to sustain Rawls's accounts of the relationship between the right and the good and his construction of the original position. I am sympathetic to Sandel's critical claim that it would be difficult to imagine that these Rawlsian subjects of justice would, given the accounts of community and agency involved, be inclined to share one another's fate in the way Rawls's principles of justice demand. Moreover, I believe that the central features of Sandel's analysis and critique largely survive Rawls's disavowal of dependence upon any specific metaphysic and his hermeneutic turn to political liberalism: that is, Sandel's concerns remain pertinent to Rawls's "freestanding normative conception" of democratic persons. In short, I find the transcendental analysis and critical contentions of Sandel's first book generally persuasive, even if I find somewhat frustrating the relative absence there of a concrete sense of what Sandel believes to be the implications of his argument for liberal practices, policies, or institutions.

My disagreements with Sandel begin to mount when he moves to remedy this silence regarding the implications of his argument in *Democracy's Discontent*. I agree with his argument there that contemporary American liberal public philosophy has largely abandoned the political economy of citizenship that had a civic republican provenance and was an important liberal ideal up to and through the New Deal. I also concur with his view that this abandonment represents a significant loss—a concurrence reflected in my inclusion of a neorepublican political economy within my own model social agenda. I find somewhat unconvincing, however, Sandel's attempt to explain what he believes was responsible for the changes he sees and deplores. And because his prescriptions are related to these critical and diagnostic claims, I also disagree with some of the recommendations he offers regarding how we ought to deal with these problems.

Sandel attributes the move away from a political economy of republican citizenship principally to two causes: the triumph of Keynesian economics and the growth of a constitutional jurisprudence devoted to the expansion of personal civil liberties and to state neutrality about conceptions of the human good—what he calls a jurisprudence of "the procedural republic." This argument I find eccentric, both in the sense of being odd and in the sense of being off target. Take first the claim about the role of Keynesian economics in this story. Sandel construes Keynesian economics as complicit in the rejection of an economy of citizenship because of Keynes's insistence that "it is important to develop a high-consumption economy so that we can achieve full employment." On the basis of that quotation, Sandel attributes to Keynes the view "that consumption is the sole end of all economics activity"—an insistence he sees as "counter to one of the main assumptions of republican political thought" regarding the role of economic activity in producing conditions conducive to self-rule.[28] But the inference Sandel draws regarding the larger implications for social goals allegedly resident within Keynes's analysis of the requisites

AFTERWORD

for sustaining full employment in an advanced economy seems to me a non sequitur: Keynes was undertaking to make no such general claim about confining social purposes or economic arrangements to the promotion of unconstrained consumerism, and no such claim is necessarily implicit in what he said. Sandel's causal and critical argument here amounts to a political version of what philosophers call a category mistake—that is, a conflation of and therefore a confusion regarding logically distinct issues. Keynes's question is not "What are the social purposes of economic activity?" It is "What are the conditions necessary for maintaining full employment?" His general analysis of employment equilibria and his recommendations for macroeconomic policies needed to deal with the potentially damaging consequences of phenomena such as liquidity preference and planned savings/planned investment time lags seem to me logically discrete from and irrelevant to the norms and concerns that inform a political economy of citizenship. One can, in short, simultaneously endorse Keynesian macroeconomics and a republican political economy without contradiction.[29]

Sandel's critique of constitutional jurisprudence in the area of civil liberties is, to my mind, equally unconvincing. He tells us that, jurisprudentially speaking, "the procedural republic"—that is, a rights-based and state neutrality (vis-à-vis conceptions of the good life) form of liberal political association—arrived about 1943 and has continued to develop and expand unabated to the present day.[30] He critically scrutinizes a long line of judicial opinions from *West Virginia v. Barnette*[31] to *Bowers v. Hardwick*[32] to substantiate his related claim that this important area of constitutional jurisprudence incorporates and depends upon the conception of the person "as a freely choosing unencumbered self" that he criticized in his first book.[33] Finally, although at times he seems more concerned about the spread of this constitutional logic into the larger political culture than about its effect on the content of civil liberties law per se,[34] Sandel suggests that a better constitutional logic of civil liberties would be based not on the notion of a sphere of free choice open to autonomous selves but instead upon the Court's and hence the state's explicit recognition and affirmation of what it deems to be "important human goods."[35] To provide a specific example of what this abstract claim would mean in practice and in law, Sandel would prefer that a constitutional proscription of state attempts to criminalize and interfere with homosexual relations not be based upon the "voluntarist" principle "that people should be free to choose their intimate associations for themselves" but instead upon an explicit "substantive" legal affirmation of the "virtues" of homosexual intimacy and the "important human goods" realized therein.[36]

My views on these matters diverge from those of Sandel both hermeneutically and normatively in the following ways. First, regardless of occasional rhetorical flourishes that may appear in judicial dicta, what the Court has been doing in the civil liberties decisions that Sandel examines and criticizes is not, in my view, the institutionalization of some "new understanding of freedom,"[37] much less the reading into constitutional law of some metaconception of selfhood or of the nature of the human good. In this context, at least, Rawls's protestation about the importance of distinguishing the political from the metaphysical is valid and pertinent. What the Court has in fact been doing in these cases—and quite properly so—is defending the specifically political autonomy of individual democratic citizens to pursue their own conceptions of the humanly good life, doing so by preserving a domain of private action within which individuals are protected against oppressions and legal coercions imposed by the state/majority on the basis of its own views about what a humanly good life consists in.

Normatively, I would also resist Sandel's revisionist suggestions on behalf of bringing the good back into the foundations of constitutional jurisprudence in the area of civil liberties. Instead of seeing it as an improvement, I would regard it as both improper and dangerous for the Court to base its rulings regarding the scope and content of civil liberties upon its own judgments about what is and is not an "important human good." To undertake to do this is improper because it violates fundamental liberal and democratic norms by implicitly depending upon the quasi-Platonic idea that judges are some kind of omnibus moral experts whose putative knowledge of the Good is entitled to trump any contrary views of the larger public. Encouraging such a form of constitutional jurisprudence is dangerous, moreover, because such counsel seems to embody an obliviousness to the old truism that the Court follows the election returns—not only in its decisions in the short run but also in its composition in the longer term. Any belief that a more "substantive" and less "procedural" constitutional jurisprudence would in its content turn out the way Sandel envisions and desires—for example, in institutionalizing "a kind of toleration" that "cultivates a pluralism of mutual appreciation"[38]—depends upon the overly sanguine assumption that the judges' substantive views about good and bad lives will be the same as those of Sandel and his enlightened friends. That seems to me the same kind of delusion of insularity reflected in the famous expression of astonishment by *New York Times* film critic Pauline Kael in 1968 that she couldn't believe that Richard Nixon had won the presidential election because "no one I know voted for him."

Two final general differences between Sandel's views and my own deserve mention here. First, Sandel seems to imply that American liberalism needs to choose between embracing the civic republican liberty of the ancients and the liberal freedom of the moderns. At least he construes the procedural republic he criticizes as an embodiment of the belief that "our liberty depends not on our capacity as citizens to shape the forces that govern our collective destiny but rather on our capacity as persons to choose our values and ends for ourselves."[39] I would argue that our liberty depends upon both our capacity to engage in collective self-rule and our having the capacity and the social latitude to pursue lives of our own choosing. And if Sandel does not intend to reject the latter in favor of the former, he at least, in my view, would tip the balance too far in that direction—as seen in the logic of his revisionist jurisprudence. Second, although Sandel criticized the neo-Kantian philosophical assumptions packed into Rawls's argument for his principles of justice, he never extended that critique to include the content of the difference principle. He seems essentially sympathetic to the latter, wanting not to revise or replace it so much as to reground it philosophically within a neo-Hegelian conception of communally constituted selves and politically within a civic republican formative project. In contrast, I worry a good deal less about problems allegedly produced by assumptions about "socially unsituated" and "antecedently individuated" selves, and more about the naturalistic conception of agency required to defend the moral intuitions informing the high liberal account of social justice and about the destructive impact of both of these upon the principles, the policies, and the political fortunes of American liberalism.

The principal point of tangency between my argument and Richard Rorty's view of American liberalism is our common invocation of Whitman and Dewey as sources of inspiration. I cite them for the ways in which they exemplify the type of populism and perfectionism I want liberalism to recapture; Rorty writes that "Whitman and Dewey gave us all the romance and spiritual uplift we Americans need to go about our public business" and tells the American left that "it should ask the public to consider how the country of Lincoln and Whitman might be achieved."[40] So in seeking to resurrect some of the moral intuitions and social aspirations of "Democratic Vistas," am I merely echoing and seconding what Rorty urged upon us in *Achieving Our Country*? My answer is that I welcome Rorty's eloquent testimony about the perennial vitality of Whitman's and Dewey's democratic hopefulness. But his reading and mine of Whitman, Dewey, and their political visions are not exactly the same. My sense is that Rorty may have been dancing to the right music, but he didn't get the lyrics quite right.

Rorty's reading of Whitman and Dewey is driven by his complaints about the politics of the cultural left (which he sees as "haunted by ubiquitous specters" and as unwarrantedly pessimistic about the possibilities of American democracy) and is constructed through the prism of Rorty's own postmodernist conception of what he calls neopragmatic bourgeois liberalism. That is, he portrays both Whitman and Dewey as championing a democratic society composed of a public sphere devoted to achieving social justice and to the protection of a private sphere with sufficient free space for unbounded aesthetic selves—"strong poets"—to pursue a wide variety of private quests for personal happiness. My own sense is that this interpretation winds up misrepresenting Whitman and Dewey on both sides of the public/private divide because of Rorty's insistence upon seeing them as avatars of himself.

Regarding the public sphere, it seems somewhat eccentric and misleading to maintain as Rorty does that Whitman and Dewey "wanted the struggle for social justice to be the country's animating principle, the nation's soul."[41] The claim is misleading in part simply because the term *social justice* in the context of contemporary deontological liberalism means something both more determinate and more demanding than what Rorty understands it to mean: "the liberation of the weak from the strong" or "decent wages and working conditions and the end of racial prejudice."[42] Whitman and Dewey both, no doubt, would have endorsed social justice in this rather general and limited sense. But neither of them offered a more specific account of distributive justice, and neither made it the centerpiece of his social vision. This is particularly true of Whitman, who spoke often about civic equality and solidarity but rarely if at all about social justice. And this reading of Dewey, as Robert Westbrook points out, seems to ignore altogether what he calls "the communitarian side of Dewey's thinking" and Dewey's depiction of democracy as a "way of life" that "must affect all modes of human association."[43]

On the private side of the ledger, the democratic characters celebrated by Whitman and Dewey were certainly expected to display great diversity in the plans of life they created in order to flourish in their unique personal particularity, but these democratic persons were not conceived as the wholly unbounded selves of postmodernist moral aestheticism. However variegated, they were all to be members of a democratic community and were accordingly expected to exhibit the competencies and to abide by the norms intrinsic to that mode of political association. Whitman expressed this dialectic of freedom and principled constraint in saying things such as "Indirectly, but surely, goodness, virtue, law . . . follow freedom. These, to democracy, are what the keel is to the ship, or saltiness to the ocean." In the same vein, he celebrated "the simple, unsophisticated Conscience, the primary moral element" as an essential "part of any model fit for the future personality of America." He would, he continued, not leave democratic persons morally unbounded but would instead "demand the invariable application to individuality, this day and any day, of that old, ever-true plumb-rule of persons, eras, nations."[44] In similar fashion, the "higher capacities of individuals," the development of which Dewey enshrined as one of the "enduring values" of liberalism, include those competencies and character traits that enable and motivate democratic selves to participate in the process of collective practical reasoning he sees as constitutive of the democratic way of life and democratic decisionmaking. By leaving this essential feature of democratic persons out of the hermeneutically constructed Dewey he appropriates, Rorty exhibits—to cite Robert Westbrook's well-chosen words once more—his "refusal to accept the ethical postulate conjoining self-realization and the social good which was at the heart of Dewey's ethics throughout his career."[45] So even if I am willing, like Westbrook, to "grant Rorty a halfway covenant with Dewey," I would want to insist that a more intact and less gerrymandered Dewey—one that retains some of the features Rorty leaves on his cutting-room floor—is closer to being a populist perfectionist of the sort I favor than he is to being a "postmodernist bourgeois liberal" of the sort Rorty commends to us.

AFTERWORD

ONE FINAL NOTE

When writing about contemporary politics, the world continues to change beneath our feet. I began writing this book during the second presidential term of George W. Bush. I did not then and do not now believe that America is a Center-Right country, even if more of the American public characterizes itself as conservative rather than liberal. But I did worry that the Madisonian electoral coalition of cultural and economic conservatives skillfully cobbled together by Karl Rove and others might well continue regularly to produce electoral victories unless American liberalism could get beyond what I consider its self-inflicted wounds. My hope was to encourage those necessary correctives by helping American liberals take a critical look in the mirror. I was completing my final revisions of the manuscript just as the election of 2008 came to its spellbinding conclusion. The exhilaration of the diverse yet unified crowd that flooded Grant Park as Barack Obama gave his victory speech provided an amazing reminder of and contrast to the conflicts seen there forty years before when competing liberal constituencies did fratricidal battle.

Did that remarkable occasion represent the arrival of the kind of liberal reformation I have advocated here? That seems to me quite impossible to say at this time. One swallow does not make a spring. And "change you can believe in" does not a public philosophy make. But several features of Obama's unexpectedly successful campaign seem to correspond to aspects of the anticipatory sketch of liberal reformation I set out in my final chapter. These include the important strategic role of a younger generation whose political imaginations and reflexes are not driven by perceptions, experiences, and passions from several decades past; the centrality of a political rhetoric of civic agency and self-governance; a policy agenda directed toward the development of social capital; and an electoral map that roughly conformed to the one envisioned in my account of the building of a new liberal majority. Only time will tell. The performance of the new administration will matter a great deal, of course, and as Machiavelli would have insisted, uncontrollable fortune will have its say in the future course of events. Nevertheless, apart from my widely shared dismay at the financial crisis inherited by the incoming administration, I send my complete manuscript off to press in considerably better spirits than when I first put pen to paper. Perhaps the reformation of American liberalism I depict here as a hopeful possibility may be somewhat closer at hand than I thought.

Notes

INTRODUCTION

1. Donald G. Macrae, *Max Weber* (New York: Viking Press, 1974), p. 97.
2. Theodore Roszak, *The Making of a Counter Culture* (Garden City, N.Y.: Doubleday, 1968), p. 137.
3. Ibid., p. 136.
4. Charles Reich, *The Greening of America* (New York: Random House, 1970), p. 342.
5. Ibid., p. 24.
6. Ibid., p. 85.
7. Michael Tomasky, *Left for Dead: The Life, Death, and Possible Resurrection of Progressive Politics in America* (New York: Free Press, 1996), p. 34.
8. Good craftsmanship here means essentially what the Greeks meant by *arete*, excellence in the sense of fittedness to purpose. The two best recent expositors of this norm for social life are Alasdair MacIntyre and Charles Anderson, with their conceptions of "practice" and rational enterprises. See MacIntyre's *After Virtue* (Notre Dame, Ind.: University of Notre Dame Press, 1981) and Anderson's "How to Make a Good Society," in *The Constitution of Good Societies,* ed. Karol Soltan and Stephen Elkin (University Park: Pennsylvania State University Press, 1996), pp. 103–117.
9. Benjamin Barber, *Strong Democracy* (Berkeley: University of California Press, 1984), p. 142.
10. Harry C. Boyte and Nancy N. Kari, "Unsung Heroes," *New Democrat* 9, 4 (July–August 1997): 15–16.
11. See John Tomasi, *Liberalism beyond Justice* (Princeton, N.J.: Princeton University Press, 2001), pp. 111–114. Tomasi acknowledges appropriating this phrase from Samuel Freeman.

CHAPTER 1: MY / TRADITIONAL AMERICAN LIBERALISM

1. Hartz's magnum opus is *The Liberal Tradition in America* (New York: Harcourt, Brace and World, 1955). See also Carl Becker, *The Declaration of Independence* (New York: Vintage Books, 1958).
2. See Bernard Bailyn, *The Ideological Origins of the American Revolution* (Cambridge, Mass.: Harvard University Press, 1967), and J. G. A. Pocock, *The Machiavellian Moment* (Princeton, N.J.: Princeton University Press, 1975). See also Gordon Wood, *The Creation of the American Republic* (Chapel Hill: University of North Carolina Press, 1969).
3. Steven M. Dworetz, *The Unvarnished Doctrine: Locke, Liberalism, and the American Revolution* (Durham, N.C.: Duke University Press, 1990).
4. John Dunn, *The Political Thought of John Locke* (Cambridge: Cambridge University Press, 1969), pp. xi–xii.
5. For useful reflections on the problematic quality of the liberal/republican dichotomy, see Jeffrey Isaac, "Republicanism vs. Liberalism: A Reconsideration," *History of Political Thought* 9, 2 (Summer 1988): 349–377. It is also noteworthy in this context that recent students of political thought who examine the ideas of figures such as Locke, Sydney, and Smith find there a rather promiscuous intermingling of both liberal and republican norms. See, for example, Ruth Grant, *John Locke's Liberalism* (Chicago: University of Chicago Press, 1987); Alan Houston, *Algernon Sydney and the Republican Heritage in England and America* (Princeton, N.J.: Princeton University Press, 1991); Jerry Muller, *Adam Smith in His Time and Ours* (New York: Free Press, 1993).
6. The quoted phrases are from the "Author's Introduction" to *Democracy in America,* trans. Henry Reeve and ed. Richard Heffner (New York: New American Library, 1956), pp. 28–29.
7. Edmund Burke, *Reflections on the Revolution in France* (New York: Liberal Arts Press, 1955), p. 56.
8. Walt Whitman, "Democratic Vistas," in Whitman, *Poetry and Prose* (New York: Penguin Books, 1996), pp. 970–971.
9. Ibid., p. 967 (capitals in original).
10. Cecelia Kenyon, "Men of Little Faith: The Antifederalists on the Nature of Representative Government," *William and Mary Quarterly,* 3rd ser., 12 (1955): 3–43.
11. Jean-Jacques Rousseau, *The Social Contract and Discourses,* trans. and ed. G. D. H. Cole (New York: E. P. Dutton, 1950), bk. 1, chap. 3, p. 7.
12. Ibid.
13. John Locke, *Two Treatises of Civil Government* (London: J. M. Dent, 1955), p. 118.
14. Rousseau, *Social Contract,* bk. 1, chap. 4.
15. Thomas Jefferson, "Letter to Roger Weightman," June 24, 1826,

in *Great American Political Thinkers,* vol. 1, ed. Bernard Brown (New York: Avon Books, 1983), p. 366.

16. Rousseau, *Social Contract,* bk. 1, chap. 4.

17. All the quotations in this paragraph are taken from Tocqueville, *Democracy in America,* pt. 1, chap. 2.

18. David Hackett Fisher, *Albion's Seed* (Oxford: Oxford University Press, 1989), pp. 177–178.

19. Tocqueville, *Democracy in America,* pt. 1, chap. 2.

20. Ibid.

21. Thomas Jefferson, Letter to John Adams, October 28, 1813, in *Great American Political Thinkers,* pp. 351–352.

22. Whitman, "Democratic Vistas," p. 971.

23. Tocqueville, *Democracy in America,* pt. 2, chap. 5.

24. John Trenchard and Thomas Gordon, *Cato's Letters,* 6th ed. (New York: Da Capo Press, 1971), p. 249.

25. Adam Smith, *An Inquiry into the Nature and Causes of the Wealth of Nations* (New York: Modern Library, 1985), p. 80.

26. Ralph Waldo Emerson, "Self-Reliance," in *Emerson: Essays and Lectures* (New York: Library of America, 1983), p. 276.

27. Emerson, from "Character" and "Politics," in ibid., pp. 500 and 569.

28. Thomas Jefferson, "Notes on the State of Virginia," in *Great American Political Thinkers,* p. 328.

29. Aristotle, *The Nicomachean Ethics,* trans. J. A. K. Thomson (Baltimore, Md.: Penguin Books, 1955), bk. 1, chap. 7.

30. Whitman, "Democratic Vistas," pp. 970–971.

31. One way to conceptualize this process and its significance is to see it as a historically occasioned shift from the "hypothetical" toward the "actual" column in the typology provided by James Fishkin in the context of what he calls "the quest for consent" in *The Dialogue of Justice* (New Haven, Conn.: Yale University Press, 1992), p. 51.

32. Melancton Smith, "Speech to the New York Convention, June, 1788," in *The Debate on the Constitution, Part II,* ed. Bernard Bailyn (New York: Library of America, 1993), pp. 761–762. These remarks echo the views of Aristotle and civic republicans about the benefits and propriety of grounding a political regime on the middling classes, and they anticipate Mill's remarks in his *Considerations on Representative Government* (Chicago: Henry Regnery, 1962) about the inability of "almost any of the members" of Parliament to "ever for an instant look at any question with the eyes of a working man" (p. 60).

33. Tocqueville, *Democracy in America,* pt. 1, chap. 5.

34. Michael Levy, ed., *Political Thought in America* (Chicago: Dorsey Press, 1988), p. 43.

35. Whitman, "Democratic Vistas," pp. 968–970.

36. Ibid., p. 970.
37. Ibid., 983 and 980.
38. Ibid., pp. 974–975.
39. See Philip Pettit, *Republicanism* (Oxford: Oxford University Press, 1997), esp. chap. 1, for a useful discussion of the distinction and contestation between these alternative conceptions of liberty.
40. Whitman, "Democratic Vistas," pp. 972, 988.
41. See Pettit, *Republicanism*, chap. 4.
42. Michael Walzer, *Spheres of Justice* (New York: Basic Books, 1983), chap. 1, p. 3.
43. George Orwell, *Homage to Catalonia* (New York: Harcourt Brace, 1938), pp. 5, 104, and 113.
44. See Don K. Price, *The Scientific Estate* (Oxford: Oxford University Press, 1965).
45. He spoke disparagingly, for example, of "a parcel of dandies and ennuyées, dapper little gentlemen from abroad, who flood us with their thin sentiment of parlors, parasols, piano-songs, tinkling rhymes, the five-hundredth importation—or whimpering and crying about something, chasing one aborted conceit after another, and forever occupied in dyspeptic amours with dyspeptic women." See Whitman, "Democratic Vistas," p. 999.
46. Abraham Lincoln, "Fragments on Slavery," in *Lincoln on Democracy*, ed. Mario Cuomo and Harold Holzer (New York: HarperCollins, 1990), p. 63.
47. As Condorcet wrote in the context of his optimistic expectation of the progress of equality, social equality "must constantly diminish without ever disappearing altogether: for it is the result of natural and necessary causes which it would be foolish and dangerous to wish to eradicate"; see Condorcet, *Sketch for a Historical Picture of the Progress of the Human Mind*, trans. June Barraclough (London: Weidenfeld and Nicolson, 1955), p. 179.
48. Wilson Carey McWilliams, *The Idea of Fraternity in America* (Berkeley: University of California Press, 1973), pp. 95 and 3.
49. Aristotle, *Nicomachean Ethics*, bk. 8, chap. 7, p. 241.
50. John Winthrop, "A Model of Christian Charity," in *Political Thought in America*, ed. Michael Levy, 2nd ed. (Chicago: Dorsey Press, 1982), p. 12.
51. Jefferson, "First Inaugural Address," in *Great American Political Thinkers*, p. 339.
52. Abraham Lincoln, Letter to James H. Van Allen, April 14, 1865, in *Lincoln on Democracy*, ed. Mario Cuomo and Harold Holzer (New York: HarperCollins, 1990), p. 349.
53. George Bancroft, "On the Progress of Mankind," in *Great American Political Thinkers*, pp. 426–427.

54. Whitman, "Democratic Vistas," pp. 972–973.

55. "Yet what a shabby dream it was, that vision of Whitman's. Sentiment without reference to person, a profusion of superficial contacts without depth or meaning. Whitman's fraternity is typified by the 'brotherhood' George Babbitt found among salesmen in railway club cars"; McWilliams, *Idea of Fraternity in America*, p. 421.

56. John Stuart Mill, *Utilitarianism* (Indianapolis, Ind.: Liberal Arts Press, 1957), p. 40.

57. Tocqueville, *Democracy in America*, pt. 1, chap. 16; Mill, *Considerations on Representative Government*, chap. 3.

58. Tocqueville, *Democracy in America*, pt. 1, chap. 12.

59. Ibid., pt. 1, chap. 14.

60. The quoted passages all are found in the selections from Bancroft's writings in *Great American Political Thinkers*, pp. 414–424.

61. Ibid., pp. 419–420.

62. See, for example, Gertrude Himmelfarb, *On Liberty and Liberalism: The Case of John Stuart Mill* (New York: Alfred Knopf, 1974).

63. Whitman, "Democratic Vistas," p. 953.

64. Ibid.

65. Bancroft, "The Office of the People," in *Great American Political Thinkers*, p. 419; Mill, *Considerations on Representative Government*, pp. 55 and 32.

66. Mill, *On Liberty* (Indianapolis, Ind.: Bobbs-Merrill, 1956), p. 71; Whitman, "Democratic Vistas," p. 971; Mill, *Considerations on Representative Government*, p. 57.

CHAPTER 2: THE NEW FACE OF AMERICAN LIBERALISM

1. I first encountered this phrase in John Tomasi's *Liberalism beyond Justice* (Princeton, N.J.: Princeton University Press, 2001), chap. 6. Tomasi accords pride of authorship of the term, however, to Samuel Freeman, a legal and political theorist who identifies with the orientation the term references.

2. John Rawls, *A Theory of Justice* (Cambridge, Mass.: Harvard University Press, 1971), p. viii.

3. John Rawls, "Justice as Fairness: Political Not Metaphysical," *Philosophy and Public Affairs* 14, 3 (Summer 1985): 225 and 229.

4. Ibid., pp. 225–226.

5. For a useful summary, see the data that George Klosko gathers and assesses as they relate to Rawls's claims in his *Democratic Procedures and Liberal Consensus* (New York: Oxford University Press, 2000).

6. This quotation comes from a working paper presented at a conference at Texas A&M University. The revised version appeared as

Connolly's "Secularism, Partisanship and the Ambiguity of Justice," in *Political Theory and Partisan Politics,* ed. Edward Portis, Adolf Gundersen, and Ruth Shively (Albany, N.Y.: SUNY Press, 2000), pp. 149–172.

7. Tomasi, *Liberalism beyond Justice,* pp. 114–115.
8. Rawls, *Theory of Justice,* pp. 3, 4, and 7.
9. *The Federalist Papers,* #51.
10. Matthew Arnold, "Equality," in *Essays Religious and Mixed,* ed. R. H. Super (Ann Arbor: University of Michigan Press, 1972), p. 289.
11. Ronald Beiner, *What's the Matter with Liberalism?* (Berkeley: University of California Press, 1992), pp. 159–161.
12. Rawls, *Theory of Justice,* p. 62.
13. Ibid., p. 83.
14. Ibid., p. 102.
15. Ibid., p. 101.
16. Ibid., p. 107.
17. Ibid., p. 141 (emphasis added).
18. Ibid., p. 100.
19. Bruce Ackerman, *Social Justice in the Liberal State* (New Haven, Conn.: Yale University Press, 1980), pp. 246, 248.
20. Iris Marion Young, *Justice and the Politics of Difference* (Princeton, N.J.: Princeton University Press, 1990), pp. 53–55.
21. Ibid., p. 38.
22. Rawls, *Theory of Justice,* p. 141.
23. Jean-Jacques Rousseau, "A Discourse on the Origins of Inequality," in *The Social Contract and Discourses,* trans. and ed. G. D. H. Cole (New York: E. P. Dutton, 1950), p. 193.
24. Michael J. Sandel, *Liberalism and the Limits of Justice* (Cambridge: Cambridge University Press, 1982).
25. Rawls, "Justice as Fairness: Political Not Metaphysical," p. 232n15 and p. 240n22.
26. Rousseau, "Discourse on the Origin of Inequality," pp. 207–209.
27. Immanuel Kant, "The Critique of Pure Practical Reason," in *The Philosophy of Kant,* ed. Carl J. Friedrich (New York: Random House, 1949), pp. 261–262.
28. John Rawls, *Political Liberalism* (New York: Columbia University Press, 1993), p. 19.
29. Rousseau, "Discourse on the Origin of Inequality," p. 208.
30. Ibid., pp. 207–208.
31. Rawls, *Political Liberalism,* pp. 31–33.
32. Here, viewing ourselves as free, Rawls himself says, is tantamount to regarding ourselves "as being entitled" to make claims. The idea, rather garbled in its rendering, seems to be that we can claim this entitlement on the grounds of our human dignity, which in turn is grounded in our political status as free persons.

33. Rawls, *Theory of Justice*, p. 104.
34. Rawls, *Political Liberalism*, pp. 19 and 189.
35. High liberals would likely challenge this characterization by pointing to (1) the "lexical priority" Rawls accords to "basic liberty" among the social primary goods, and (2) Rawls's invocation of what he calls "the Aristotelian principle," which he defines as the empirical supposition that human beings possess a natural inclination to develop their personal capacities. The short answer to these demurrals is that the construction of moral agency/responsibility embodied in Rawls's conception of democratic persons makes it impossible for him to mean by the term *liberty* what Kant meant by it and impossible for him to include among our human capacities some of those that Aristotle considered most essential.
36. Plato, *The Republic*, iv, 441.
37. Aristotle, *The Politics*, trans. Ernest Barker (New York: Oxford University Press, 1958), p. 181.
38. Ibid., pp. 181–182.
39. Jean-Jacques Rousseau, *The Social Contract and Discourses*, trans. and ed. G. D. H. Cole (New York: E. P. Dutton, 1950), bk. 2, chap. 11.
40. Melancton Smith, "Speech before the New York Ratifying Convention: June 21, 1788," in *The Debate on the Constitution, Part II*, ed. Bernard Bailyn (New York: Library of America, 1993), pp. 761–762.
41. Thomas Jefferson, *Notes on the State of Virginia*, quoted in *Great American Political Thinkers*, vol. 1, ed. Bernard Brown (New York: Avon Books, 1983), p. 328.
42. Ibid., p. 329.
43. Walt Whitman, "Democratic Vistas," in Whitman, *Poetry and Prose* (New York: Penguin Books, 1996), pp. 979 and 974–975.
44. David Tappan, Hollis Professor of Divinity at Harvard in the eighteenth century, quoted in John R. House Jr., *The Changing Political Thought of John Adams* (Princeton, N.J.: Princeton University Press, 1966), p. 34.
45. Rawls, *Theory of Justice*, p. 104.
46. Walt Whitman, "Democratic Vistas," pp. 978–979.
47. These are all phrases used by Rawls to characterize the relevant social group in *A Theory of Justice*.
48. Ibid., p. 98.
49. Smith, "Speech before the New York Ratifying Convention," p. 762.
50. Rawls, *Theory of Justice*, p. 91.
51. Ibid., p. 80.
52. Christopher Lasch, *Revolt of the Elites* (New York: Norton, 1995), pp. 28–29.
53. Thomas R. Dye, in Dye and Harmon Zeigler, *The Irony of Democracy*, 2nd ed. (Belmont, Calif.: Wadsworth Publishing, 1972), pp. 365–366.

54. Amy Gutmann, *Liberal Equality* (Cambridge: Cambridge University Press, 1980), pp. 176–177.

55. Rawls, "Justice as Fairness: Political Not Metaphysical," pp. 225–226.

56. Ibid., p. 229.

57. As it happens, my own substantive policy judgments broadly overlap with those reached by representatives of high liberalism. What I find problematic is any attempt to place these judgments beyond legitimate contestation by the whole body of citizens, as if our judgments were somehow privileged by our intellectual expertise or by some presumed moral superiority.

58. Quoted in Harry Boyte and Nancy Kari, *Building America: The Democratic Promise of Public Work* (Philadelphia: Temple University Press, 1996), p. 186.

CHAPTER 3: WHY DID IT HAPPEN?

1. Jürgen Habermas, "Popular Sovereignty as Procedure," in *Deliberative Democracy: Essays on Reason and Politics*, ed. James Bohman and William Rehg (Cambridge, Mass.: MIT Press, 1997), p. 39.

2. Ronald Dworkin, "Liberalism," in *Public and Private Morality*, ed. Stuart Hampshire (Cambridge: Cambridge University Press, 1978), p. 116.

3. John Dewey, *Liberalism and Social Action* (New York: G. P. Putnam's Sons, 1935), excerpted in Michael Levy, ed., *Political Thought in America* (Chicago: Dorsey Press, 1988), p. 412.

4. For a useful overview, see Daniel Rogers, "In Search of Progressivism," *Reviews in American History* 10 (1982): 113–132.

5. Dewey, in Levy, *Political Thought*, p. 412.

6. Jane Addams, quoted in Gary Hart, *Restoration of the Republic: The Jeffersonian Ideal in 21st Century America* (Oxford: Oxford University Press, 2002), p. 198.

7. Eldon J. Eisenach, *The Lost Promise of Progressivism* (Lawrence: University Press of Kansas, 1994), p. 5.

8. Henry Steele Commager, ed., *Lester Ward and the Welfare State* (Indianapolis, Ind.: Bobbs-Merrill, 1967), p. xxxviii.

9. Michael Sandel, *Democracy's Discontent* (Cambridge, Mass.: Harvard University Press, 1996), p. 263. Sandel cites Hubert Humphrey as providing "one of the last sustained statements of the civic argument" for a decentralized republican political economy, but he argues that Keynesian political economy abandons the older republican political economy of citizenship and helps usher in what Sandel calls "the procedural republic." And Franklin Delano Roosevelt (FDR) is depicted as inconsistent

in his leanings, holding on to the work ethic and its conception of agency, and at times appealing to "an expansive sense of national community" (p. 280) but also as leaving behind the "formative project" of republican citizenship and casting many of his arguments "in terms of individual rights and the voluntarist conception of freedom" (p. 282).

10. Franklin Delano Roosevelt, "Annual Message to the Congress, January 4, 1935," in *The Public Papers and Addresses of Franklin D. Roosevelt*, vol. 4, ed. Samuel Rosenman (New York: Random House, 1938), pp. 19–20.

11. Harry C. Boyte and Nancy N. Kari, "Unsung Heroes," *New Democrat* 9, 4 (July–August 1997): 15–17.

12. Rawls, *Theory of Justice*, p. viii.

13. Samuel Scheffler, "Responsibility, Reactive Attitudes and Liberalism in Philosophy and Politics," *Philosophy and Public Affairs* 21, 4 (1992): 299–323.

14. Frank Norris, *McTeague: A Story of San Francisco* (Oxford: Oxford University Press, 1995), p. 181.

15. Ibid., pp. 45, 72–73.

16. William Connolly, *Identity/Difference: Democratic Negotiations of Political Paradox* (Ithaca, N.Y.: Cornell University Press, 1991), p. 97.

17. Scheffler, "Responsibility, Reactive Attitudes, and Liberalism," p. 303.

18. Max Weber, "Objectivity in Social Science," in *The Methodology of the Social Sciences*, trans. and ed. Edward Shils and Henry Finch (New York: Free Press, 1949), pp. 111 and 81.

19. Max Weber, "The Meaning of Ethical Neutrality," in ibid., p. 18.

20. Alasdair MacIntyre, *After Virtue* (Notre Dame, Ind.: University of Notre Dame Press, 1981) p. 103.

21. The phrase *value slope* is taken from Charles Taylor's illuminating analysis of the relationship between beliefs about reality and endorsements of social goals. See his "Neutrality in Political Science," *Philosophy, Politics, and Society,* ed. Peter Laslett and W. G. Runciman (Oxford: Blackwell, 1967), pp. 25–57.

22. John DiIulio, "Men at Work," *Public Interest* 143 (Spring 2001): 111–112.

23. Walt Whitman, "Democratic Vistas," in Whitman, *Poetry and Prose* (New York: Penguin Books, 1996), p. 967.

24. Roberto Michels, *Political Parties* (New York: Free Press, 1915), p. 421.

25. Whitman, "Democratic Vistas," p. 968.

26. As Bernard Berelson wrote, "Lack of interest by some people is not without its benefits." In the case of "the least interested voters, . . . here again is an instance in which an individual 'inadequacy' provides a positive service for the society." See Bernard Berelson, Paul Lazarsfeld,

and William McPhee, *Voting* (Chicago: University of Chicago Press, 1954), pp. 311ff.

27. Lester Milbrath, "The Functional System," in *Frontiers of Democratic Theory*, ed. Henry Kariel (New York: Random House, 1970), p. 87.

28. All quotations and data are found in James W. Prothro and Charles M. Grigg, "Fundamental Principles of Democracy: Bases of Agreement and Disagreement," *Journal of Politics* 22, 2 (May 1960): 276–294.

29. Herbert McClosky, "Consensus and Ideology in American Politics," *American Political Science Review* 58, 2 (June 1964): 361–382. (Quotations here are taken from pp. 365, 366, and 374.)

30. John B. McConahay, "Self-Interest versus Racial Attitudes as Correlates of Anti-busing Attitudes in Louisville: Is It the Buses or the Blacks?" *Journal of Politics* 44, 3 (August 1982): 714–715.

31. See, for example, Paul M. Sniderman and Edward G. Carmines, *The Scar of Race* (Cambridge, Mass.: Harvard University Press, 1993).

32. See Mary R. Jackman, *The Velvet Glove: Paternalism and Conflict in Gender, Class, and Race* (Berkeley: University of California Press, 1994).

33. See, for example, David O. Sears and Tom Jessor, "Whites' Racial Policy Attitudes: The Role of White Racism," *Social Science Quarterly* 77 (1996): 751–759, and Donald R. Kinder and Lynn M. Sanders, *Divided by Color: Racial Politics and Democratic Ideals* (Chicago: University of Chicago Press, 1996).

34. A good overview is provided by Howard Schuman, Charlotte Steeh, Lawrence Bobo, and Maria Krysan, *Racial Attitudes in America: Trends and Interpretation*, rev. ed. (Cambridge, Mass.: Harvard University Press, 1997).

35. Theodor Adorno, Else Frenkel-Brunswik, Daniel Levinson, and R. Nevitt Sanford, *The Authoritarian Personality* (New York: Harper and Brothers, 1950).

36. These various propositions were designed to tap into clusters of personality traits designated by the researchers as conventionalism, authoritarian submission, authoritarian aggression, anti-intraception, superstition and stereotypy, power and toughness, destructiveness and cynicism, and projectivity. See Adorno et al., *Authoritarian Personality*, pp. 255–257.

37. Ibid., p. 974.

38. Ibid., p. 269. The actual mean score on the F (authoritarian) scale of their sample group of working-class men was 4.19. The sample group of California service club men had a mean score of 4.08, and the overall mean score for all those taking the same form of the questionnaire was 3.76. Working-class women had a mean score of 3.86.

39. Seymour Martin Lipset, *Political Man: The Social Bases of Politics* (New York: Anchor Books, 1963).

40. Ibid., p. 92.

41. Ibid., pp. 94, 115.
42. Ibid., pp. 106–108, 114.
43. DiIulio, "Men at Work," p. 112.
44. Connolly, *Identity/Difference*, p. 78.
45. John Stuart Mill, *Considerations on Representative Government* (Chicago: Henry Regnery, 1962), p. 32. (In Mill's words: "The most important point of excellence which any form of government can possess is to promote the virtue and intelligence of the people themselves.")
46. See Richard H. Rovere, *Senator Joe McCarthy* (Cleveland, Ohio: Meridian Books, 1960), p. 104.
47. Richard Hofstadter, "The Paranoid Style in American Politics," *Harper's Magazine,* November 1964, pp. 77–86.
48. Alan Brinkley, "Richard Hofstadter's *The Age of Reform*: A Reconsideration," *Reviews in American History* 13 (September 1985): 462.
49. David Brown, "Redefining American History: Ethnicity, Progressive Historiography and the Making of Richard Hofstadter," *History Teacher* 36, 4 (August 2003): 529. This essay provides a very useful review of this episode in American historiography, along with intimations of its political implications.
50. Richard Hofstadter, "Democracy and Anti-intellectualism in America*,*" *Michigan Alumnus Quarterly Review* (Summer 1953): 286.
51. Richard Hofstadter and C. DeWitt Hardy, *The Development and Scope of Higher Education in the United States* (New York: Committee on Financing Higher Education, 1952), p. 107.
52. Hofstadter, "Democracy and Anti-intellectualism," p. 286.
53. Letter from Curti to Hofstadter, November 20, 1953, Box 34, Richard Hofstadter Papers, as cited in Brown, "Redefining American History," p. 537.
54. As Bricker once allegedly said to McCarthy, "Joe, you're a dirty son of a bitch, but there are times when you've got to have a son of a bitch around, and this is one of them." See Rovere, *Joe McCarthy*, p. 65. As Rovere characterized the Taft et al. view of McCarthy's usefulness to them: "He was crude, he was unwashed, he was unversed in the theology, but what did any of this matter so long as he had the ear of the people and was able to be heard when he said the stables needed cleaning?" (p. 136).
55. *Rectification* means to provide compensation for wrongs inflicted upon someone. The logic of rectification is the logic of the law of torts. Even libertarians such as Robert Nozick acknowledge the legitimacy of demands for rectification. This is pure conjecture, of course, but one might speculate that Rawls chose the term *redress,* consciously or unconsciously, precisely to trade upon the moral slope of its definitional penumbra—which gets into the logical terrain of rectification. In any case, my dictionary uses terms such as *reparation* and *retribution* among its definitions for

redress. It would be hard to claim, however, that the notions of reparation, retribution, and righted wrongs are really appropriate for all the circumstances to which the difference principle would apply. For example, if you happened to stumble upon a lost $20 bill and I had no such morally arbitrary good fortune, you would likely consider it both odd and inappropriate for me to demand a share of it as a "reparation."

CHAPTER 4: THE DEONTOLOGY TRAP

1. See in this regard John Rawls, *A Theory of Justice* (Cambridge, Mass.: Harvard University Press, 1971), pp. 7–11.
2. Ibid., p. 141.
3. "The general conception is simply the difference principle applied to all primary goods including liberty and opportunity. . . . In one form or another the difference principle is basic throughout." See ibid., p. 83.
4. Ibid., p. 101.
5. Ibid., p. 100.
6. Bruce Ackerman, *Social Justice in the Liberal State* (New Haven, Conn.: Yale University Press, 1980), p. 248.
7. "The sense of injustice revolts against whatever is unequal by caprice." See Edmond Cahn, *The Sense of Injustice* (Bloomington: Indiana University Press, 1949), p. 14.
8. Rawls, *Theory of Justice*, p. 102.
9. Kurt Vonnegut, "Harrison Bergeron," in *Welcome to the Monkey House* (New York: Dell Publishing, 1968). The opening paragraph reads: "The year was 2081, and everybody was finally equal. They weren't only equal before God and the law. They were equal every which way. Nobody was smarter than anybody else. Nobody was better looking than anybody else. Nobody was stronger or quicker than anybody else. All this equality was due to the 211th, 212th, and 213th Amendments to the Constitution, and to the unceasing vigilance of agents of the United States Handicapper General."
10. Martha Nussbaum, *Frontiers of Justice* (Cambridge, Mass.: Harvard University Press, 2006), p. 194.
11. Ibid., pp. 194–195.
12. Ibid., p. 194.
13. It is directly pertinent here to note that Kant found himself driven to endorse this dubious argument to paper over the inadequacy of his principles otherwise to justify construing the receipt of poor relief as a right. See Samuel Fleischacker, *A Short History of Distributive Justice* (Cambridge, Mass.: Harvard University Press, 2004), p. 70.
14. For further elaboration of the moral and political dilemmas presented by uneliminable or morally valuable gratuitousness in human life,

see my essay on "The Antinomies of Social Justice," *Review of Politics* 55, 2 (Spring 1993): 193–216.

15. Rawls, *Theory of Justice*, p. 3.

16. David Hume, *A Treatise of Human Nature,* ed. L. H. Selby-Bigge (Oxford: Clarendon, 1896), pt. 2, sec. 2.

17. Michael J. Sandel, *Liberalism and the Limits of Justice* (Cambridge: Cambridge University Press, 1982), pp. 32–35.

18. Rawls, *Theory of Justice*, p. 442.

19. Ibid., p. 426.

20. Ibid., p. 429.

21. Aristotle would surely not accept the characterization of friendship as a "nonmoral value," for example. See ibid., p. 434.

22. There seems here a striking similarity to the equally utopian supposition of libertarians such as Friedrich von Hayek and Charles Murray that we need only create a laissez-faire contract society and the institutions and associations of civil society will then arise by "spontaneous order." Sociologists such as Alan Wolfe would almost surely argue—and with good reason—that these parallel utopianisms about human behavior represent characteristic delusions of statist liberals, on the one hand, and conservative market liberals, on the other, about the omnicompetence of their most favored social institution. See Wolfe, *Whose Keeper? Social Science and Moral Obligation* (Berkeley: University of California Press, 1989).

23. Some arguments in support of these claims can be found in my *Civic Liberalism: Reflections on Our Democratic Ideals* (Lanham, Md.: Rowman and Littlefield Publishers, 1999), esp. chap. 7.

24. The description of the parties in his account of the contract situation, he says, "invites misunderstanding. In particular, the description of the parties may seem to presuppose a particular metaphysical conception of the person. . . . I believe this to be an illusion caused by not seeing the original position as a device of representation." See John Rawls, *Political Liberalism* (New York: Columbia University Press, 1993), p. 27.

25. Ibid., pp. 86–87.

26. Ibid., p. 18n20.

27. Ibid., p. 18.

28. John Locke, *Two Treatises of Civil Government* (London: J. M. Dent, 1955), p. 136.

29. Rawls, *Theory of Justice*, p. 3.

30. Ibid., p. 107.

31. Ibid., p. 104.

32. Rawls, *Political Liberalism*, p. 34.

33. Ibid., p. 280.

34. Ibid., pp. 186 and 190.

35. Ibid., p. 189.

36. Rawls, *Theory of Justice*, p. 74.

37. Thomas Hobbes, "Introduction" to *Leviathan* (New York: E. P. Dutton, 1950), p. 5.

38. Rawls demonstrates his awareness of the problems associated with at least one-half of his social division of responsibility and its enabling assumption that we have power over our choice of ends when he writes: "Taking responsibility for our tastes and preferences, whether or not they have arisen from our actual choices . . . is something we must learn to deal with. . . . We don't say that because the preferences arose from upbringing and not from choice that society owes us compensation. Rather, it is a normal part of being human to cope with the preferences our upbringing leaves us with." See Rawls, *Political Liberalism*, pp. 185 and 185n15. In other words, even if we don't really have the third moral power he attributes to us regarding our choice of ends, we nevertheless are required to "cope with" and accept responsibility for those ends visited upon us rather than chosen. The obvious question that he ignores is why it is not, pari passu, incumbent upon us to cope with and accept responsibility for our propensity or lack thereof to work. And the obvious explanation of this omission is that any compromise of the blanket excuse he insists upon in this instance would force abandonment of his principles of justice.

39. See Sandel, *Liberalism and the Limits of Justice*, pp. 89–91; Bonnie Honig, *Political Theory and the Displacement of Politics* (Ithaca, N.Y.: Cornell University Press, 1993), p. 139; and Samuel Scheffler, "Responsibility, Reactive Attitudes and Liberalism in Philosophy and Politics," *Philosophy and Public Affairs* 21, 4 (1992): 306n7.

40. Rawls, *Theory of Justice*, p. 315.

41. Rawls, *The Law of Peoples* (Cambridge, Mass.: Harvard University Press, 1999), p. 117.

42. Alternatively, Rawls could renege on his recognition/concession that the values people affirm and the life goals they pursue play a causal role in their economic results and thereby logically accept the claims of critics such as Thomas Pogge that difference-principle-style redistributive norms should apply across national boundaries. And with regard to the contradiction between his accounts of distributive and redistributive justice, Rawls could abandon mens rea along with his endorsement of a retributive component in criminal punishments. The logic behind his original principles of justice would thus remain intact. But the price then would be the explicit abandonment of widely accepted moral beliefs about criminal responsibility and about responsibility for actions predicated upon one's beliefs and values. For Pogge's argument, see his essay, "An Egalitarian Law of Peoples," *Philosophy and Public Affairs* 23, 3 (Summer 1994): 195–224.

43. Rawls, *Theory of Justice*, p. 312.

44. Robert Nozick, *Anarchy, State, and Utopia* (New York: Basic Books, 1974), p. 214.

45. Ibid., p. 228.

46. On the contrary, I would argue that Nozick winds up inadvertently putting on display some of the disabling aporia within libertarian rights arguments: his admission that these rights claims (to property and self-ownership) cannot be based upon moral desert "all the way down," the difficulties he has in trying to cope with the Lockean proviso, and his failure to take with any seriousness the practical implications of his norms of "rectification."

47. John Rawls, *Justice as Fairness: A Restatement* (Cambridge, Mass.: Harvard University Press, 2001), p. 79.

48. Ibid.

49. See Rawls, *Political Liberalism*, p. 148.

50. Ibid., p. 145.

51. Ibid., p. 134.

52. If we kept following the train of argument Rawls would likely offer on the basis of other claims and moral intuitions he expresses elsewhere, the ultimate justification for this seemingly irrational and improper grant of authority would be that people did nothing to deserve their talents and hence their owning them is morally arbitrary. That ultimate answer works, however, only if it is assumed that no moral rights can inhere in ownership that was undeserved. The collective society, moreover, has no claims of desert over such undeserved holdings either. According them that power as a default outcome is itself morally arbitrary. And we might doubt that reasonable people who reflected that their very lives and existence are themselves undeserved would agree to such a default rule.

53. Rawls, *Justice as Fairness: A Restatement*, p. 75.

54. Ibid., p. 76.

55. Rawls, *Theory of Justice*, p. 102.

56. Ibid., p. 106.

57. Aristotle, *Nicomachean Ethics*, bk. 8, chap. 9.

58. Ibid.

59. Rawls, *Theory of Justice*, p. 106. Regarding the impossibility of a pluralistic democracy being a community or association, see his *Political Liberalism*, pp. 40–43. Rawls has a specific and somewhat restrictive definition of community. But his basic point is clear: if a pluralistic society is to have a moral "common aim," it can only be one of "insuring that political and social institutions are just" (p. 146n13).

60. Patrick Neal, *Liberalism and Its Discontents* (New York: New York University Press, 1997), pp. 195–196.

61. Immanuel Kant, "Metaphysical Foundations of Morals," in *The Philosophy of Kant: Immanuel Kant's Moral and Political Writings,* ed. Carl J. Friedrich (New York: Random House, 1949), p. 207.

62. Ibid., pp. 159, 175n12.

63. Rawls, *Theory of Justice*, p. 103.
64. Kant, "Metaphysical Foundations," p. 159n4.
65. Paul W. Kahn, *Putting Liberalism in Its Place* (Princeton, N.J.: Princeton University Press, 2005), pp. 45, 24.
66. Richard Rorty, *Contingency, Irony, and Solidarity* (Cambridge: Cambridge University Press, 1989), p. xvi.
67. Ralph Waldo Emerson, "Self-Reliance," in *Emerson: Essays and Lectures* (New York: Library of America, 1983), p. 262.
68. Rorty, *Contingency, Irony, and Solidarity*, p. xvi.
69. Emerson, "Self-Reliance," p. 262.
70. Todd Gitlin, *The Twilight of Common Dreams* (New York: Henry Holt, 1995).
71. William Galston, *Liberal Purposes* (Cambridge: Cambridge University Press, 1991), pp. 160, 162.
72. See among many available treatments of these developments David G. Lawrence, *The Collapse of the Democratic Majority* (Boulder, Colo.: Westview Press, 1996); Thomas B. Edsall, *Chain Reaction* (New York: W. W. Norton, 1991); Jacob S. Hacker and Paul Pierson, *Off Center* (New Haven, Conn.: Yale University Press, 2005); Jeffrey C. Isaac, *The Poverty of Progressivism* (Lanham, Md.: Rowman and Littlefield, 2003).
73. Kaus would shift the focus of liberal concern away from material equality to a concern for "civic equality." Young seeks to expand and reinterpret the concept of justice in a way that would center it on social inclusion and the removal of structured social impediments to fulfilling lives. See Kaus, *The End of Equality* (New York: Basic Books, 1992), esp. chaps. 2 and 3, and Young, *Justice and the Politics of Difference* (Princeton, N.J.: Princeton University Press, 1990), esp. chap. 1, and *Inclusion and Democracy* (New York: Oxford University Press, 2000). In the latter book, Young goes so far as to try to incorporate the teleological goods of self-determination and personal development into her conception of justice.
74. Thomas Frank, *What's the Matter with Kansas?* (New York: Henry Holt, 2004), p. 109.
75. Quoted by Sandel, *Democracy's Discontent* (Cambridge, Mass.: Harvard University Press, 1996), pp. 213–214.
76. Ronald Beiner, *What's the Matter with Liberalism?* (Berkeley: University of California Press, 1992), p. 67.
77. Ibid., p. 63. Beiner specifically references here Charles Larmore's account of liberal neutrality vis-à-vis the good. But the same puzzle arises in Rawls's account of the well-ordered society. In the latter part of *A Theory of Justice*, Rawls seems to suggest that the citizens of a just society will spontaneously pursue a program of personal development because of the "natural fact" that "human beings enjoy the exercise of their realized capacities" (p. 426). As I noted earlier in this chapter, however, this hopeful speculation seems to be a piece of free-floating romantic utopianism:

the assumption that the capitalist bazaar when regulated by the difference principle can be expected to generate people who exhibit the liberal virtues and spontaneously seek to develop their personal talents rather than, say, people who pursue life careers of self-centered consumerist hedonism.

78. See in this connection Matthew S. Holland, *Bonds of Affection: Civic Charity and the Making of America* (Washington, D.C.: Georgetown University Press, 2007).

79. In this context, liberals who more commonly invoke lyrics from Bob Dylan or hip-hop to plumb the moral intuitions of the popular mind could profitably take closer stock of pop sermonizing about the moral significance of work found in lyrics such as those in the country rock group Alabama's "Forty Hour Week," where "people in this country who work hard every day" are saluted for "working together like spokes inside a wheel to keep this country turning around."

80. See note 79.

81. Michael Tomasky, *Left for Dead: The Life, Death, and Possible Resurrection of Progressive Politics in America* (New York: Free Press, 1996), p. 96.

82. Abraham Lincoln, *Lincoln on Democracy*, ed. Mario Cuomo and Harold Holzer (New York: HarperCollins Publishers, 1990), pp. 90, 62, and 135.

83. Michael Graetz and Ian Shapiro, *Death by a Thousand Cuts: The Fight over Taxing Inherited Wealth* (Princeton, N.J.: Princeton University Press, 2005). The quotations come from the authors' presentation of their findings at the Brookings Institution on March 24, 2005.

84. Andrew Carnegie, "Wealth" (1889), in *Political Thought in America,* 2nd ed., ed. Michael Levy (Chicago: Dorsey Press, 1992), p. 334.

85. The practical imperatives here include the traditional republican concern—one that animated Jefferson's successful legislative efforts to eliminate primogeniture and entail—for creating a middle-class society and constraining extreme inequality among the democratic citizenry.

86. Graetz and Shapiro's Brookings briefing, March 24, 2005; see note 83.

87. Kaus, *End of Equality*, p. 178.

88. Steven M. Teles, *Whose Welfare? AFDC and Elite Politics* (Lawrence: University Press of Kansas, 1996), p. 53.

89. Ibid., pp. 75–76.

90. Peter Edelman, "The Worst Thing Clinton Has Done," *Atlantic Monthly* 279, 3 (March 1997): 43–58.

91. Quoted by Russell Shorts, "All Politics Are Local," *New York Times Sunday Magazine,* October 2, 2005.

92. Tomasky, *Left for Dead*, p. 12.

CHAPTER 5: NEW DEMOCRATIC VISTAS

1. Thomas S. Kuhn, *The Structure of Scientific Revolutions*, 2nd ed. (Chicago: University of Chicago Press, 1970).
2. Quoted in ibid., p. 151.
3. Iris Marion Young, *Justice and the Politics of Difference* (Princeton, N.J.: Princeton University Press, 1990).
4. John Rawls, *A Theory of Justice* (Cambridge, Mass.: Harvard University Press, 1971), pp. 3–4.
5. Richard Rorty, "The Priority of Democracy to Philosophy," in *Objectivity, Relativism, and Truth: Philosophical Papers*, vol. 1 (Cambridge: Cambridge University Press, 1991), p. 187.
6. 372 U.S. 335 (1963).
7. See *United States v. Carolene Products Company*, 304 U.S. 144 (1938), footnote 4.
8. Mill, "Epigram" to *On Liberty* (Indianapolis, Ind.: Bobbs-Merrill, 1956).
9. Walt Whitman, "Democratic Vistas," in Whitman, *Poetry and Prose* (New York: Penguin Books, 1996), pp. 972, 953, 968.
10. See, inter alia, A. K. Sen, *Commodities and Capabilities* (Amsterdam: North-Holland, 1985), and Martha Nussbaum, *Women and Human Development* (Cambridge: Cambridge University Press, 2000).
11. This account of a (significant) threshold requirement of public investment in principled public purposes above and beyond which the further allocation of goods is a matter of public discretion and also likely for many practical, prudential, and moral reasons to give wide play to free acquisition and exchange in the marketplace resembles the model offered by Michael Walzer in *Spheres of Justice* (New York: Basic Books, 1983). Walzer's argument there is that the provision of goods necessary for all to participate in the common life of a society is a common responsibility: "The social contract is an agreement to reach decisions together about what goods are necessary to our common life, and then to provide those goods for one another." Beyond this realm of common provision, given the presence of "the right blocks"—i.e., prohibition of commodifying things like personal freedom and political office—"there is no such thing as a maldistribution of consumer goods. It just doesn't matter [morally speaking] that you have a yacht and I don't, or that the sound system of her hi-fi set is greatly superior to his, or that we buy our rugs from Sears Roebuck and they get theirs from the Orient" (pp. 65, 107–108).
12. Jonathan Kozol, *Savage Inequalities: Children in America's Schools* (New York: Crown Publishers, 1991).
13. Thomas Jefferson, "Notes on the State of Virginia" (1982), quoted in *Great American Political Thinkers*, vol. 1, ed. Bernard Brown (New York: Avon Books, 1983), p. 321.

14. Ibid.

15. Milton Friedman, *Capitalism and Freedom* (Chicago: University of Chicago Press, 1962), pp. 101–107.

16. Bruce Ackerman and Anne Alstott, *The Stakeholder Society* (New Haven, Conn.: Yale University Press, 1999).

17. Marie Jean Antoine Nicolas Caritat de Condorcet, *Sketch for a Historical Picture of the Progress of the Human Mind*, trans. June Barraclough (London: Weidenfeld and Nicolson, 1955), p. 181.

18. The *locus classicus* of this argument is in Mill's *Considerations on Representative Government*. The prudential significance of the development of social capital to the successful functioning of democratic regimes is also a central theme of more recent work. See in this context Robert Putnam, *Making Democracy Work* (Princeton, N.J.: Princeton University Press, 1993), and Francis Fukuyama, *Trust: The Social Virtues and the Creation of Prosperity* (New York: Free Press, 1995).

19. See Richard Dagger, "Neo-republicanism and the Civic Economy," *Politics, Philosophy, and Economics* 5, 2 (2006): 151–173, and Michael Sandel, *Democracy's Discontent,* pt. 2 (Cambridge, Mass.: Harvard University Press, 1996).

20. Sandel, *Democracy's Discontent*, p. 124.

21. In the afterword, I specify some of my agreements and disagreements with Sandel's views.

22. Richard Dagger offers his own model in his previously referenced article, "Neo-republicanism and the Civic Economy." The model I sketch here overlaps but is not identical with his.

23. John Adams, Letter to James Sullivan of May 26, 1776, quoted in John R. Howe Jr., *The Changing Political Thought of John Adams* (Princeton, N.J.: Princeton University Press, 1966), p. 86.

24. John Rawls, *Justice as Fairness: A Restatement* (Cambridge, Mass.: Harvard University Press, 2001), pp. 138–139.

25. See Walzer, *Spheres of Justice*, pp. 97–103.

26. Alexis de Tocqueville, *Democracy in America,* trans. Henry Reeve and ed. Richard Heffner (New York: New American Library, 1956), pt. 1, chap. 3, p. 50.

27. Dagger—and others—have suggested the use of a progressive consumption tax instead or in addition. I will not explore the relative merits of income and consumption taxation here. It is the progressivity in either case that is the point at stake.

28. My use of Social Security as an exemplar here does not imply that I consider its current provisions sacrosanct. Changing demographics and life expectancy may well warrant changes in a program that was never intended to fund early retirement of the healthy. It is not any specific details of the current system that make it an appropriate model in this

context, but it is instead its basic functions and its general criteria for participation and distribution of benefits.

29. Theda Skocpol, *The Missing Middle: Working Families and the Future of American Social Policy* (New York: W. W. Norton, 2000), pp. 27, 30.

30. Stuart White, *The Civic Minimum* (Oxford: Oxford University Press, 2003), p. 59. In his final restatement of his theory of justice, Rawls states his own general endorsement of this expectation in reaction to the claim by proponents of an unconditional basic income that full-time surfers who spurn gainful employment nonetheless should be supported economically. This expectation in Rawls is hinged upon his interpretation of the proper application of the difference principle to this hypothetical case, however, so it is unclear how he might respond to a surfer who pleaded that he had simply been unfortunate in being given a character that incapacitated him for productive labor. See Rawls, *Justice as Fairness: A Restatement*, p. 179.

31. Whitman, "Democratic Vistas," p. 970.

32. Skocpol, *Missing Middle*, pp. 142, 168.

33. Tocqueville, *Democracy in America*, p. 193.

34. Friedman, *Capitalism and Freedom*, p. 31.

35. See Robert Nozick, *Anarchy, State, and Utopia* (New York: Basic Books, 1974), p. 177.

36. Putnam, *Making Democracy Work*.

37. Whitman, "Democratic Vistas," pp. 992–993.

38. Condorcet, *Sketch for a Historical Picture*, p. 100.

39. Ibid., p. 102.

40. For elaboration of these suggestions, see Benjamin Barber, *Strong Democracy* (Berkeley: University of California Press, 1984), esp. pp. 267–281, and Bruce Ackerman and James Fishkin, *Deliberation Day* (New Haven, Conn.: Yale University Press, 2005).

41. One way to flesh out this contrast is to juxtapose Rawls's account of what he calls the "political virtues" with the considerably more capacious account of liberal civic virtues found in chapter 8 of my *Civic Liberalism* (Lanham, Md.: Rowman and Littlefield, 1999)—or in chapter 10 of William Galston's *Liberal Purposes* (Cambridge: Cambridge University Press, 1991). The political virtues incumbent upon Rawls's good citizens are those that follow logically from construing them as "subjects of justice": theirs are passive virtues of forbearance and accommodation, to wit, "the virtues of civility and tolerance, of reasonableness and the sense of fairness"; see Rawls, *Political Liberalism* (New York: Columbia University Press, 1993) p. 194. The conceptions of civic virtue—tantamount to the responsibilities of democratic citizens, ideally speaking—in my account and in Galston's also incorporate more active and affirmative virtues.

42. George Klosko provides a very useful compilation and assessment of relevant studies in his *Democratic Procedures and Liberal Consensus*

(Oxford: Oxford University Press, 2000). See also the experimental results reported by Norman Frolich and Joe Oppenheimer in their "Choosing Justice in Experimental Democracy with Production," *American Political Science Review* 84 (1990): 461–480, and the interview data in Jennifer Hochschild, *What's Fair? American Beliefs about Distributive Justice* (Cambridge, Mass.: Harvard University Press, 1981).

43. The relative tone-deafness of many liberals to the potential support these sentiments of common identity and civic friendship can provide for their own goals stems from a variety of factors. Among these are their overestimation of the power of rights discourse to generate their preferred distributive norms, their tendency to see patriotism as ineluctably tinged with xenophobia and cultural imperialism, their tendency to see communitarian sentiments as having historically functioned in the service of social exclusion and political dominance, and the fact that many liberals are more cosmopolitan than particularistic in their own political identity. Important exceptions to this pattern include people such as Michael Walzer, Alan Wolfe, Robert Bellah, Philip Selznick, Amitai Etzioni, Charles Anderson, and Harry Boyte.

44. Samuel Lubell, *The Future of American Politics* (New York: Harper and Brothers, 1952).

45. Jeffrey Isaac, *The Poverty of Progressivism* (Lanham, Md.: Rowman and Littlefield, 2003). Isaac also expresses some reservations about the desirability as well as the feasibility of a Progressive restoration.

46. See Ruy Teixeira and Joel Rogers, *Why the White Working Class Still Matters* (New York: Basic Books, 2000), esp. pp. 34–38.

47. See, for example, Harry Boyte, *Everyday Politics: Reconnecting Citizens and Public Life* (Philadelphia: University of Pennsylvania Press, 2004), and *Commonwealth: A Return to Citizen Politics* (New York: Free Press, 1989); Charles Anderson, *Pragmatic Liberalism* (Chicago: University of Chicago Press, 1990).

AFTERWORD

1. Richard Rorty, *Achieving Our Country* (Cambridge, Mass.: Harvard University Press, 1998); Michael Sandel, *Democracy's Discontent* (Cambridge, Mass.: Harvard University Press, 1996).

2. Walt Whitman, "Democratic Vistas," in Whitman, *Poetry and Prose* (New York: Penguin Books, 1996), p. 971.

3. See here Walzer's *Spheres of Justice* (New York: Basic Books, 1983), chap. 3.

4. Whitman, "Democratic Vistas," p. 972.

5. John Rawls, *Political Liberalism* (New York: Columbia University Press, 1993), p. 152.

6. Ibid., p. 194.
7. Ibid., p. 197.
8. John Stuart Mill, *On Liberty* (Indianapolis, Ind.: Bobbs-Merrill, 1956), p. 76.
9. Whitman, "Democratic Vistas," pp. 992–993, 982, and 953.
10. Rawls, *Political Liberalism*, p. 18n20.
11. Ibid., p. 194.
12. The specific parameters of the distributive principles and policies Rawls establishes are most explicitly and candidly set out in his "Introduction to the Paperback Editions" of *Political Liberalism*, especially pp. lviii–lix. Rawls opines that only this narrow range of substantive conceptions of distributive justice satisfies the criterion of reciprocity, but he offers inadequate argumentative warrant for that claim. Populist perfectionists, it may be noted, might well support some of the distributive norms here mentioned by Rawls on the basis of their own conception of democratic purposes—even if they are unpersuaded by his insistence that these norms are derivable from norms of reciprocity per se.
13. John Tomasi, *Liberalism beyond Justice* (Princeton, N.J.: Princeton University Press, 2001), p. 45.
14. See, for example, Benjamin Page and Robert Shapiro, *The Rational Public* (Chicago: University of Chicago Press, 1992), and Samuel Popkin, *The Reasoning Voter* (Chicago: University of Chicago Press, 1991).
15. See, for example, Jennifer Hochschild, *What's Fair? American Beliefs about Distributive Justice* (Cambridge, Mass.: Harvard University Press, 1981); Adolf Gundersen, *The Environmental Promise of Democratic Deliberation* (Madison: University of Wisconsin Press, 1995); and Alan Wolfe, *One Nation, After All* (New York: Penguin Books, 1998).
16. John DiIulio, "Men at Work," *Public Interest* 143 (Spring 2001): 111–112.
17. Wolfe, *One Nation, After All*, pp. 298, 158.
18. Robert Dahl, *A Preface to Democratic Theory* (Chicago: University of Chicago Press, 1956), p. 101.
19. A few examples taken from the literature can serve to illustrate this point. The public opinion survey used as the database for Herbert McClosky's "Consensus and Ideology in American Politics," *American Political Science Review* 58, 2 (June 1954): 361–382, includes the following propositions to which the respondents are asked to agree or disagree: "Freedom does not give anyone the right to teach foreign ideas in our schools" and "A book that contains wrong political views cannot be a good book and does not deserve to be published." In all, 45 percent of "influentials" and 56 percent of the general electorate agreed with the first proposition. And 18 percent of influentials and 50 percent of the general electorate agreed with the second proposition. Agreement was taken to indicate a failure to understand and support democratic liberties.

Both propositions are so indeterminate in their meaning and referents, however, that it is hard to know what the respondents understood them to mean and hence to know what their response indicated in terms of their "attitudes." "Freedom" or any other abstract concept cannot "give people rights." It is not clear that respondents differentiated "having a right" from "doing the right thing." Who knows what respondents thought "foreign ideas" meant. And who knows whether "teach . . . in our schools" meant to inform high schoolers or to catechize first graders. Regarding the second proposition, who knows what respondents thought a "wrong political idea" was—e.g., whether it was something on the order of "we should have government-provided health care" or "the separation of powers should be abolished" or "Iraq is in Latin America." And agreeing that what has been stipulated to be a "wrong" idea does not "deserve" publication is certainly not the same thing as asserting that the government should prohibit its publication. Similarly, how are we to know exactly what the proposition used as a basis for the "F-Scale" in *The Authoritarian Personality* to the effect that "obedience and respect for authority are the most important virtues children should learn" signifies to respondents? Do they interpret it as meaning that all children should be taught slavish subordination and unquestioning acceptance of all political leaders? Or do they think it means that children heading off to school for the first time should be admonished to comply with their teacher's instructions and to do what the street-crossing guard tells them to do? Or when respondents agree to another proposition from the F-Scale survey to the effect that "if people would talk less and work more, everybody would be better off," are we to suppose that this indicates enthusiasm for suppressing the chattering classes? And if not, how does indulging the interviewer with agreement provide evidence of protofascist sympathies?

20. Another example from the tolerance literature, this one from Herbert McClosky and Alida Brill's *Dimensions of Tolerance: What Americans Believe about Civil Liberties* (New York: Russell Sage Foundation, 1983), illustrates this point. The authors reported there considerable discrepancy between the response of political elites, on the one hand, and the mass public, on the other, to the question: "If a news photographer takes a picture of a famous person entering a house of prostitution, should publishing the photos be permitted or forbidden as an invasion of privacy?" Most of the elite respondents favored permitting publication, and most of the general public favored forbidding it. McClosky and Brill took this discrepancy as a confirmation of their general thesis that elites understand and support civil liberties more than the mass public. But as reviewers in the *Michigan Law Review* observed, that interpretation and assessment is not incontestable: "What is interesting," they note, "is that the question requires a choice between two values—a free press versus

the right to privacy—each of which might be seen as libertarian." Since the pattern of responses "suggests that the general public values the right to privacy more than [the elite respondents] . . . this might suggest that both the law and the community elite are behind, rather than ahead of, the general public in appreciating this libertarian value." See *Law and Society* 83 (February 1985): 909.

21. Paul Sniderman, Joseph Fletcher, Peter Russell, Philip Tetlock, and Marcus Prior, "The Theory of Democratic Elitism Revisited," *Canadian Journal of Political Science* 33, 3 (September 2000): 575.

22. As Christopher Lasch wrote in *The Revolt of the Masses* (New York: W. W. Norton, 1995), p. 90: "The thinking classes seem to labor under the delusion that they alone have overcome racial prejudice. The rest of the country, in their view, remains incorrigibly racist. . . . But whether it springs from self-righteousness or panic or a mixture of the two, the assumption that most Americans remain racists at heart cannot stand up to close examination."

23. For useful commentary, see Paul Sniderman and Philip Tetlock, "Symbolic Racism: Problems of Political Motive Attribution in Political Analysis" and "Reflections on American Racism," *Journal of Social Issues* 42 (1986): 129–150 and 173–188, respectively.

24. Sniderman and Tetlock, "Reflections on American Racism," p. 184.

25. Anna Greenberg, "Defending the American People," *Responsive Community* 9, 4 (Fall 1999): 57–58.

26. "The Making of the President—of Sixth Grade," *Atlantic Monthly* 294, 3 (October 2004): 62.

27. Michael Sandel, *Liberalism and the Limits of Justice* (Cambridge: Cambridge University Press, 1982); Sandel, *Democracy's Discontent*; Rorty, *Achieving Our Country*.

28. Sandel, *Democracy's Discontent*, p. 268.

29. To put this point another way, recall that the central theoretical and polemical purpose of Keynes's argument was to deny the validity of Say's Law, the venerable proposition fundamental to classical political economy that held that supply creates its own demand. So the logically pertinent rhetorical question here becomes: in what way would a reaffirmation of Say's Law and macroeconomic policies contingent upon it be more compatible with or conducive to projects of forming good democratic citizens than would accepting Keynes's explanation of how a less than full employment equilibrium is a real possibility? I cannot come up with any credible answer to that question, and Sandel would seem to have to do so in order to make plausible his own indictment of the larger consequences of Keynesianism.

30. See Sandel, *Democracy's Discontent*, p. 54.

31. 319 U.S. 624 (1943).

32. 478 U.S. 186 (1986).

33. Sandel, *Democracy's Discontent*, p. 103.

34. As when he worries that these assumptions he claims to find in our constitutional discourse about the nature of selves, autonomy, and the grounds of toleration "increasingly set the terms of moral and political debate in general." See ibid., p. 108.

35. Ibid., p. 105.

36. Ibid., p. 104.

37. Ibid., p. 275.

38. Ibid., p. 119.

39. Ibid., p. 275.

40. Rorty, *Achieving Our Country*, pp. 97, 92.

41. Ibid., p. 51.

42. See Richard Rorty, "Trotsky and the Wild Orchids," reprinted in Rorty, *Philosophy and Social Hope* (New York: Penguin Books, 1999), and Rorty, *Achieving Our Country*, p. 59.

43. Robert Westbrook, *John Dewey and American Democracy* (Ithaca, N.Y.: Cornell University Press, 1991), p. 541.

44. Whitman, "Democratic Vistas," pp. 974, 988.

45. Westbrook, *John Dewey and American Democracy*, p. 541.

Index

Achieving Our Country (Rorty), 264, 286, 291
Ackerman, Bruce, 49, 61, 62, 64, 156, 161, 237, 251
Adams, Henry, 285
Adams, John, 6, 105, 206, 240
Addams, Jane, 74, 99, 100
Adorno, Theodore, 119
African Americans, 137, 138–39, 149, 211, 216–17, 231, 278, 279, 280–81
Age of Reform (Hofstadter), 128–29
Aid to Families with Dependent Children (AFDC), 209–10
Ailes, Roger, 198–99
Albion's Seed (Fisher), 19
Alstott, Anne, 237
American Civil Liberties Union (ACLU), 92, 247
American Jewish Committee, 119
American Revolution, ideological origins of, 4–5, 7–8
Anderson, Charles, 261
Anti-Intellectualism in American Life (Hofstadter), 128–29
Apology (Plato), 132
Aquinas, Thomas, 224
Aristotle, 16, 24, 25, 107, 148, 190, 191, 226, 303n35
   civic friendship and, 35, 55, 187–88
   egalitarian justice and, 169, 171
   human good and, 55, 189, 191
   on middle class, 76, 77, 240
   phronimoi and, 53, 106, 142, 272

Arnold, Matthew, 58
Authoritarian Personality, The, 119

Bailyn, Bernard, 4
Bancroft, George, 36, 41–42, 45, 74
Barber, Benjamin, 25, 133, 251, 272
Bates, Katherine Lee, 32
Beard, Charles, 129
Becker, Carl, 3
Beiner, Ronald, 58, 200, 201, 202
Bell, Daniel, 80
Bentham, Jeremy, 24, 102, 134, 141, 151, 226
Berger, Victor, 129
Berlin, Sir Isaiah, 9, 151
Bloom, Allan, 131
Bowers v. Hardwick, 288
Boyte, Harry, xviii–xix, 101, 261
Brandeis, Louis, 200
Bricker, John, 132, 307n54
Brinkley, Alan, 128
Brown v. Board of Education, 133, 135
Buckley, William, 132
Burke, Edmund, 10, 27, 39, 77, 155
Bush, George W., 284
Byrnes, James F., 125

Cahn, Edmund, 156
capitalism, 80, 95, 207, 313n77
Carnegie, Andrew, 207
Chatauqua movement, 99
civic (neorepublican) economy, 238–40, 241–44, 254, 287

INDEX

civic friendship, 35–36, 38, 55, 187–88, 190, 195, 317n43
civic republicanism, 4, 6–7, 32, 43, 67, 76, 105, 127, 133, 202, 203, 238, 242, 287, 291
civil rights, 132–36, 137–38, 143, 144, 147–48, 149, 211, 222, 224, 230, 253–54
Clinton, Bill, 211–12
Clinton, Hillary, 216
Closing of the American Mind, The (Bloom), 131
Commager, Henry Steele, 100–101
common people (American public), xvi, 11–12, 27, 28–30, 85–86, 113–14, 117, 121, 142–43, 282–83. *See also* working/middle class
Comte, Auguste, 98
Condorcet, Marquis de, 9, 15, 25, 67, 105, 237, 250, 251, 275, 300n47
Congregationalism, 29
Connolly, William, 51, 109, 122
consent, principle of, 13, 15, 17–18, 25–26, 43, 61–62, 89, 274–75, 276, 285
conservatives, 197, 212, 246, 256, 257–58, 294
Considerations on Representative Government (Mill), 18
Constant, Benjamin, 1, 31
contemporary (high) American liberalism
  rights-based theory and, 94, 100, 144, 152, 196, 209, 216, 255, 264
  traditional liberalism and, 53, 67–68, 74, 76, 79–80, 81, 84, 90, 92, 95–97, 101–3, 110–11, 143–44
  welfare of least advantaged and, 51, 82–83, 84–85, 86, 88, 91, 144, 161, 203, 205–6, 255, 264
  See also under self-realization, principle of; self-rule, principle of; social (distributive) justice; working/middle class
Curti, Merle, 129–30, 131, 259

Dagger, Richard, 238
Dahl, Robert, 278–79
Daily Worker, 127–28

Darwin, Charles, 106, 107–8, 217
Debs, Eugene, 129
decisionism, 104–5, 110–11, 140, 141, 151
democracy
  majority rule and, 115–16, 231
  Rawls and, 66, 68, 83, 103
  Whitman on, 11, 13–14, 21, 26, 27, 32, 43, 44–45, 67, 93, 99, 100, 203, 220, 229, 239, 285, 291–93
Democracy in America (Tocqueville), 18
Democracy's Discontent (Sandel), 264, 286, 287
democratic citizenship, 219, 228–29, 230, 233, 236, 253, 271, 272, 274
democratic good, conception of, 225–28, 248, 253, 274
Democratic Party, xvi, 215, 216, 257, 259
democratic personhood, 66–67, 68, 69, 70, 166, 167–69, 171–73, 176, 180–81, 214, 227, 271, 286, 293, 303n35
democratic revisionism, 142–43
"Democratic Vistas" (Whitman), 14, 44, 67, 227, 269–70, 291
development, principle of, 13, 24, 43, 45. *See also* self-realization, principle of
Development and Scope of Higher Education in the United States, The (Hofstadter), 131
Dewey, John, 95, 99, 101, 103, 268, 291–92, 293
DiIulio, John, 112–13, 121, 205, 277
Discourse on the Origins of Inequality (Rousseau), 68
distributive justice. *See* social (distributive) justice
Dred Scott case, 207
Dunn, John, 5
Dworetz, Steven, 5
Dworkin, Ronald, 49, 94, 95, 103, 141
Dye, Thomas, 85–86
Dylan, Bob, xv

Earned Income Tax Credit, 243
Edelman, Peter, 211–12
education, 34, 42, 78–79, 86, 121, 131, 159, 235–36

egalitarianism
  deontology and, 146, 147, 148, 149, 152, 169, 171, 175, 176, 180, 187, 247
  distributive justice and, 50, 111, 204, 215, 219, 247, 255–56
  pre-1960s, 19, 32, 34, 127, 152, 169
  Rawls and, 50, 51, 90, 172, 204
  rights-based, 90, 93–94
Eisenach, Eldon, 100
Eisenhower, Dwight, 126
elites, 45–46, 86
  academic, 283
  conservative, 210
  liberal, 85, 88, 89, 92, 132, 139, 144, 205, 206, 210, 283–84
  political, 33, 115, 117, 143, 283–84
  social and economic, 8, 77, 122, 252
Emerson, Ralph Waldo, 22, 42, 194, 195
Engels, Friedrich, 62
Enlightenment rationalism, 105
equality
  civic, 32–33, 43, 198, 204, 209, 219, 231, 238, 243, 248, 256, 273, 292
  economic, 59, 129, 142–43, 149, 154, 169, 209, 221, 229, 264
  moral, 222, 226, 230
  of opportunity, 254
  racial, 118, 129, 138
  social, 32, 59, 129, 137, 138, 142–43, 149, 154, 155, 169, 173, 187, 198, 200, 203, 209, 229, 264, 267, 268, 285
Ethics (Aristotle), 35
exploitation, 61–62, 64, 103

fairness, 156
  distributive, 57, 58–59, 161–62, 173, 198, 200, 201, 221, 266, 271, 285
  justice as, 54, 57, 67, 137, 161–62, 167, 183–84, 187, 188, 214, 220
Federalist #10 (Madison), 23
Federalists, 8, 10, 27–28
Filmer, Sir Robert, 31
First Treatise of Civil Government (Locke), 16
Fisher, David Hackett, 19
Fishkin, James, 251
Fourteenth Amendment, 222
Frank, Thomas, 199
Frankfurter, Felix, 274

Franklin, Benjamin, 36, 39
fraternity, 34–37, 38, 187–88, 190
French Liberal Thought in the Eighteenth Century (Martin), 35
Frenkel-Brunswik, Else, 119
Freud, Sigmund, 106, 107, 108
Friedman, Milton, 236, 246
Frontiers of Justice (Nussbaum), 158

Galston, William, 196, 197
Gibbon, Edward, 1
Gideon v. Wainwright, 231
Gilbert, W. S., 192, 193–94
Gingrich, Newt, 211
Gitlin, Todd, 195
Godwin, William, 273
Gordon, Thomas, 4
Gore, Al, 284
Graetz, Michael, 207, 208
Greenberg, Anna, 283–84
Greening of America, The (Reich), xiv–xv
Grigg, Charles, 115, 116
Gutmann, Amy, 86–87

Habermas, Jurgen, 40, 93, 245, 250, 272, 274
Halevy, Elie, 110
Hamilton, Alexander, 28, 77
Hamiltonians, 8, 27–28
happiness, pursuit of, 23–24
Harrington, James, 4, 32, 77
Hartz, Louis, 3, 14
Hayek, Friedrich von, 38–39
health care reform, 235, 243–44
Hegel, G. W. F., xi, 9, 10, 11, 14, 24, 27, 43, 46, 53
high liberalism, 49. *See also* contemporary (high) American liberalism
Hillquist, Morris, 129
Hiss, Alger, 132
Hobbes, Thomas, 26, 31, 148, 176, 190
Hofstadter, Richard, 126–27, 128–31, 132, 259
human capital, development of, 230, 231, 234–35, 236–37, 254, 267
human good, concept of, 59–60, 105, 108, 109–10, 111, 140, 141, 151–52, 166, 189, 268, 285, 287, 289–90

INDEX

Humboldt, Wilhelm von, 45, 99, 232
Hume, David, 42, 55, 149, 150, 159, 163, 190, 224
Humphrey, Hubert, 100, 200, 304n9

Idea of Fraternity in America, The (McWilliams), 34
inheritance (estate) taxes, 207–8, 209, 241–42, 256
Irony of Democracy, The (Dye), 85–86
Isaac, Jeffrey, 258

Jacksonian democracy, 9–10, 40, 41
Jefferson, Thomas, 15, 17, 27, 36, 42, 49, 67, 87, 105, 200, 206
   on democracy, 9–10, 30, 79, 235–36
   on education, 86, 235–36
   on equality, x, 17, 32, 58, 313n85
   on natural aristocracy, 34, 78–79, 90
   on respectable yeoman, 23, 78, 219, 240
   on self-rule, 20, 22–23, 235
Johnson, Hiram, 100
justice
   as fairness, 54, 57, 67, 137, 161–62, 167, 183–84, 187, 188, 214, 220
   liberal, 55–64, 153–54
   See also social (distributive) justice
Justice as Fairness: A Restatement (Rawls), 185

Kael, Pauline, 290
Kahn, Paul, 194
Kant, Immanuel, x, 9, 73, 105, 165, 173, 203, 303n35
   on basic human rights, 222
   on moral powers, 68, 69–71, 72, 74, 107, 110, 149–51, 152, 190, 192–93, 226
   on reason, 106–7, 110, 189, 190–92
Kari, Nancy, xviii–xix, 101
Kaus, Mickey, 32–33, 198, 209
Keillor, Garrison, 259
Kenyon, Cecelia, 14
Keynes, John Maynard, 52, 287–88, 320n29
King, Martin Luther, Jr., 35, 144, 224
Kozol, Jonathan, 235
Kuhn, Thomas, 215, 216

La Follette, Robert, Jr., 124, 127, 128, 129
La Guardia, Fiorello, 129
Larmore, Charles, 188–89, 190
Lasch, Christopher, 85
Lasswell, Harold, 128
Law of the Peoples, The (Rawls), 178
Laws, The (Plato), 58
Lenin, Vladimir, 23
Levinson, Daniel, 119
Liberalism and Social Action (Dewey), 95, 101
Liberalism and the Limits of Justice (Sandel), 163–164, 166, 286
Lincoln, Abraham, 33, 36, 42, 45, 49, 133, 206–7, 281
   "of the people" phrase of, 12, 15, 18, 23, 25, 26–27, 43, 275
Lipset, Seymour Martin, 120–21, 128
Locke, John (Lockean thought), 26, 74, 172
   on equality, 16
   influence on American liberalism by, 3–7, 8, 13–14, 43, 68, 73, 99
   on political authority, 13, 15, 16
   on property rights, 6, 171
   Protestant sensibility and, 5–6
   self-rule and, 13, 14, 18
London, Jack, 108
Lubell, Samuel, 257
Luther, Martin, 9, 27

Machiavelli, Niccoló, 27, 295
MacIntyre, Alasdair, 110
Macpherson, C. B., 5
Madison, James, 23, 32, 56, 88, 102, 105, 191
Marcuse, Herbert, xiv
market economy, 58, 61, 186, 222, 236, 256, 287–88
Marshall, George, 126
Martin, Kingsley, 35
Marx, Karl, 62, 74, 75
Massachusetts Bay Colony, 19–20
McCarthy, Joseph, 124–28, 130, 307n54
McCarthyism, 123–32, 143–44
McClosky, Herbert, 116–17
McKinley, William, 257
McTeague (Norris), 108–9
McWilliams, Carey, 34–35, 37

INDEX

Medicaid, 243
Michels, Roberto, 114
middle class. *See* working/middle class
Mill, James, 105
Mill, John Stuart, 14, 18, 105, 143
   on happiness, 134
   on mental and moral development, xi, xix, 26, 30, 42, 45, 55, 99, 111, 122, 123, 141, 232, 270, 274
   perfectionism and, 43, 271
   on representative government, 39, 44–45, 238, 274
   theory of democracy of, xiii, 43–45, 226, 239
Minnesota Farmer-Labor Party, 261
"Model of Christian Charity, A" (Winthrop), 6
moral powers, 69–70, 71, 72, 73, 74, 141–42, 168, 174, 179–80, 184
morals, metaphysic of, 104–6, 109, 111, 122, 140
Myrdal, Gunnar, 133

NAACP Legal Defense and Educational Fund, 118, 135
National Welfare Rights Organization (NWRO), 211
naturalism, 104–11, 140–41, 183, 217
Neal, Patrick, 188, 189, 190, 191
neorepublican political economy, 238–40, 241–44, 254, 264, 287
New Deal liberalism, xviii–xix, 99, 100–103, 127, 138, 144, 196, 209–10, 257, 258, 259, 261, 267
New Left, xii, xiii–xv, xvi
Niebuhr, Reinhold, 130
Nixon, Richard, 259
Norris, Frank, 108–9
Nozick, Robert, 180–81, 204, 205, 247, 311n46
Nussbaum, Martha, 158, 159–60, 232

Obama, Barack, 216
Old-Age, Survivors, and Disability Insurance (OASDI), 242
On Civil Disobedience (Thoreau), 281
On Liberty (Mill), 26, 44, 45, 67, 99, 269–70
Origin of the Species (Darwin), 217

O'Rourke, P. J., 246, 247, 248
Orwell, George, 33

Paine, Tom, 105
"Paranoid Style in American Politics, The" (Hofstadter), 128–29
Parks, Rosa, 211
Paul, Saint, 189
perfectionism, 143, 147
   foundation and goals of, 43, 226, 242, 244
   populism and, 227, 229, 230, 239, 240, 242, 243, 244, 254, 262, 265, 271–72, 291, 293
   Rawls and, 240, 318n12
   reform of liberalism and, 228–30, 265, 268, 270, 271–72, 285, 291, 293
   self-rule and, 239, 243
   traditional liberalism and, 43, 226, 239, 269–70, 271
Pericles, 37
Perkins, Frances, 213
Pettit, Philip, 32
Philosophical Investigations (Wittgenstein), 221
Pirates of Penzance (Gilbert and Sullivan), 192–93
Plato, 58, 75, 107, 132, 190
Plessy v. Ferguson, 133
Pocock, J. G. A., 4
political authority, 15–17
Political Liberalism (Rawls), 182
Political Man (Lipset), 120
Politics (Aristotle), 24, 76
populism, 45, 146, 282, 285
   conservatism and, 199, 256
   contemporary (high) liberalism and, xvii, 46, 52, 94, 122–23, 133, 143, 147, 282
   criticism of, 128–30, 131
   definition of, xvii
   foundation and goals of, 14, 40, 43, 207, 244
   McCarthy and, 127, 130, 131, 132, 143
   New Deal liberalism and, 127, 144
   perfectionism and, 227, 229, 230, 239, 240, 242, 243, 244, 254, 262, 265, 271–72, 291, 293

327

INDEX

populism (*continued*)
   progressivism and, 12, 27, 31, 32–33, 34, 43, 99, 122–23, 144, 261
   self-rule and, 13, 285
   Whitman and, 11–14, 43
populist perfectionism. *See* perfectionism
Progressive Party of Wisconsin, 124, 129–30, 259, 261
progressivism, 124, 127
   civic friendship and, 35, 36, 38, 165
   contemporary (high) liberalism and, 99, 100, 103, 144, 206, 219–20, 261
   criticism of, 129–30, 131
   equality and, 32–33, 34, 35
   foundation of, 1–2
   fraternity and, 34–35, 36, 37, 38
   liberty and, 31–32
   origin of, 2, 14, 43, 98, 146
   populism and, 12, 27, 31, 32–33, 34, 43, 99, 122–23, 144, 261
   reform of liberalism and, 99, 257–59, 261
   social (distributive) justice and, 134, 219–20, 267
   vision of, 14, 25, 27, 30, 31–32, 40, 42, 55, 98, 99–100, 101–3, 122–23, 134, 200
property rights, 6, 23–24, 171, 239–41
Protestantism, 5–6, 19, 29, 38, 80, 105, 217, 258
Prothro, James, 115, 116
public sphere/forum, 245–46, 250, 251–52, 254, 292
Puritanism, 19–20
Putnam, Robert, 21, 249

racism, 117–20, 128, 133, 135, 137, 144, 149, 278, 280, 281, 282, 283, 320n22
Rawls, John, 140
   on chain-connectedness, 83–84, 262
   conception of good and, 219, 226
   criticism of, 50, 51, 167, 177–81, 184–85, 187, 188–89, 190, 196, 204–5, 286, 291
   on democracy, 66, 68, 83, 103
   democratic personhood and, 66–67, 68, 69, 70, 166, 167–69, 171–73, 176, 181, 227, 228–29, 286, 303n35
   difference principle of, 155–56, 161, 177–78, 185, 187–88, 192, 205, 247, 310n42, 312–13n77, 316n30
   egalitarianism and, 50, 51, 90, 172, 204
   on fraternity, 187–88
   influence on contemporary (high) liberalism of, xx, 49–51, 52
   international distributive justice and, 178–79, 310n42
   moral desert and, 180, 181–83, 184, 186–87
   on moral powers, 69–70, 71–72, 74, 86, 179, 184
   on natural inequality, 61, 64, 84, 155–56, 157–58, 161, 173, 181, 185–87, 223
   on political virtues, 269, 271–72, 316n41
   on property ownership, 240
   redress, principle of, 61, 62, 64, 137, 154–57, 254, 266, 307–8n55
   retributive justice and, 177–78
   self-realization and, 164–65, 234
   social (distributive) justice and, 50, 54, 56–61, 64, 67, 70, 88–90, 103, 137–38, 150, 159, 162–63, 166–67, 173–75, 177, 178–79, 182–83, 191–92, 220, 310n42
   on social responsibility, 73, 171, 174–75, 179, 254, 310n38
   toleration and, 268–69
   welfare of least advantaged and, 51, 59, 82–83, 84–85, 86, 88, 161
Reich, Charles, xiv–xv, xvi
Republic, The (Plato), 75
republicanism, 6–7, 10. *See also* civic republicanism
Republicans, 128, 197, 257, 258
respectable yeomanry. *See* working/middle class
Rogers, Will, 48
Roosevelt, Franklin, 101, 304n9
Rorty, Richard, 194, 227–28, 263–64, 286, 291–92, 293
Roszak, Theodore, xiii, xiv
Rousseau, Jean-Jacques, 15, 16–17, 26, 37, 65, 68–69, 70, 71, 74, 77, 102, 105, 107, 193
Rove, Karl, 257

INDEX

Sandel, Michael, 66, 101, 163, 166, 200, 238–39, 264, 286–91
Sanford, R. Nevitt, 119
Sartre, Jean-Paul, 17, 71, 246
Scheffler, Samuel, 108, 109
Second Treatise of Civil Government (Locke), 6, 13, 18
self-realization, principle of
   contemporary (high) liberalism and, 92, 95, 110–11, 122, 129, 141, 143, 147, 164–65, 197, 203
   reform of liberalism and, 215, 224, 225, 230, 231, 233–34, 243, 244, 255, 263, 268, 270, 272, 285, 293
   traditional liberalism and, 13, 15, 24, 90, 93, 102, 105, 108, 110, 152, 201
self-rule, principle of
   contemporary (high) liberalism and, 53, 86, 88, 92, 95, 110–11, 121–22, 129, 130, 136, 141, 142, 147, 152, 197, 200, 203, 275
   Darwin's theory and, 107–8
   McCarthyism and, 143–44
   personal, 21–22
   reform of liberalism and, 203, 224, 225, 226, 227, 230, 231, 233, 234, 238, 250, 253, 263, 265, 272, 274–76, 282, 285
   traditional liberalism and, 13–14, 15, 18, 20, 21, 22, 26, 31–32, 38, 43–45, 90, 99–100, 102, 110, 121–22, 142, 200, 201, 235, 239, 261
   See also democratic self-rule *under* Whitman, Walt
Sen, A. K., 232
Shalala, Donna, 91, 93, 103
Shapiro, Ian, 131, 207, 208, 209
Skocpol, Theda, 242, 244–45
Slaughterhouse cases, 133
Smith, Adam, 22, 67, 105
Smith, Melancton, 28, 30, 77, 81, 83, 205
Sniderman, Paul, 280, 282
socialism, 75–76, 129
social (distributive) justice
   as contemporary (high) liberalism goal, 53–54, 55–64, 67, 93–94, 95–96, 133, 134, 136, 137, 144, 147–48, 151–52, 153, 166, 169–70, 198, 203–4, 218, 219, 220, 247, 261, 264

   definition of, 51, 54, 55, 56, 59, 93, 264
   deontology and, 149, 150
   reform of liberalism and, 264–69, 271, 273, 285, 292
   welfare of disadvantaged and, 82–83, 84–85, 86, 88, 161, 221–22
   See also under Rawls, John
Social Security, 237, 242, 315n28
Social Statics (Spencer), 6
Socrates, 132
Spencer, Herbert, 6
Stalin, Joseph, 23
Strauss, Leo, 5
student loan programs, 236–37
Sunstein, Cass, 49
Sydney, Algernon, 4, 22, 77

Taft, Robert, 132
Taylor, Charles, 282
Teles, Steven, 210
Terkel, Studs, 259
Tetlock, Philip, 282
Theory of Justice, A (Rawls), 54, 73, 103, 149, 166, 182, 183, 191, 312n77
Thoreau, Henry David, 281
Thucidydes, 16
Tocqueville, Alexis de, 1, 10, 18–19, 20, 21, 29, 33, 39–41, 127, 241, 246
tolerance, 269, 277, 278–80, 283, 318–19n19, 319n20
Tomasi, John, 54, 272
Tomasky, Michael, xvi, 206, 213
traditional American liberalism
   contemporary (high) liberalism and, 53, 67–68, 74, 76, 79–80, 81, 84, 90, 92, 95–97, 101–3, 110–11, 143–44
   equality and, 16–17, 32
   foundations of, 1–3, 15, 105
   human development and, xi, xix, 30, 37, 42, 45, 53, 55, 99, 111, 122, 123, 141, 200–201, 232
   principles and goals of, 13, 53, 67–68, 93, 105, 110
   See also perfectionism; populism. *See also under* self-rule; self-realization; working/middle class
Trenchard, John, 4
trickle-down economics, 83–84
Truman, Harry, 124

INDEX

Vietnam War, 139
Vindication of the Governance of New England Churches, A (Wise), 29
Vonnegut, Kurt, 158, 308n9

Wallace, George, 260
Walzer, Michael, 32, 266, 314n11
Ward, Lester Frank, 100–101, 103
Watts, Alan, xiv
Weber, Max, xiii, 17, 110, 141, 151, 205
Welcome to the Monkey House (Vonnegut), 308n9
welfare system, 87, 209–10, 211–12
Westbrook, Robert, 292, 293
West Virginia v. Barnette, 288
White, Stuart, 243
Whitman, Walt, xiii, 42, 264
    on common people, 11–12, 27, 29–30, 79, 81–82, 113–14, 244
    on community, 249
    democratic self-rule and, 13–14, 21, 26, 27, 32, 43, 44–45, 67, 93, 99, 100, 203, 220, 229, 239, 285, 291–93
    on fraternity, 37–38
    perfectionism and, 271
    on personal freedom/development, 24–25, 53, 55, 74, 143, 227, 232, 266, 267, 268, 270
    on political elitism, 33
    populism and, 11–14, 43
    Rorty on, 291–92
    on universal suffrage, 21, 275

Winthrop, John, 6, 35
Wise, John, 29
Wittgenstein, Ludwig, 2, 155, 219, 221
Wolfe, Alan, 277
Wood, Gordon, 4
working/middle class (respectable yeomanry), 261–62
    authoritarianism of, 84–85, 119–21, 128
    contemporary (high) liberalism and, xvi, 79–80, 81–82, 83, 133, 139, 111–13, 144, 196, 198–99, 205–8, 207, 210, 258–62
    definition of, 77
    history of, 18, 19, 38, 76, 80, 240
    praise for, 23, 28, 46, 76, 77–78, 112
    restoration of, 244
    rift with liberalism of, 79–80, 81–82, 83, 133, 139, 144, 111–13, 144, 196, 198–99, 205–8, 207, 210, 258–62
    social justice and, 84, 123, 137, 144, 206, 210, 212–13, 260, 261–62
    social scientists on, 111–23
    traditional liberalism and, 23, 28, 30–31, 46, 76, 77, 78–81, 83, 84, 90, 123, 127, 138, 200, 205, 212–13, 313n85
    unflattering depictions of, 92, 113–14, 120, 121–22, 141, 277–81
"Worst Thing Bill Clinton Has Done, The" (Edelman), 211–12

Young, Iris, 63–64, 198, 220